'Somebody Had To Do It'
The story of notorious 'Union Buster' Christopher Pole-Carew

Barrie Williams

In 1939, Great Walstead School was run by a remarkable headmaster, Mr. R.J. Mowll. In Dickensian tones, he would say constantly and repetitively to any passing boy: " **Get something definite to do.** *" The boys were simply never, ever, for so much as one minute during any waking hour, allowed to do* **nothing....**

AuthorHouse™ UK Ltd.
500 Avebury Boulevard
Central Milton Keynes, MK9 2BE
www.authorhouse.co.uk
Phone: 08001974150

© 2010 Barrie Williams. All rights reserved.

No part of this book may be reproduced, stored in a retrieval system, or transmitted by any means without the written permission of the author.

First published by AuthorHouse   8/25/2010

ISBN: 978-1-4520-2952-8 (sc)

This book is printed on acid-free paper.

Contents

1: PREFACE 1
*' I didn't expect to **like** him…'*

2: MAKING THE MAN 3
' In those uncomplicated days of Empire, before jealousy and greed crept in, people still enjoyed the wonderful things that life had to offer.'

3: A NEW WORLD 37
The newspaper industry is a ruthless business and it seemed that I was getting acclimatised remarkably quickly!'

4: A TIGER BY THE TAIL 49
' Daddy, there's a man on the phone who says he wants to kill you.'

5: BLOODY BATTLES 77
' A hero to his employees; the envy of his gutless contemporaries and a hate figure to the unions.'

6: THE MAN FOR MURDOCH 120
*Q:'Would you mind if I put machine guns on the roof?'A:' I think you **would** too!'*

7: THIS MAN POLE-CAREW 165
' Christopher Pole-Carew is not a man about whom either friends or enemies have ever harboured doubts.'

8: RETIREMENT - SORT OF! 227
Was it just luck that brought so many of you, with the skills to save my life, to where we had crashed ?'

9: THE POEMS OF POLE - CAREW 269
Carpentry, bricklaying, plumbing, beekeeping. Many and surprising are the skills of Pole- Carew. But poetry?

10: THE THOUGHTS OF POLE-CAREW 286
*He's been called outspoken, blunt, belligerent, forthright, infuriating, amusing. But **never** boring…*

11: HE DID IT HIS WAY 295
*Controversial and enigmatic, people love him or hate him, but **what** a man!*

About the Author

BARRIE WILLIAMS is a journalist and author who spent more than 40 years in the newspaper industry. His successful newspaper career began in 1961 when he joined the Shrewsbury Chronicle as a 16-year-old trainee reporter. He then worked for national newspapers before returning to regional journalism as the News Editor of the Shrewsbury Chronicle. He went on to become a Sub Editor on the Wolverhampton Express & Star; News Editor of the Stoke-on-Trent City Times and Diary Editor of the Nottingham Evening Post before moving to the Kent Evening Post , where he was News Editor and Associate Editor before being appointed Editor. After five years as Editor of the Kent Evening Post, he was appointed Editor and Editorial Director of the Nottingham Evening Post. Fourteen years later, he moved to the West Country as Editor of the Western Morning News, a position he held for 10 years. In nearly 30 years as a top regional newspaper Editor, Barrie Williams established a reputation as a formidable campaigning journalist, winning countless awards, including the coveted Newspaper Of The Year title four times. His exceptional newspaper career is described in outspoken and entertaining style in his autobiography 'Ink In The Blood' published by Woodfield - www.woodfieldpublishing.com Barrie Williams lives in Cornwall with his wife Pauline.

1
PREFACE
*' I didn't expect to **like** him…'*

SO began a national magazine article written after one of very few interviews given by Christopher Pole - Carew.

It was an understandable reaction.

A whole generation of British journalists had grown up learning to loathe the " terrible toff " who broke the powerful print unions and blazed the bloody trail that was eventually to destroy trades union power in the United Kingdom.

In the 1970s and 1980s Christopher Pole - Carew had a major influence on the direction of British industrial relations. As the hugely controversial boss of T.Bailey Forman, publishers of the *Nottingham Evening Post* , he tackled the enormous issues of new technology and union domination in the print industry a decade before anybody else dared to try. Then he went on, under a blanket of total secrecy, to mastermind much of the tactically brilliant "military" operation that was *Times, Sun* and *News Of The World* mogul Rupert Murdoch's seismic move from Fleet Street to Wapping and to head up the infamous *Daily Mirror* proprietor Robert Maxwell's ill-fated attempt to launch a new evening newspaper for London.

Both the regional and national print industry battles involving Christopher Pole - Carew were among the bloodiest industrial conflicts of the 20th Century and when the revolution he started had run its course thousands of jobs had been wiped out. To this day, in trades union folklore, he is a hate figure with which to frighten the children. When union folk speak the name of the dreaded ***"Pole - Carew"*** it is spat out with revulsion. To them, he is a capitalist ogre; an evil enemy of the working class.

The left wing newspaper *Socialist Worker* called Pole-Carew: "The most notorious union buster in the print industry"

Little wonder, then, that when journalist Kate Macmillan ventured into the monster's den (otherwise known as Shute Barton, the stately Devonshire family home of the Pole-Carews) to do that magazine interview she was so disarmed by this enigmatic fellow's good humoured charm, infectious enthusiasm and irresistible likeability.

It would have come as no surprise, however, to the comparatively small number of people who know the man better than the myth.

What follows - and told for the first time - is the remarkable life story of an extraordinary man.

2

MAKING THE MAN

' In those uncomplicated days of Empire, before jealousy and greed crept in, people still enjoyed the wonderful things that life had to offer.'

IF you're looking for the archetypal villain in a tale of class hatred they don't come any more tailor made than Christopher Pole-Carew.

The roots of his aristocratic family tree are 32 generations deep.

He is proud of, yet at the same time humorously self-deprecating about, his place in the historic Pole (originally pronounced Pool) family of English landed gentry.

He says: "Our records go back, father to son, for 32 generations which, provided you lived in an area of England clear of marching armies and preferably far enough away from your liege lord for his messenger to arrive late with his summons to battle, was not too remarkable. South Devon was clearly far enough away!"

One of the earliest recorded ancestors is one Robert Le Hare at the beginning of the 12th Century." This was pre-surnames so I reckon he either had very long ears or he was a pretty fast mover."

Robert Le Hare acquired the manor of Pool in the Wirral of Cheshire from two Pole (also spelt Pool or Pull) heiresses. The Poles were a powerful local family. Almost certainly, Le Hare was a close relative; valuable manors with their land didn't pass out of families in those days, unless there was a special reason. A later descendant became Vice Admiral of the West, moved down to the West Country, married a local girl and stayed. Hence the Devon connection. In 1560 William Pole (*" he was a sharp lawyer who made a lot of money - time for another one in the family!"*) bought Shute.

" We conducted our affairs in the way that that section of society habitually did: caring for one's estate, carrying out one's local duties, occasionally extending that to standing as an MP ; every so often providing someone with wider interests or ambitions. On the way (in 1730) we picked up the Carew estate at Antony (in south east Cornwall) when a distant Carew relative died, whilst insisting that his heir took the name and coat of arms of Carew.

" So, we Poles became Pole-Carews. And why not!

" Meanwhile,the younger sons of the Pole- Carews (pronounced Pool-Careys in those days) went away and succeeded (not often!), disappeared (ie. failed) or got killed. There were plenty of wars across the centuries to provide opportunities for the first and third of these options!"

One notable 18th Century success was Reginald Pole-Carew who, according to Christopher's account, " went on the Grand Tour, as one did, but instead of heading for Italy turned left and went to Russia, in the time of Catherine The Great. He was a spy for the British Government and reported back in immense detail on their military and naval installations. It was suggested that he became Ambassador to Russia but he turned that down because he thought an Englishman's place was on his estate at home. So he came home and became an MP."

Then there was Christopher's Great Uncle Reggie: " He married late and he married Beatrice Butler, daughter of the Marquis of Ormande. When he went to ask the Marquis for his daughter's hand in marriage, as one did, the reply was: 'Go away, my boy, and make yourself worthy of her.' So off he went, came back knighted and a General from the Boer War, married her, had two sons and a couple of daughters and lived happily ever after."

In Victorian times, a fourth option for the future of younger sons was added... that of a career in the colonies.

"Which takes us to my grandfather, Charles Edward Pole-Carew, a second son who went tea planting in Ceylon - as the name Sri Lanka was corrupted into in those days - made money and managed somehow to lose it!"

Neither was Christopher's father, Gerald, to be counted among the Pole-Carew successes.

"My father never achieved very much: the highlights of his life were the two World Wars. He survived, whilst his brothers died, in the First War because his battalion, the Duke Of Cornwall's Light Infantry, spent most of its time on garrison duties in India.

"It was said that his uncle, General Reginald Pole-Carew, made sure Gerald was in India because the General wanted to look after his brother's only surviving son but I don't think that was true. A more accurate explanation is that the War Office deliberately sent different battalions of regiments to different places in order to avoid the destruction of too many sons from one single place in the country. There was a classic example early in the war of terrible losses when the Kings Own Yorkshire Light Infantry were wiped out devastating street after street of homes in Sheffield, where they had come from, and the lesson was learned. Anyhow, my father survived."

It is evident that Christopher Pole-Carew had little time for his father.

With considerable understatement, he explains it thus : " To say that I was close to my father would give a totally wrong impression. My father got through all his money and he then got through all my mother's money."

In 1916 Gerald had married Eileen O'Callaghan, from an old Irish Protestant family, who lived in Newquay in Cornwall.

"Our family moved to London where Gerald failed to achieve much at all, except to spend all his wife's money. My mother had inherited quite well because both her brothers had been killed during the First War. Brother Duncan, just 18, was sent out to fight in France on the Saturday and was killed on the Sunday. Can you imagine that? How the hell was that sort of thing ever allowed to happen? Brother Denys survived the Battle of Jutland only to be killed in a car accident in Newfoundland. Those tragedies resulted in a considerable inheritance for my mother but my father, while fiddling around with various jobs, got through it all."

While in the process of squandering his wife's inheritance, Gerald Pole-Carew had fathered three children - Geraldine, Oliver and Loveday - before Christopher was born in 1931.

His parents' marriage was foundering (" *but in those days, marriages didn't just fall apart. Couples from a rural background just didn't divorce. It just didn't happen.*") They separated for a time " while my mother tried frantically to recoup what was left of her money and my father was spending his way steadily through it" until the Second World War " solved the problem, in a way, because it gave him a meaning and a purpose to life again. He joined up, with considerable difficulty because he was over- age. He spent his time doing those things that they needed someone to do: he was the executive officer of a troop ship, responsible for the troops while they were on board. So he had a rather lovely war sailing all around the world, fortunately without ever getting sunk."

In 1935, because their parents' marriage was "a mess", Loveday and Christopher had been "packed off out of the way to Mrs Dyson's boarding school in Golders Green." Sister Loveday was five years old. Christopher was only four.

Such establishments as Mrs Dyson's were no 1930s equivalent of today's tender, loving nursery schools. This was not playschool. This was intense, concentrated schooling and strict discipline,with no home to go to at the day's end, no mother and father to provide love and comfort. And at an age which nowadays would be considered cruelly unacceptable.

It was, of course, normal for upper class children to be boarded out but at four and five? Today, Pole-Carew and his sister insist they "didn't mind at all" and it meant that the four-year-old Christopher began serious learning much earlier than most, giving him a head start in the education stakes.

"The younger you start learning, the quicker you can assimilate stuff," he says " You sat in the classroom and worked through the alphabet. At four I was reading - and I mean properly. Just as an adult would read. No problem"

Little Christopher would help the cooks at Mrs Dyson's school, running errands, carrying dishes, generally trying to be helpful and each time he helped, the kindly ladies gave him a marble.

Seventy five years later he recalls: "I built up a collection of around 100 marbles then (*and I'm deeply upset here!*) my mother gave things for the war effort and one of the things she gave was a large silver cup that one of her brothers had won and in which I kept my marbles. I never saw those marbles again. It's been a running sore in our family ever since!"

By the age of six, he had moved to a more normal preparatory school Hill Crest in Haywards Heath, Sussex... and was learning Latin!

"At Hill Crest they were doing their initial learning- to- read thing but I'd done that so they gave me something else to do and I added Latin. I'm not saying I was fluent at six, but I was certainly well on. The master who taught me Latin had a very simple method. Every time I got something wrong he would make me go back and do it again and again and again, until I got it right. Very effective."

This period in the life of Pole-Carew must have had an intense influence on him and must surely have been a very early mould for the incredibly strong character which was to make him so fiercely determined and single minded as an adult and a top businessman. He is not a man who subscribes readily to such theories but he does concede that the sort of family support and love which it is reasonable to expect at four, five and six years old was, for him, " extremely limited."

"How often did my family come to see me at school at half term or whatever? Almost never." In fact, for 12 years, from the age of four to 16, while he was in various educational boarding establishments his parents visited him just four times.

That must have been tough?

"No. It's not tough if you don't expect it. One just accepted it. I spent the holidays at school because my mother was with my father who was wherever and it suited her just to leave us at school. One should remember that there was a war on and travelling was not at all easy for civilians; few families had cars and petrol was rationed almost to extinction. But boarding school was fun. A school with 300 acres of woods and its own swimming pool has got a lot of attractions. There were four or five of us left at school for the holidays and we had a whale of a time."

He recalls japes like " we allocated each one of us a personal apple tree. That tree was yours and the apples on it were yours to eat. There was a boy called MacNamara, whose home was in Ireland, whilst his father was in the army. We ate all the apples on his tree but without picking them so that when he went to his tree they were all hanging as cores!"

He roars with laughter as he tells the tale, as he does with others, such as… "One of the older boys, who'd have been 10 or 11, alleged one day that the headmaster's car, a blue/grey Ford, was made out of biscuit tins because, he claimed, that was what Ford made their cars out of! This seemed to us to be a quite reasonable assumption, because Fords were known as cheap cars in those days, but we weren't too sure and there was only one way to find out:

With our penknives (*which in those days every sensible boy carried - and I still do*) we scraped the paint off a mudguard, expecting to find Huntley & Palmer and Peak Frean biscuit tin labels underneath. We were disappointed, but it didn't matter; our expert pronounced the metal to be of biscuit tin quality, so we assumed they had soaked the labels off before making the car. Fortunately, the headmaster never found out by whom, or why, his car had been scraped!"

Seven decades on, is there still an element of contrived, self-defensive schoolboy bravado about these fun time stories? " No. It's hard to explain," he says " but if you haven't got any family ties of any strength you don't miss them. It must have affected me but I'm not aware of what the effect was."

Pressed again, he finally allows:" Well. OK. Yes. I suppose it must have given me self-reliance."

Hill Crest closed when the Second World War broke out. The headmaster, a Mr Wrigley, was an RAF Reserve pilot. He simply called all his young charges, including the then eight-year-old Christopher Pole-Carew together and told them he was closing the school and going off to fight the war.

Most of the pupils then transferred to a nearby school, Great Walstead, which was run by a remarkable man named R.J.Mowll. In Dickensian tones, he would say constantly and repetitively to any passing boy :*" Get something definite to do!"*

The boys were simply never, ever for so much as one minute during any waking hour allowed to do ***nothing.***

So ingrained is the discipline that induced that at 79 years of age, Christopher Pole-Carew still adheres to it. You will never, ever catch him doing ***nothing.*** At the end of every day he calls himself to account for the manner in which he has succeeded in *getting something definite to do* throughout that day. And anyone who ever worked with the man will confirm that the creed never left him!

R.J.Mowll's boys were taught, among other subjects, Greek and Latin, at which young Christopher was now so advanced that he topped forms of much older pupils. But they also learned "fun things" like ferreting in the school's rambling acres of woodland; rifle and shotgun shooting.

At the tender age of 11, Christopher Pole-Carew was regularly using a 12 bore shotgun (which will probably not surprise some of the trade union officials he was to encounter in later life!)

"Health and Safety had yet to be invented," he observes wryly, "but no-one got shot! Come to think about it, Health and Safety is a lot to do with running scared of what *could* happen and has little to do with reality. So we were perfectly safe and we never shot each other."

But the extraordinary R.J.Mowll's most eccentric additions to his boys' essential learning were bricklaying and plumbing. He had concluded that there was going to be so much egalitarian social change after the war that the upper classes would no longer be able to get domestic help so they had better learn to do things for themselves. Thus, R.J.Mowll's Great Walstead produced, in the incomparable Christopher Pole-Carew, not just mastery of the Classics but of building, carpentry and plumbing - trades which he continued to employ for himself throughout his life and still does today.

By now, Britain was again at war with Germany and in the skies over Great Walstead the Battle Of Britain raged every day.

Young Pole-Carew and some 50 other boys watched intently at all hours as German bombers streamed over their school. The excitement of this free show reached its zenith the day they were provided with the spectacular memory of watching wide-eyed and open-mouthed as a deadly Doodlebug (German flying bomb) was pursued by a Spitfire (RAF fighter plane) which caught up with it and lifted the Doodlebug's tail with its wing, causing it to dive into the countryside rather than continuing on to hit the massed homes of London.

With such fantastic feats of bravery happening around their school, it was the hope of every boy at Great Walstead that the war would continue long enough for them to get into uniform and have a go themselves.

When Christopher was 12, his father told him:" I have decided that I shall put you into the Army." The boy replied: "Thank you, but I would like to go into the Navy." Why the Navy? When he was four, he had been a page boy at his nanny's wedding, dressed in a white sailor suit complete with genuine silver naval bosun's whistle which had belonged to his Uncle Denys and remains, to this day, among his most prized possessions. From then on there was only **one** choice of military service for him.

It's difficult to comprehend the eagerness of a boy of 13 to devote himself to military service but that's not the way Pole- Carew sees it:

" The war was on. There was a war environment all round. In London there was a blackout and bombs were dropped nightly. You saw huge areas of devastation. My brother was in the Army; my sister was in the Wrens; my father was in the Army. Anybody of military age was in the services - no nonsense. It was total war. It was a way of life. Perhaps 13 was a young age at which to want to be involved but maybe because I had learned self-reliance so early I made my mind up earlier."

So, in 1944, Christopher took the Common Entrance Exam for Public Schools and qualified for the Royal Naval College , Dartmouth - except the college was temporarily **not** at Dartmouth, but at Eaton Hall, Chester and he delights in telling the story of how that came about:

" Dartmouth College had been evacuated because the Germans had decided that it would be a very sound move to send an aircraft down the Channel, turn right at Dartmouth, turn left up the hill to the college and bomb it. The best time to do that, they resolved, was Evening Quarters on a Sunday, which was when we fell in before marching off to supper. If they timed it right they could kill off four years' worth of potential Navy officers with one bomb. The German High Command put this cunning plan into operation, but unfortunately for them they had not worked out the illogical

English way of doing things. Dartmouth had the normal boarding school holiday periods but because it was a naval college we had them to specific weeks which meant that every four years the summer holidays were one week out so we had eight weeks instead of seven weeks, to get us back into line with other schools. Trust the Germans to choose *that week* to go and bomb the college and drop a bomb smack in of the middle of it when there were no cadets there at all and they killed one pensioner!"

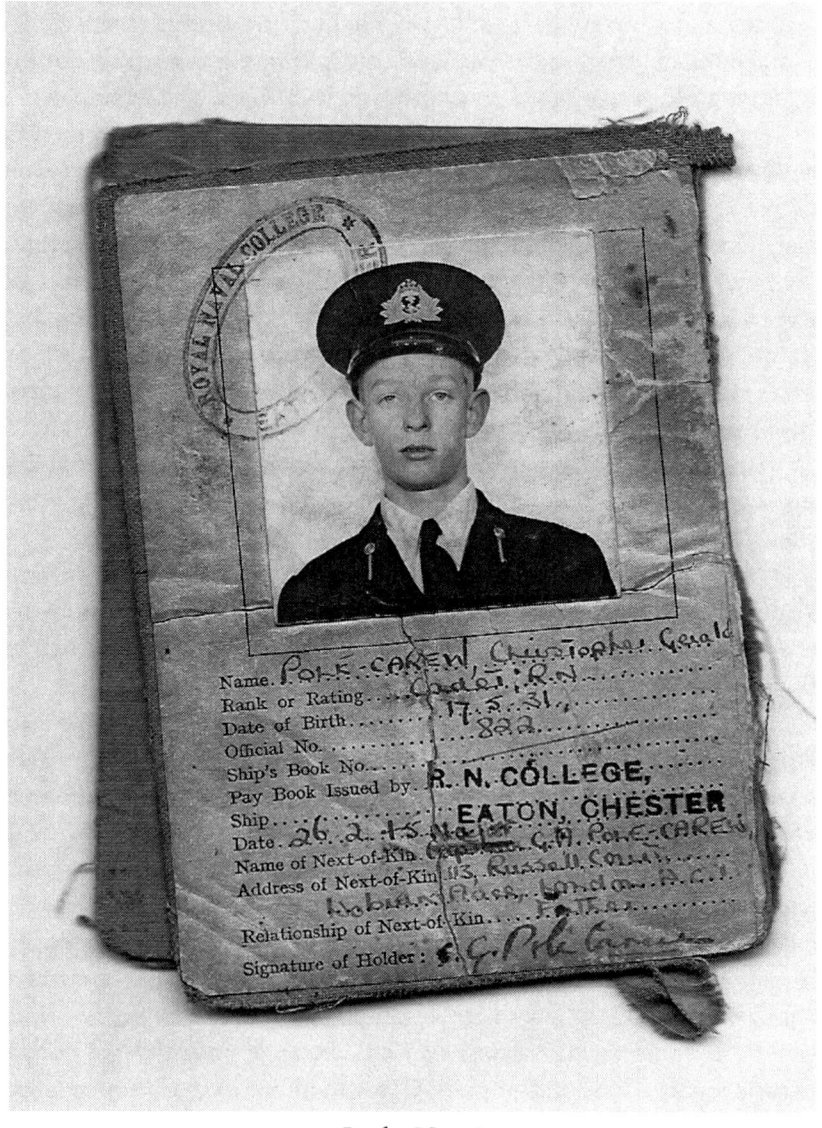

In the Navy!

In January, 1945, having passed rigorous medical and psychiatric tests, as well as the academic entrance exam, Christopher Pole-Carew became a Naval Cadet at the age of 13. He was one of only 44 out of more than 1,000 applicants to make it. The days that followed, with the college back at Dartmouth, are etched indelibly in his memory: "Dartmouth in those days was a kind of distortion of a normal public school because although the education was standard for boys aged 13 to 17, it was interlarded with naval and military activities.

Having been in boarding schools since I was four years old there seemed nothing odd about going off yet again, but Dartmouth **was** different. There was no possibility of misunderstanding: it was a Royal Naval establishment through and through with the sole objective of turning out a steady supply of thoroughly well grounded officers for the Royal Navy. Since this had been going on for over half a century, the system did just that.

"The source of pupils were mainly private preparatory schools, plus a few boys from grammar school. I suspect the reason for the proportions was that there was always a good supply of sons following officer fathers into the Navy and these would have been educated privately. Also, for a boy to get into Dartmouth was seen by prep school headmasters as the equivalent in status of a good scholarship to an ordinary public school. I doubt if the average grammar school boy would have valued it quite so highly.

"The war was still on when we sat the Common Entrance exam in December 1944, with the medical interview just before Christmas at Oxford. My father took me down; we stayed at Campion Hall, which I seem to remember was a hot bed of Roman Catholicism with someone reading something to us in Latin throughout the evening meal!

"Your first two terms were in Drake House, where you found your feet before going on to one of the proper houses - Blake, Hawke, Exmouth (I was in Exmouth) , Grenville and St. Vincent. Drake was inside the massive Eaton Hall home of the Dukes of Westminster, as were all the classrooms, whilst the other houses were sited in army huts in the grounds.

"We were taught the usual subjects - Maths, Science , French, etc but also Navigation and Seamanship.

Navigation was hard: Spherical Trigonometry, which is Trigonometry but with the circumferences of circles - the surface of the earth - as the sides of the triangles; the theory behind sun and star sights; how to use a sextant. In those days, navigation was all about taking sun and star sights, clouds permitting.

"Seamanship was much more fun: How to drop and weigh anchor, tying knots, sending away seaboats, what to do in a hurricane - all taught by Chief Petty Officer Marks.

"Chief Petty Officer Marks had joined the Navy in the days of sail. He was a huge, fat amiable Westcountryman with massive hands and fingers like bananas, with which he spliced enormous bits of rope with the greatest of ease. Spelling had largely passed him by - the Admiralty having acknowledged that he was skilful enough to serve the Navy without having to waste his time reading things, which he had officers to do for him - and the cadets used to tease him, asking him how to spell things like " oid beckert " (*hide becket ,to those outside the Westcountry! It was a leather strip that joined the rope to the lead weight on a depth sounding line*) He would reply that 'lettering weren't much use in a storm at sea.' Another favourite saying of his was:' Them 'aint barrels, them's ca-rr-sks.' He was a lovely man.

"Dartmouth was also remarkable for the outstanding visiting lecturers it attracted: Peter Scott, of bird fame, who was also a very gallant Motor Torpedo Boat captain; Earl Mountbatten, the last Viceroy of India; Louis Ketner, on classical music - to say nothing of Royal visits and being inspected by the King.

"Drill was carried out before breakfast in winter in the dark.If you need to learn to obey orders without thinking, doing it when you couldn't see where you were going was no bad way!

"Every moment was disciplined, nor was any minute left unoccupied: starting with cold baths at 7am; breakfast served by Wrens (*Yes! And they made our beds too!)* followed by Divisions (' *Parade will close for Prayers' to the tune of Lillibolero played by the Royal Marines Band*) It was :" Fall out the Roman Catholics, which meant all non-Anglicans, including the occasional Sikh or Muslim from the "Benbows", the 17 year entry.

"As a Christian Scientist I was tempted to join Lou Brotherton and Basil Longy of our term (busily crossing themselves) but I preferred to stay incognito, muttering "forgive our debts" instead of trespasses in the Lord's Prayer, to confirm my secret upholding of the real true faith!

" Instruction (lessons) started, when you fell in outside the classroom, were brought to attention (*'Class 3/2 E French ready for Instruction*, **Sir!***)* and marched in to sit at your desk to attention, arms folded. In the afternoon it was Compulsory Games. Prep finished at 2030 with Rounds at 2100 with all cadets lying in bed **to attention** (*it's true – honestly!*);

their clothes laid out in their sea chests, open for inspection. Right. Keep silence. And sleep until cold bath time.

" Sundays were different. We would have a first inspection by your Cadet captain (prefect) then fall in for Division, inspected by your House Officer *(much more important than a Housemaster)* then inspected by the Captain of the College. Then you would march off to chapel, which filled the time nicely till lunch. In the afternoon we had spare time and we'd bicycle out to nearby farms to gorge ourselves on Devonshire cream teas. After tea it was Evening Quarters and another quick inspection before being marched off to supper. Then it was back into normal routine, lying to attention in bed for Rounds except that, being Sunday, your sea chest was allowed to be shut, although you couldn't relax because it was always likely to be opened for a spot check. And then… Right. Keep silence. And sleep until cold bath time."

Dartmouth College in those days was run with a rigid, almost overwhelming discipline in which beatings (with a cane) were frequent. The punishment rituals would, in today's totally different society, lead to *shock/horror/scandal* headlines but Pole-Carew recalls that the disciplinary methods were totally acceptable to everyone.

He says: " Something like 1200 boys had applied for the 44 places in the term that started on January 18th, 1945 and we all knew that we were the select elite few who were good enough. There wasn't a hoop made that we wouldn't have jumped willingly through. The education was outstandingly good and that was helped even more by the pupils' total dedication. Even at 13, we believed that if you didn't give of your best at all times it would 'affect your future career': virtually every one of us was determined to become an Admiral (after a few inevitable intervening years, of course!) All in all, it was not a bad basis for pushing knowledge into us.

"There was very little spare time. A 'log' was kept of whatever exercise we took of an afternoon; the requirement was three and a half 'logs' a week. Football, rowing and sailing counted as one. Squash was a half. Failure to achieve the three and a half automatically meant being beaten by the House Cadet Captain, most of whom prided themselves on their whipping strength and accuracy.

"Beatings were routine and frequent as was the lesser (but considered worse) punishment of 'Slack Party' which was keeping silence at all meals; spending every moment of cherished spare time picking up rubbish;

even more kit inspections at inconvenient times and some brutally violent Physical Training in the afternoons.

" I ran an 'insurance book' to 'insure' my fellow cadets (premium 2d a week) against punishments: the pay-out was 3d for a beating, or 1d a cut, three being the minimum; 2d for a Slack Party. This went well for a time but eventually fizzled out amid much recrimination because I happened to be the most punished cadet in my term and therefore the main beneficiary!

"At some early point you had to make a decision whether to play cricket in the summer or opt for the 'River', which was rowing and sailing. I chose the 'River' and this was where Dartmouth was the most wonderful of all places to be for a teenage boy. We would run down the steps (about 200 of them) in fours to Sandquay where the boats were; boats of a seemingly unlimited number and variety; naval sea boats; cutters and whalers and gigs; dinghies, 35ft, 50 square metre yachts (reparations from the Germans) ,various motor boats and occasionally a frigate in harbour to sail around.

"I became Head of the River for my House and got my sailing colours, which together brought immense privileges : I could take out any boat I liked (no checks on manning or anything so pathetic as today's health 'n safety - just the assumption that you knew what you were doing); I could take a yacht or a sea boat out into the open sea, take a motor boat up to Totnes, organise sailing races up on the open waters at Dittisham. In my time, my House, Exmouth, won every cup for sailing and rowing and I got the Amaryllis Cup, awarded to the cadet in any year who showed the most seamanlike qualities. On the river, my happiness was total.

"Also at Sandquay were the engineering workshops: all cadets did a week's engineering each term, working their way through the various processes: machine shop, foundry, pattern making, tin smiths (I still have the box I made there), drawing office (" *It'aint symmetrical about the centre line - do it again."*) and lectures on the internal combustion engine.This was another haven of Heaven in that most wonderful of schools.

" Dartmouth had its own pack of beagles, for hunting hares, known as the Britannia Beagles. In the House of Commons, the traditional way of raising a question about Dartmouth was to ask the Minister of Defence whether the Britannia Beagles were paid for by the Admiralty (they weren't: the cadets, or rather their parents, paid for them). Having received that standard reply, the next step was to ask a Supplementary Question, eg. 'Is it true that the cadets sleep with the Wrens ' or whatever!

" We were paid one shilling a week, for which we had to Pay Parade in alphabetical order: One pace forward March, off cap, pay book placed on top :'Pole-Carew, 822E, Sir." On cap, double away. *Next…*

"Incidentally, the number was my Dartmouth number and no more. In those days Naval Officers didn't have numbers, ratings did and so did Army and Air Force officers but we were considered to be individuals, not numbers. Nice touch!

"Another number of great importance was the one given to you before joining Dartmouth by Gieves, the naval outfitters, who seemed to know all about you before even the Admiralty had managed to tell you! Gieves made all naval officers' uniforms and held them in an iron grip throughout their careers - largely through an amazingly tolerant policy regarding the paying of their bills (two or even three years late was not uncommon!)

"Nowadays people whinge about too many exams. For heaven's sake - they don't know the half! We had monthly orders pinned up on the House notice boards, half term reports with your Tutor (one of the masters who was specifically concerned with your non-Naval education and end of term exams.)

"If you stepped out of line from a disciplinary point of view you were in trouble with your House Officer and this could go to the Commander of the College or even to the Captain - at which point, God help you! This probably meant' Bye, bye Dartmouth' with as much humiliation as possible.

"They also had the ultimate punishment of 'Official Cuts.' This only happened to one cadet in my time there…for getting caught in a compromising position with one of the Wrens (he was obviously well developed for his age!) The offender reported to the gym where the Commander of the College and all the House Officers, all wearing swords and medals, were lined up in the gallery. The offender was held down over a vaulting horse by two burly PT instructors while the punishment was administered by the Chief PT Instructor.

After each stroke of the cane he reported to the Commander :
'One cut delivered, Sir'
'Carry on with the punishment.'
'Aye, aye, Sir'
"And so on until the punishment had been meted out.
"Who says we haven't gone soft!
"Punishments for educational failing were, frankly, non - existent, except for a talking to by one's tutor, but there was always the ultimate

sanction of being put down a term – ie. marking time for one term. On the face of it, this was not too serious, though you were left behind educationally while all those you had joined with went on, but there was one built-in sting:the time taken for the unfortunate cadet to become an Admiral was extended by four months; in one's early teens, a very serious delay!

"We had a Gunroom,which is the name of the midshipman's mess in a ship, which was simply lockers on the wall and tables where we read and did prep every evening finishing at 8.30pm, which gave half an hour to get washed and into bed, lying to attention with your sea chest open for inspection at 9pm. Then lights out.

"Our block was up the hill at the back of the College, looking straight out to sea with no land until you reached South America. In summer, all windows in the dormitories were opened at the top on both sides, thus allowing plenty of health giving fresh air. In winter, we were permitted to have every other window shut so the fresh air blew through the dormitory diagonally, thus slowing it down a bit!

"The time cadets customarily spent at Dartmouth was eleven terms but the war having ended and the Navy reduced in size there were more junior officers than ships for them to go to and some genius civil servant found a solution - make cadets do 12 terms instead. My year was the first to have to do 12 terms. It was brought in suddenly, with no warning, so there was no education syllabus for us and we were given the option of a series of special subjects with which to occupy the extra term. I chose 'The Evolution of the Fighting Ship' (gripping stuff!) and Heraldry, which I also studied at Greenwich (in those days the Navy's equivalent of a bit of university experience and suitably sited within easy reach of London's fleshpots!) Heraldry remains an interest and fascination of mine to this day."

So how much talent and potential did young Pole - Carew show at Dartmouth Naval College?

" Not enough to indicate a future Admiral!" he says.

" There was one period when I was accused of organising a gang - no doubt, they thought, with nefarious aims. Astonishingly, this was considered a heinous act, but what greater demonstration of leadership qualities could you show in a college designed solely to turn out military leaders?"

Nevertheless his time at Dartmouth Naval College is etched indelibly in Pole-Carew's memory as a great experience:" Yes, the discipline at Dartmouth was harsh and the routine and pressure unrelenting but we didn't mind that and I now count the joys and benefits of those of us who had the good fortune to have gone there.

" We all knew we were special and that from there we were to become officers in the finest Navy in the world - so great was it that to this day the **Royal** Navy is called just that, while every other nation with a navy is obliged to put their country in their title."

Of the many and varied experiences in such a remarkable life, being an officer cadet at Dartmouth College in the 1940's remains among the most indelible and fond of his memories.

When he was 17, young Pole-Carew headed for sea at last. His term became cadets in the training cruiser HMS Devonshire. They joined her in Devonport in 1949. It was a rude awakening to some of the realities of seaborne life, such as scrubbing ice-covered decks in bare feet at 6.30 in the morning. However, that was to change dramatically for the better when they sailed for the West Indies, first stop Trinidad; the joy of the warmth of the Tropics and not a little excitement, such as the day they were painting the ship's side off Barbados on a stage lowered over the bows.

Two of the cadets, Pole-Carew and John Ford, painted happily, though every so often a wave washed over them and took off the paint, so that they had to start again.

Pole-Carew recalls : "Suddenly, shouts from above told us to finish painting, which we did reluctantly and taking our time. Then the shouts became more urgent. We were not allowed to climb up the stage ropes to return on board because that would have spoiled the paintwork, so we had to swim to the gangway at the stern of the ship, some five minutes distant, which we did - to be greeted with curses for having taken so long.

" When we reached the upper deck we discovered the urgency for our return…there below us, cruising to and fro off the side of the ship, were three very healthy and no doubt hungry sharks!

" The Captain of HMS Devonshire was St John Cronyn, a man with a fine war record and something of a martinet – but also a martyr to gout! In harbour, the Watch was kept by an officer and various seamen on the Quarter deck, the stern of the ship, below which the Captain's cabin was situated. And God help anybody who dared disturb him! The area directly above was roped off and all hands who used the Quarter deck wore gym shoes (trainers) and talked in hushed, muttered voices. Quite right, too!"

At 18, Pole - Carew became a Midshipman in the flagship of the America & West Indies Squadron, HMS Glasgow: "Naval life in those days had so very much to offer. No student today could possibly envisage a gap year to compare - and all paid for by Her Majesty's Government at the rate of 7s 6d a day, or the cost of a rum and coke in a smart bar in Nassau, Bahamas! Sixpence in Jamaica!

"Imagine being in command of a ship's motor boat with your crew of four sailors, all about the same age, to-ing and fro-ing from ship to shore. Imagine, with a bunch of friends, taking a sailing boat away to camp over a weekend on a desert island in the West Indies, catching your food by netting it from the sea; knocking down coconuts to drink the milk then eventually sailing warm, tired and happy back to your ship.

"Sure, they did some perfunctory exercises with the Americans, but our main aim was to " show the flag" to our many possessions - in our case the islands of the West Indies, bringing much pleasure and great parties to so many people."

He laments: *" In those uncomplicated days of Empire, before jealousy and greed crept in, people still enjoyed the wonderful things that life had to offer."*

Midshipmen had to keep a journal of their sea time. This was obligatory, the object being to train the young sailors in "the power of observation; the power of expression and the habit of orderliness."

The journals were subject to frequent inspection by officers and occasionally by the Captain.

A glance through Pole-Carew's journal of his time aboard HMS Glasgow reveals a young man in love with the sea and the life it afforded; a confident, able young man taking all in his stride and enjoying every minute of the sort of social life, especially ashore, of which landlubber contemporaries back home must have been deeply envious.

For example, he describes an idyllic Christmas in Bermuda (though, today, he denies any memory of appearing in HMS Glasgow's pantomime, a "hugely successful" production in which he played the Fairy Godmother!). His journal tells how after the final performance the cast went on to a cocktail party still wearing their costumes. Sadly there are no pictures of this event. Had there been, they would have fetched a pretty penny among those who worked with him later in his life!

That Christmas Day he went swimming in the warm, welcoming sea and his journal recalls the joy of it all.

The next move in his naval career was to Greenwich Naval College as a sub- lieutenant. He describes Greenwich as " a reward given to junior officers who had missed out on a spell at a university by being at sea and so were given their own potted equivalent, complete with adjacent fleshpots up the road in London."

He recalls "many a trip with my good friend Bill Swinley who owned a car - rare in those days - and welcomed the running costs being shared.

"Greenwich was two terms of genuine fun, interspersed with some serious work and thought- provoking study, such as writing a thesis on Jane Austen, plus sessions called The Junior Officers' War Course which were aimed mainly at teaching junior officers to make accurate decisions quickly under pressure; no bad thing.

"The constant round of training led next to technical courses:

Gunnery, Torpedoes and Anti-submarines' Flying, Navigation, Signals and so on; the bread and butter knowledge of the Navy behind the also unremitting training to lead and to command, which in civilian life is called Management, but is never actually taught there."

The next step for junior officer Pole-Carew was to volunteer for submarines, which he describes as " that secret navy within the Navy."

Why did he join submarines? He says he's not quite sure but, as he stands **6ft 5ins** tall, it could not have been for comfort!

The fact that it meant a four month course in England, which would keep him near a certain Gill Burton (who had become rather important to him) must have had some influence on the decision; maybe the extra pay submariners got also helped make up his mind.

"More to the point," he says, "was the fact that in a changing Navy, sea going opportunities - and particularly the chance of commanding ships - were getting more and more scarce.

" Certainly, submariners took on much greater responsibilities in their duties than did their equivalents in age and rank on the surface in the General Service. So, if you took your career seriously it made sense to go for the specialisation with the best prospects."

There followed four months at Gosport, across the water from Portsmouth, in HMS Dolphin, the Naval Submarine Headquarters where he " learned all about trimming a boat (adjusting its weight of ballast until it weighed 'nothing' in the sea); navigating under water (which meant taking tides and currents *very* seriously) and knowing where to point a torpedo so that it hits its moving target…and still within range of evening visits to London!"

Much as he enjoyed, as have so many young men, the attractions of an occasional night out in London it was not to the metropolis that Christopher Pole - Carew was drawn on leave.

Since he was 13 he had spent most of his leaves with Uncle Herbert and Aunt Joan Hudson at their beautiful home, Great Ruffins at Wickham Bishops in Essex. Perhaps it was because here, in the company of the wonderfully eccentric Hudsons, he found the warmth and jollity he had missed out on as a boy or maybe it was the sheer unbridled fun he had staying with the madcap couple who were not real uncle and aunt " but such close family friends as to be considered relatives." Whatever the reason, he made for the magical Great Ruffins with its 11 acres of gorgeous gardens at every opportunity.

Uncle Herbert was an eccentric from the days when England specialised in them. Unspecifically old, he had a shock of wild white hair, as did Aunt Joan. They were surrounded by pets; dogs sleeping in their bedrooms; cats constantly having kittens under their billiard table, Polish bantams wandering around the house. So naïve were this dotty duo that when one of her King Charles Spaniel bitches ,Tina, kept getting pregnant Aunt Joan professed surprise and bewilderment because the suspected dog, Jamie. slept on a separate sofa.

Uncle Herbert used to say that he had inherited three fortunes and been taxed out of two of them. He told of having been in California when Los Angeles was still a village. He had served his Queen (and King) and country three times…the 1896 Ashanti Expedition , the Boer War and the Great War – incidentally in the Duke of Cornwall's Light Infantry with the Pole-Carew brothers.

By 1939, Uncle Herbert considered he had done his bit, but he might have taken up arms again had he known that because his house had a lookout tower from which you could see over the surrounding countryside and because he was so overtly eccentric he was seriously, but totally erroneously, investigated by the police who thought he could well be a German spy! Fortunately, he never did learn of this. Aunt Joan firmly suppressed it.

Later, when the Home Guard was using Great Ruffins' tower as a look-out post, Uncle Herbert insisted that while the officers could use a lavatory in the house, other ranks had to use a bucket in a room at the top of the tower, but took no account of the need to empty it.The other ranks' revenge for this discriminatory treatment was to empty the bucket by tipping it over the side of the tower, with no regard for whatever or whoever happened to be below. This would occur without the knowledge of Uncle Herbert and to the great amusement of his young friends.

Keeping suitably acclimatised in such a vast old house was difficult and the Hudsons' solution was to move around the interior in deference to the season. Thus, Uncle Herbert had his winter bedroom, his summer bedroom and so forth. So did Aunt Joan. For some reason known only to himself, Uncle Herbert's winter billet was a dank room next to the scullery in the servants quarters and when the old boy eventually went to meet his maker many years later, his wife was adamant that he would never have done so had he not refused an electric blanket because he thought that was too risky.

Christopher Pole-Carew recalls:" To celebrate the end of the war, the Hudsons gave a dance. It was a great excitement - the first party of its kind for six years!

"Everybody brought food and drink. Rationing was still very much in full swing and it would have been impossible for any family to provide them from their own resources so it was very much a pooled effort. There was dancing in the library, with little parties gathered in different parts of the house and carefully hoarded alcohol flowed freely. One unfortunate younger guest was given a weak gin and orange, which he topped up from a water bottle standing nearby. When he was eventually too drunk to stand, someone noticed that the water bottle actually contained a secret supply of neat gin. My goodness. The scandal!

"The Montgomeries (cousins) were blamed and were all but banned from Great Ruffins for ever. Indeed, whenever their name was mentioned the incident was cited by Aunt Joan as evidence of their dissolution and carelessness."

On one of his first visits to Great Ruffins young Christopher met Gill Burton, the 13- year- old daughter of a local fruit farmer, Clive Burton. Her father was getting in his apple crop and used two young volunteers, Christopher and 'Ginge', the local solicitor's son, to strip the trees after the piece workers had been through. The boys were paid 4d a bushel for hard apples and 5d for soft ones.

He takes up the story: "This was difficult, hard work - for pennies, so much of our time was spent lying under the apple trees eating the crop! On one such occasion we were surprised by Gill riding quietly up to us through the grass on her smart pony, all properly turned out in jodhpurs and hard hat. As the farmer's daughter, she hardly deigned to notice the two boys now reduced to casual labourers and swept by with her pretty nose firmly in the air. Shamefaced, we went hurriedly back to work, dreading that we might be reported. I think this might have been when Cupid's dart first struck. After that, we met socially and played tennis together."

Gill says that it was while staying with Aunt Joan and Uncle Herbert in 1947 that she first met Christopher properly:"Aunt Joan and Uncle Herbert gave marvellous parties for all ages with guests bringing jellies, sandwiches and drink, mostly soft. There was dancing to a gramophone operated by Moore, the gardener, dressed in Uncle Herbert's family footman's uniform of blue tail coat, yellow and black striped waistcoat and breeches.

"I was dancing 'Strip the Willow' with my father, who was tone deaf, when Uncle Herbert got bored with the party and wanted to go to bed so he told Moore to change the record to 'God Save The King.' To my great embarrassment, my father went on dancing, not noticing the change of tune.

"Christopher was there for the summer and as there were several of us we played tennis and picnicked. Then in 1948 my family emigrated to South Africa."

Clive Burton was a very interesting and innovative man. He pioneered farmers' co-operatives in Britain, particularly applicable to fruit farmers, giving them joint packing facilities and when South Africa was building up its fruit export trade after the war, he was invited to go out there to give the benefit of his expertise and experience. This led to the creation of Outspan, the huge citrus co-operative. Clive Burton was to spend 25 years in South Africa - a business acumen and talent lost to Britain after he got seriously frustrated with the new Labour Government which decided to import plums from Holland, thus wrecking the value of his own, particularly good, crop which was left to rot on the trees.

The Burtons had been mid 19th Century tobacco importers and manufacturers of pipe tobacco (Alfred Burton, at 21, having married into the Pritchard family of tobacco importers in 1853) and being made a partner in what became Pritchard and Burton, a company which had, among many interesting distinctions, given Charlie Chaplin his first job as a boy. When Chaplin revisited the firm's Farringdon Road factory as a world famous Hollywood film star in the 1920's he was told by the Foreman of the cutting room :"You're the lad I kicked out for always acting the fool!" A very successful fool, it had transpired!

Soon after being made a partner, young Alfred Burton made a spectacular buy of raw tobacco which had a dramatic impact on the future prosperity of the firm. He heard that a ship had arrived at London Docks with a cargo of Indian tobacco reputed to be damaged by sea water, which was to be auctioned as salvage. He bought the entire cargo at a very low price and when it was delivered to the factory it was found that the water damage was only superficial but the quality of the leaf, very dark in colour with a strong aroma, was totally different to tobacco usually bought from Virginia. To utilise this bargain buy, small quantities were blended into an existing pipe mixture that had been on the market for many years. The new blend - *Boar's Head Shag* - became hugely popular, the firm's best selling line, and could still be obtained in London 150 years later, being manufactured by the company which took over the family business in 1954.

Descendant Clive Burton brought that same entrepreneurial flair to the fruit business and South Africa's gain was definitely Britain's loss.

Daughter Gill went with him to South Africa in 1947 and was thrilled to be flown low over giraffes to their new home in that beautiful country.

Her budding romance with young Pole - Carew would have been put on hold, anyway because by this time he was in the West Indies with the Navy.

The youngsters wrote letters to each other for three years then, when Christopher was at Greenwich, Gill returned to England and they were reunited in London. Says Gill: "I came back to the UK in 1951 and we met up again. I did a secretarial course at Queens Secretarial College in London and had a variety of jobs then went back to South Africa for eight months.

"I returned in 1953 for the Queen's Coronation, which Christopher and I saw from the Farmers' Club in Northumberland Avenue, running up to Trafalgar Square, as my father, who was a member, gave us tickets. We had wonderful seats on a balcony.

"It was drizzling so everyone in the procession of coaches and cars huddled under cover to keep dry - except for the Queen of Tonga! She, as a real queen, was quite close up to the front of the procession and she sat waving happily to everyone and totally ignoring the rain. She got tremendous cheers from everybody. She shared her coach with a very elderly Raja or Nizam or whatever, who looked utterly miserable, getting wetter and wetter in all his finery."

In 1953, Christopher was appointed to HMS Trespasser, a T-class wartime submarine, as Third Hand. She was in dry dock in Portsmouth, refitting, with no Captain yet appointed but in the charge of Gervase Frere-Cook, the First Lieutenant.

This first job in submarines was an eye-opener: there was a shortage of submarine officers due to the sinking, first of the Truculent in the Thames

Estuary followed shortly after by the loss of the Affray, in the English Channel.

So Christopher Pole-Carew wasn't just another officer in Trespasser, he was the *only* other one which meant being Torpedo officer, Gunnery officer, Navigation, Confidential Books and Captain's Secretary, as well as being 50 per cent of the watch keeping officers.

When they sailed from Portsmouth to join the Third Submarine Squadron at Rothesay, Frere-Cook told him:" If you haven't got a watch keeping ticket, I'm watch-on-stop-on for the next two days, so you've just qualified!

"You've got the first watch. See you in four hours. You'd better learn fast or I'll make your life a misery."

He did learn fast – very fast.

Pole-Carew observes: " In those days, following on from the war, and with Governments still obsessed with the idea that Britain was still the great power it had once been, we still had five squadrons of submarines plus almost unlimited surface ships. The First Squadron at Malta, the Second at Portland, the Third at Rothesay (with special duties keeping an eye on the Russians based in the Kola Inlet in the north), the Fourth in Singapore and the Fifth at Gosport. There were also one or more each with the Canadians and Australians and constant advanced training for aircraft and surface ships, from Londonderry. Sadly, the number was unsustainable whilst also funding a Welfare State, but in those days, no-one was prepared to admit it."

The new Captain of the Trespasser was Lieutenant Commander Leo Temple-Richards. Pole-Carew remembers him as " a lovely person but suffering from worry that he might not get promoted to Commander and his time for doing so was running out (sadly, he didn't make it). This invariably caused strain because everybody was driven that much harder to prove that the Captain was that much more efficient."

Young Pole-Carew got on very well with Temple-Richards - which was just as well, as later events were to show.

The Engineer Officer, Harry O'Dell was a Commissioned Warrant Officer. He had made his way up from the lower deck to Commissioned rank, wearing the single gold stripe of a sub-lieutenant. He had been conscripted into submarines in 1931 (the year Pole-Carew was born!) had hated them from the beginning and still did. " Be that as it may," says Pole-Carew," there was nothing he didn't know about submarines and he'd survived the war."

Life in submarines back then was " hard "

Nowadays, although it's still no picnic, submariners enjoy considerably more comforts, much more time and labour saving technical equipment and comparative luxuries such as Sat- Nav.

Pole-Carew's generation navigated the hard , time-honoured way by the sun and the stars, plotting their own courses "in longhand."

The demand of the watches meant two hours on watch, four off, which (including the time to turn over your watch meant, in effect, three hours on/ three hours off) made the maximum sleep break being just three hours.

"We used to reckon that if you managed four and a half hours sleep in a 24 hour period, you were lucky. One of the side effects of this was that one ate a tremendous amount. We had what they called 'submarine comforts' which we highly prized… lots of soup, especially during night watches, or extra 'Ki', which was a particularly virulent form of immensely thick and quite delicious cocoa beloved by all who kept cold watches. We used to have fruit juice, which was to make up for our not seeing any daylight, at least that's what those who knew about such things thought. Nobody in a submarine saw daylight, except for officers when they kept watch. They used to say you could always tell the officers when they came ashore because they were the only ones with sun-burned eye balls from looking through the periscope.

" Occasionally we ran on the surface and in Trespasser - which was a 1939/45 war submarine, with the old fashioned bridge, no streamlined fin over the periscope standards - being on the surface was an experience. I can remember seas so strong they smashed part of our casing (the outside structure) and you went up there with a safety belt and you lashed yourself on and every now and then waves would break right over you. So, you could spend time at sea wet, damp, lacking sleep, keeping interminable watches and in between trying to get all your other work done."

For young Pole-Carew, the physical discomforts were not helped by being six feet five inches tall in a working environment in which even short men had to stoop and having to grab what little sleep he got in a bunk five inches shorter than him, with a high pressure air valve protruding into its precious sleeping space : "I could only lie on my left side because where my knees bent was where the valve came in behind!

" But if you're tired enough - and I was - you'll sleep. No problem. And generally, when you're in your twenties you don't notice discomfort too much. But, yes, it was a hard life.

" You were deeply dependent on each other and that inter-dependence was one of the best things about being in submarines. For example, we didn't have any of the normal, formal discipline that the Navy had in the sense of the distance between officers and ratings. We used to go for runs ashore and there would be officers and sailors all together. No pointless distinctions."

Christopher Pole - Carew was later to take " a tremendous amount" of his experience in submarines into his business life:" I believed absolutely in the way that submariners conducted their relations with each other, particularly communication. Life in submarines taught you to care genuinely about the problems and difficulties of those around you and you learned that when things went wrong that inter-dependence was crucially important."

He enjoyed his entire time in the Navy, he says, though " there were certain inefficient things, which I didn't like. There was a carelessness about the treatment of people which was unnecessary. OK, you're messed about because of the rigours of the service (*rights hadn't been invented then and when your parents signed you on at 13 you were in for life to do the Navy's bidding - end of subject*). That's one thing. But when you're messed about because of the incompetence of the staff officers that's another. And I saw quite a lot of that.

" For example, the whole Fleet's been out on exercises and it's coming home and just to sharpen them up, all submarines are sent out to sea to wait around and carry out 'attacks' on them to see if their anti-submarine defences are sound, etc. Right. Everybody knows when the Fleet is going to be where it is so the submarines don't have to go to sea for an entire weekend beforehand, hanging around doing absolutely nothing just because that suits the convenience of some staff officer when they could easily have gone out much later. So why mess up the lives of 80 people per submarine and their families just because someone didn't think things through."

Part of Trespasser's role was day running from Gosport, taking potential submariners out to exercise areas off the Isle Of Wight to practise diving and handling emergencies, generally getting back by dusk. This was a pleasant routine for Christopher Pole-Carew, especially since it was convenient for meeting Gill in London at weekends and in late 1953, "egged on by Gill" he decided to get married.

Before he could marry, however, there was a big hurdle to be cleared. He needed permission from his Captain. The Navy didn't really approve of officers getting married and most certainly not if they were under 25.

'Somebody Had To Do It'

In the Navy's eyes, Christopher Pole-Carew, at just 22, had no business getting married at all and should have been settling instead for an eight year engagement.

However, Captain Leo, with whom the young officer had such a good relationship, had a warm heart and felt that young love should have its way. So, after a lecture on the folly of taking on such responsibility at such a young age (which fell on totally unreceptive ears) he agreed and in due course the announcement "appeared in the respectable newspapers."

The Navy, however, felt differently.

One evening, as young Christopher was enjoying a glass of refreshment in the boat after Rounds, Captain Leo came down to tell him that he had just received a draft for him to be sent to Australia and what, he asked, did he think of that? Since this was just two months before his wedding day, the answer, not surprisingly, was *not a lot!*

His Captain then divulged that since Christopher's engagement had been announced, he had already turned down drafts for him to be sent first to Malta then to Canada. Now they wanted him out to Australia!

" Look here," Captain Leo told his young officer,"You are the onlyofficer left who started the commission with me and we've always got on well so as far as I am concerned, you will stay till we pay off."

The conflict and Captain Leo's winning of it, illustrates an interesting dichotomy in that while the Navy in those days was so regimented that it could conspire to prevent a young couple in love from marrying, it also vested so much power in the captain of a ship that he was very much his own master and could reject a call from his admiral on the disposal of one of his officers

So in 1954 the wedding of Christopher Pole-Carew and Gillian Burton went ahead and their married life started with flats in Portsmouth.

1954 - Wedding Day

Gill recalls: " First of all, we lived at Southsea in an apartment. The address was The Fernery, The Thicket, Southsea. It was owned by a lady with bright bottle- red hair and a face to match.

" We had a kitchen, sitting room and bedroom and shared a bathroom with the other tenants. The hot water came in at 5pm and if you were lucky the water was hot enough for the first bath - otherwise, you had had it! The kitchen had only cold water.

" We stuck it for a month then moved to more salubrious surroundings, still in Southsea. Our landlady here was an artist and she thought she'd try her hand at abstract painting, which she thought was a load of rubbish but others were making good money daubing colours around so why shouldn't she? I don't know whether she was successful or not; she certainly deserved to be!

" I remember the loneliness of Christopher being away at sea and going down to Southsea Front with the other wives, waiting for them to come into harbour so that we could wave to them.

" I gave my first supper party there for Leo and Geraldine Temple-Richards. He was Christopher's submarine Captain and I was rather nervous as they were so old (26 and 29) We were both 22!"

Then Pole-Carew transferred to Chatham after Trespasser paid off in Sheerness.

It is stark evidence of the way in which Britain's armed forces have been decimated since the 1950s to record that the Navy then had no fewer than **five** dockyard ports in the UK : Devonport, Portsmouth, Chatham, Sheerness and Rosyth, plus operating depots at Portland, Londonderry and Rothesay.

Christopher Pole- Carew, who served in all of them,today laments:" Oh, dear. Where *have* they all gone!"

The next step in his Naval career was to join HMS Thermopylae, one of the latest T- Conversion submarines " originally like Trespasser but cut in half, lengthened, streamlined (fewer torpedo tubes and no lovely 4 - inch gun!) with a fin streamlining the conning tower. So much faster, but fewer torpedoes."

H.M.S/m Thermopylae passing through the Kiel-Canal

Germany June 1955

Thermopylae fitted out in Chatham. And it was in that Kent Royal dockyard town that Delia, the Pole-Carew's first child, was born in 1955.

Says Gill: " We had a flat in Gillingham, owned by a charming old bachelor called Major Le Mesurier Sinkinson. He collected antique furniture and he bought houses to put his pieces in. Fine - until I left the washing machine running and flooded him out on the floor below!"

From there they moved to Portland and lived in " a lovely cottage" on the Came Estate, outside Dorchester.

Gill recalls: " In April, 1955 we moved down to Dorset and we were lucky to get a charming cottage on the Came Estate, belonging to Lady Christian Martin, through Christopher's family connections. Thermopylae was running from Portland so Christopher was stationed there. The Navy didn't acknowledge officers being married under the age of 25 so we had to find our own accommodation. We were there for 18 months and we had quite a lot of fun because, although there was only one other young married couple, we met a lot of young people through Lady Christian, who gave a party for us to meet the locals. The locals were very kind to us and especially to me when Christopher was away at sea and we still have friends from those days to this day.

" My father had made me a small allowance so I was able to have a Mother's Help which allowed me to go out from time to time. This was Doreen (known as Dor-dor). She was the 16-year-old daughter of a farm manager, who had never been outside Dorset. Dor-dor would take Delia out in the pram for walks in deepest rural Dorset dressed to kill in high heel shoes and lots of make-up. One day she asked me :'Mrs Pole - Carew, did you have lots of boy friends when you were young?' I was 23!

" Dor-dor's father told her that if ever she went to London (he had never been there, of course) she must only look straight ahead, never sideways, especially on escalators because if a strange man caught her eye, before she knew what was happening she would be a white slave in South America! "

Christopher also remembers those Dorset days and the rurally idyllic routines and rituals of the Came Estate very fondly: " When we first arrived Lady Christian Martin, having taken advice from her butler, Metcalfe, drove us down to Came Cottage, which had been kept as a sort of grown up doll's house for her children - who had long moved on. We were shown in and Lady Christian said: 'You'll need some help in the house.' At that, she went to the nearest cottage and knocked on the door. Out came Mrs

Duncan, the cowman's wife, who actually curtsied! ' Mrs Duncan, the Pole-Carews will need some help in the house,' said Lady Christian. 'Yes, my Lady,' said Mrs Duncan. And that was that. Organised. Say what you like, the feudal system had a lot going for it!"

Church - going in a time honoured manner was an important feature of life on the Came Estate. Services, in the estate's own village church, were every third Sunday in the month.

The vicar would arrive and wait outside the church for Lady Christian to arrive before following her in. She sat on the front pew on the left, with the Pole-Carews in the pew behind her. In the pew behind us was Metcalfe, who took the collection plate round. On the right side were the serried ranks of the estate staff, with their families (except the Duncans who, it was whispered, were Roman Catholics!) On days that Lady Christian had friends staying her guests took the Pole- Carew's pew, who took Metcalfe's, who moved back one. Occasionally, I would be at sea on a 'Church Sunday' and when next we met Lady Christian would ask why I had missed church. On being told why, she would invariably reply:'Well, don't let it happen too often. I shall expect you next month!'"

In the happy domestic routine of Came Cottage, Mrs Pole- Carew had one very strict household rule:" Baby Delia was not allowed to sleep in the spare bedroom, where I kept my clothes, because Gill said the smell of submarines, a finely distilled mix of diesel, battery gas and lots of bodies in close proximity, was bad for her!"

The Captain of Thermopylae was David Scott"incredibly laid back, utterly charming and permanently relaxed.

" He had been a Submarine Commanding Officer during the war. He was one of a number of 'boy COs', so called because they were so young, some only 23, the result of the very heavy losses that submariners on both sides of the war suffered constantly.

" The first Lieutenant, Sam Fry, had the idea of applying to Marconi to give Thermopylae a television set, the first to be operated under water. And they did. Black and white, of course. but in those days a set would have cost £100, a lot of money in the 1950s. An ordinary 'H' television aerial, normally fixed to chimneys on houses, was secured to the top of the radio periscope mast and along we went at periscope depth watching TV 38 feet below!

" One day Captain Scott lay stretched full out on the glass topped chart table in the Control Room saying:' *I've always wanted to drive a submarine in a horizontal position while watching television.*'Then there was an almighty crash as the glass chart table gave way, leaving me furious, with no method of spreading out my charts to navigate the submarine!

" One of the finer arts of navigating was doing it submerged and at dead slow speeds (to conserve the electric batteries). Tides and currents assumed enormous importance, especially with no opportunities for land fixes or sun or star sights. Satnav was nearly half a century away. There were limited areas close in with the Decca Navigator system and that was fine if you knew reasonably closely where you were – and were on the surface. If not, you could be up to 100 miles out ,on the wrong direction beam. Navigating across the Atlantic required a lot of inspiration and a good dose of luck if you had an overcast sky – ie. no sights at all (and not easy if you did, from the bridge of a violently rolling submarine). In such conditions, crossing to Bermuda and actually finding it was no mean feat, which, to everybody's surprise, I achieved!"

That memorable sea going trip was to be Christopher Pole-Carew's last in the Navy.

Having married young and become a father at 23, Lieutenant Pole-Carew was giving much more thought to the future than were his unmarried contemporaries, who simply enjoyed the hardworking but exciting and fascinating life beneath the waves. It seemed obvious that there was no alternative to the contraction of the Navy. Fewer ships meant less chances of fulfilling his ambition of commanding a warship. The removal of the distinction between different types of officer (Executive - renamed Seaman, Engineer or Supply) meant that - "quite rightly" - shore establishments would be most likely to be commanded by the relevant expert (eg. an engineer for a dockyard) rather than by an Executive Admiral or Captain.

He could rationalise all this as being "very sensible and forward looking", but at the same time recognised that it would have "devastating effects" on his Naval career prospects, with decreasing opportunities for what he regarded as worthwhile jobs and dramatically reduced promotion opportunities.

Today, he says stridently: " In the new egalitarian age the Navy was changing in other ways, too. There would no longer be officers who had joined at 13; a tradition ended by the Socialist Government of the day as being too socially selective - which was, of course, perfectly true but had, nevertheless, guaranteed the Navy a constant supply of superbly trained and deeply dedicated officers.

"We were probably the last who understood and truly believed in the maxim of serving King and Country, with all that genuinely meant: a selfless giving that has now ceased to exist, almost anywhere. Certainly, we never considered that we were answerable to politicians in any way."

This new Navy was no longer to Christopher Pole-Carew's liking and one August day he went to Captain David Scott and expressed his wish to resign his commission (leave the Navy). The captain's reply was : "Come back in two months and we'll discuss it."

In those days, officers didn't just resign; they asked permission to do so, with absolutely no certainty of it being granted. Indeed, at this time, in the aftermath of the losses from the Truculent * and Affray * submarine disasters , the chances were minimal.

(* *On January 12th, 1950 HMS Truculent was returning to Sheerness having completed trials after a refit at Chatham when she sank after colliding with the Swedish oil tanker Divina. Sixty four lives were lost in the collision.*

*On Monday, April 16th, 1951 HMS Affray left Portsmouth to take part in a training exercise with a class of young officers aboard and never returned. It is said that a message was sent saying ' We are trapped on the bottom' but that after a fruitless search for the submarine no survivors were found. She was eventually located in June, 1951 with a clean break three feet above the deck and a 10 inch hole through which, it was believed, she had taken in water. The conclusion was that metal fatigue had caused the loss. **Pole-Carew, however, describes that conclusion as "rubbish" and adds:" Her snort mast - to take air from the surface - was hit by a surface ship, probably without even knowing it, resulting in a fourteen inch diameter hole into the boat with no quick operating valve to shut it. She would have filled up and they would all have been drowned instantly. There was no possible way that any signal could have been picked up even if anyone had been alive; you would have to have been within four miles of her and pointing in the right direction with the right equipment to get it. She sank in Hurd Deep, a deep channel in the bottom of the English Channel, which would have made it even harder to pin point where she was. Inevitably, all submarines were immediately fitted with emergency quick acting hand operated valves to their snort masts: known, of course, as Affray valves!"**)

It was also assumed that those who had joined the Navy at 13 had done so for life .Getting out was, to put it mildly, going to be very difficult.

But two months later, Christopher Pole-Carew asked again.

" Right," said David Scott, "You obviously mean it so we'd better work out how to succeed with this. The starting point is your letter of resignation."

The captain went on:" You must understand that there are certain things that My Lords Commissioners of the Admiralty will not accept - and things that they believe in.

" Firstly, if you insist on saying that you want to leave because the Navy is incompetent or badly run you'll never get out because the Sea Lords don't accept it as being true - how *could* it be with them running the Navy! If you insist, you can say that *in your opinion* the Navy is badly run but I wouldn't advise it - even though officers are considered entitled to hold opinions of their own.

" Secondly, all Sea Lords have a built-in horror of the possibility of a Naval officer in full uniform selling matches off a tray outside the Admiralty in Whitehall. Not surprisingly, this has not yet happened and none of them want it to happen on their watch.

" So, let's make your letter deal with those two oddities. You will say that the Navy is a fine Service and one that you will be sad to leave, with the implication that family commitments make this step a pressing one. In the past, a lot of wealthy sons went into the Navy for a short spell then left to go and run their estates. The Sea Lords understand this as a thoroughly sound reason for leaving, so you should indirectly use it. Also, get a bit in saying that you waive all possible future claims for health (like getting TB from being in submarines) or past injuries. The civil servants will like that. And put this in:*'I have ample financial resources to support myself and my family while I settle into a new career.'* Don't forget to start in the proper manner :*' Sir, I have the honour to submit my request to resign my commission.'* And address it to me."

Surely with such sound and experienced advice heeded Lieutenant Pole-Carew's request to resign could not fail. He wrote the letter, exactly as instructed and gave it to Captain Scott who took it to the Captain of the Submarine Squadron who read it and observed :'It looks like Pole-Carew's got it right.' (meaning both the letter *and* leaving the Navy) and so it was forwarded to Flag Officer Submarines...

Who turned it down!

Despite that setback, the letter continued its way to the Admiralty where it was destined to meet some good luck. It happened that they were plotting the redundancy, in a year's time, of a lot of officers, what were to become known as the 'Golden Bowlers.' The idea of getting rid of one for nothing, even though he was a submariner, who were scarce, proved irresistible...

Application accepted!

Even then, the bureaucrats made the most of the opportunity to twist the knife with the churlish announcement that ' *Lieutenant Pole-Carew will be discharged from Her Majesty's Service on July 31st 1956* (a **year** later) *and shall be landed wherever the ship in which he is serving may be and shall make his own way home.*'

That turned out to be Bermuda. And Captain David Scott told Lieutenant Pole-Carew : *'If the civil servants in the Admiralty think that I'm going to sail across the Atlantic short of one watch keeping officer and my navigator they don't know much about real life at sea. So, Pole-Carew, I'm **hiring** you to help me get Thermopylae back to England* !'

And so Lieutenant Christopher Pole- Carew completed his last trip in the Navy.

(He left just before the Suez debacle blew up and Thermopylae went to sea at three hours notice to sit in the Straits of Gibraltar for the duration of the infamous Crisis, monitoring large numbers of Russian submarines making their way into the Mediterranean, with much greater risks than the British public appreciated at the time.)

Lieutenant Pole-Carew had started his Navy career as a boy of 13 chosen, because of his class, to be a leader of men. He ended his Navy career as a young man of 25, having become an accomplished submarine officer.

Now he was to be just *Mr* Christopher Pole-Carew, husband of Gill, father of Delia.

And doing what?

3

A NEW WORLD

The newspaper industry is a ruthless business and it seemed that I was getting acclimatised remarkably quickly!'

AT 25, having left behind a 12 year career in the Royal Navy and in need of a job, Christopher Pole-Carew's introduction to the entirely different world of business and commerce was inauspicious.

He became a £650-a-year Senior Management Trainee ("a euphemism for cheap clerical labour") in the Buying Department of Unilever ("a short but incredibly boring interlude learning almost nothing except that Audrey, who ran the records section, hated trainees.")

In young Pole-Carew's case, Audrey's antipathy to budding captains of industry manifested itself in making him check, manually and meticulously, through every single one of ***32,000*** files to ensure that they were all in correct numerical sequence, a morale breaking chore which someone without Pole-Carew's training in obeying orders would probably have found impossible to tolerate.

Fortunately, means of escape from this sort of tedium did not take long to materialise. Hugh Begg, a close friend (and another submariner to have borrowed and successfully employed Pole-Carew's by now tried, tested and trusted standard letter of resignation from the Navy) had recently joined the embryonic Research and Promotions Department of Kemsley Newspapers (publishers of the Sunday Times, the Empire News and a number of regional newspapers) in Grays Inn Road, a unit of four people headed up by James Benson, author of *Above Us The Waves*. It must have seemed like London at that time was awash with dashing young submariners recently liberated from the Royal Navy by the same letter of resignation.

Hugh Begg reported that the newspaper world was interesting and lively and could represent a good career move for his friend Pole-Carew who agreed and after a successful interview with Michael Renshaw (" a charming Old Etonian who fiddled constantly with a pair of those folding spectacles that fit into a minute match box") was appointed to the City Office.

Never in his wildest dreams had Christopher Pole-Carew, product of the landed gentry, officer and gentleman, imagined that he would ever become a salesman...*"UGH!"*

But he had. And to his surprise, he found it fascinating and thoroughly enjoyable. His job in the City Office of Kemsley Newspapers was selling advertising space specialising in financial matters (Chairmans' Reports, Unit Trusts, etc) from an office up three flights of ancient wooden stairs in Old Jewry, near the Bank Of England. The daily work schedule started with checking the Financial Times to see which companies were holding their annual general meetings that day then attending one, possibly two, to try to persuade the chairman to have his speech published in the advertising columns of the Sunday Times or a relevant regional daily newspaper - "after which one repaired to Coates' Wine Bar on London Wall for much needed refreshment."

Here, young Pole-Carew's well-honed Naval drinking ability proved very valuable. All London's financial advertising reps congregated at Coates'- the most senior one being Ken Braddon of the Daily and Sunday Express who had his special place at the end of the bar where he drank gin and tonics, to which he rationed himself by keeping the lemon from each fresh drink in his glass. When there was no more room left in the glass to accommodate another gin, it was time to go back to the office and prepare to go home.

These were happy times for Christopher and Gill Pole-Carew who had gone to live with Aunt Joan and Uncle Herbert at Great Ruffins, within railway commuting distance of Christopher's new job, while they looked for a house of their own.

" The relaxed eccentricity of Great Ruffins suited us, with Uncle Herbert's armorial pennant flying over the front door in greeting and Aunt Joan's Polish bantams, with feathers on their heads instead of combs, coming downstairs as one went in. There were also snippets of excitement such as when Mrs Heron, whose daughter Elizabeth was a close friend of ours, called round unannounced one day when everyone was around the table enjoying supper, barged in, pulled up a chair, sat next to Aunt Joan and proceeded to chatter non-stop. What she said was not recorded but suddenly Uncle Herbert, his thick white moustache bristling, leapt to his feet, scattering the dogs, and roared :*' **Maarm! Get off my land! At once!**' Mrs Heron, to her great credit, didn't take offence but retired with considerable grace, leaving everyone to finish their meal as if nothing had happened. Less relaxing, however, was when our daughter Delia, by this time aged three, picked the heads off all Aunt Joan's prize black tulips on the day the garden was to be opened to the public for charity. For a vague, myopic old lady dressed like a tramp, Aunt Joan, when cross, could make her feelings known beyond any doubt!

" But all in all, Aunt Joan and Uncle Herbert were pleased to have us there. Aunt Joan liked 'a man about the house.' For instance, the dome on their house needed painting. Well, not everyone's prepared to shin up a ladder, walk around without any scaffolding and paint it - but I did. That suited her. I was happy. And it was Gill's old stamping ground from her childhood, before her parents emigrated."

Enjoyable though life was for them at the gloriously wacky Great Ruffins, it was time for the Pole-Carew's to acquire property of their own.

Christopher's salary at that time was only £750 pa. A sensible purchase would have been a semi-detached property within easy commuting distance of the City, but the only similarity between Christopher Pole-Carew and a semi-detached outlook on life was the hyphen. Instead, he bought Kingsdon Hall, a huge, dilapidated old house with 10 bedrooms and an acre and a half of garden, at Potter Street near Harlow New Town. This ramshackle pile had been owned by a Mrs McCorquadale, who had died. Her son wanted to clear up her affairs without delay and though he was asking £4,000 he accepted Pole-Carew's offer of £2, 500.

Christopher got a mortgage of £1000 from his father's solicitor and Gill's father lent them another £1000. Nevertheless, both sets of parents were shocked, both subscribing to the semi-detached solution and both thought that the young Pole-Carew's were off their heads.

It was not the last time they were to share that view and Christopher recalls how, later, at the christening of their son Peregrine, born in 1957, " the two grandfathers sat together drinking copious quantities of champagne while agreeing that we should have offered them only sherry since we clearly couldn't afford the champagne!"

Along with Kingsdon Hall, as part of the fixtures, came Edwards, the gardener. They also had a nanny and a daily.

Gill confesses: " We had delusions of grandeur as we thought we must have a dressing room and suitable rooms for the children and the staff seemed to go with the house."

The old retainer Edwards gave Pole-Carew a problem:" What could I do? I wasn't earning enough to support a wife and child in comfort, let alone a nanny, a daily help *and* a gardener so I had to do the unforgivable and give poor Edwards his notice.

"However, the timing was brilliant because the week I was to tell him, old Edwards won a large sum of money on the "Find The Ball" competition in the Sunday Empire News and had decided to end his working days anyway!"

Whether this absolutely amazing coincidence ever fully occurred to the old boy is neither here nor there because he was able to tell the new owner that he was quitting work, never knowing that he was about to be sacked.

"And that," says Christopher Pole-Carew " was just as it should be."

So was what Gill describes as " coming down to earth."

"After a couple of years we moved to a more suitable house - The Gables in Great Chesterford near Saffron Walden, which cost £4,200. We sold Kingsdon Hall to a journalist and his wife for £5,250 so we did quite well out of it. The journalist, his wife and small daughter had been living in a one roomed flat in the Grays Inn Road - so now, they were going to have plenty of room!"

Back at Pole-Carew's work, the head of the Financial Advertisement Department left and was replaced by Johnny Johnson, the Number Two. Things continued much as before, with get-togethers in the wine bar taking up even more time, this indulgence assisted by the fact that the office had moved to London Wall, where Coates' was situated.

By this time, Pole-Carew had pretty much opted out of the general run of the office and his primary job now was selling advertising for the Empire News, which he did with some success, simply by making so many calls that he couldn't fail to secure an increase in business.

"Also," he recalls, " although I enjoyed a gin and tonic , I actually felt the need to do some work as well!

" The atmosphere in the office deteriorated and one day the rep for the Sunday Times, the truly delightful ex-Eton and Guards' Ned Boldero, said to me that something should be done about it.

" His idea was that *I* should see Michael Renshaw, tell him about the state of things in the office and suggest that *I* should replace Johnny as the manager. He thought that I should be the one to do this as I was the senior but if I didn't, then he would do it instead. Well, what a choice. Sell out your boss and get promoted - or watch someone else do it!

"The next day, Friday, I went to see Michael Renshaw, whose only comment was :" What shall we do with Johnson? " to which my reply was: " It's a big company. There must be a niche for him somewhere."

" On the Monday, Renshaw sent for me and handed me the draft of an internal company circular which said that it had been decided that considerably more impetus should be given to the Empire News and to this end, Mr Johnson, as the top salesman in the City Office, was being taken off all other duties so as to concentrate on this highly important task. In order to make this possible, Mr Pole-Carew would take over as Head of the Financial Advertisement Department. So, Johnny moved out of his personal office into the general office and I moved in.

"The newspaper industry is a ruthless business and it seemed that I was getting acclimatised remarkably quickly!"

It did not take long for Christopher Pole-Carew to turn things around in that office and his promotion quickly became a success story.

What was the secret of that success?

" I just made them work!

"In a story of success there are always losers. In this case - apart from Johnny, who didn't seem too bothered - it was Coates' Wine Bar! "

So was ambition now driving Christopher Pole-Carew to succeed in his civilian business career ?

" No. I wasn't particularly ambitious. In fact I never *have* been. I would have gone soldiering on, but Ned Boldero felt something *had* to be done and being an officer and a gentleman he suggested me first!

" Money's never meant much to me either. What is important is that I cannot suffer fools. Most of the steps in my life have been taken from exasperation with a system which I knew damn well I could do better myself."

In 1960, Canadian Press tycoon Roy Thomson acquired Kemsley Newspapers, which from then on became Thomson Newspapers and his first move was to get rid of the various sons of Lord Kemsley, who were the managing directors of the provincial newspaper centres in Cardiff, Newcastle and Sheffield. They were replaced as managing directors by various senior editors of the provincial papers.

The Kemsley family interest was also removed from the Sunday Times and the Empire News was closed.

While Pole-Carew, Gill and by this time their *three* children (second daughter Camilla having arrived in 1962) were summer holidaying in Dartmouth, he was suddenly summoned to London for an interview with James Coltart, Roy Thomson's top man in charge of his UK interests.

Apparently, the appointment of editors as managing directors had proved an unfortunate move, an issue upon which Christopher Pole-Carew remains unambiguous: "Any newspaperman could have confirmed that it would. The whole ethos, certainly of provincial newspapers, had always been to shield editors from the realities of commercial life in order to protect their editorial freedom, with the result that they were invariably ignorant of those realities and tended to regard them as distasteful and clearly beneath them. To recognise this is not to criticise editors. It was and is entirely right and proper that editors should not be involved in the commercial side of the business. You cannot properly serve your community as an editor or have the right relationship with your readers as an editor if you are at the same time trying to make money out of them. That philosophy changed in later years and in my view that was ***wrong, wrong, wrong***."

Coltart's news was that Pole-Carew had been chosen for a two year course as a Thomson Management Trainee. Only four young executives had been selected for this process and it was completed by only two of them: Christopher Pole-Carew and Ian Park, who went on via the Liverpool Echo, to become the long serving Group Managing Director of Northcliffe Newspapers Ltd, the regional wing of the Daily Mail & General Trust.

(*It could be argued that Ian Park's success and very considerable achievements in the regional newspaper industry over many years conflict with Pole-Carew's theory about the suitability of editors for dealing with commercial realities because Park was a journalist…it's not an argument with which Pole-Carew concurs but he points out that 'there's always the need for an exception to prove a rule !'*)

As part of the rigours of the then remarkably enlightened Thomson Management Training Course, Pole-Carew spent the bitterly cold winter of 1962-63 in Cardiff, literally working his way through every department of the Western Mail, while back at their house in Essex, Gill tried frantically to thaw frozen pipes with a hair dryer, at one stage ringing Christopher to tell him she had just spent two freezing hours crouched in an attic only to find she was thawing the wrong pipe. Many a newspaperman's wife would confirm that such is their lot!

'Somebody Had To Do It'

Come the Spring - and what a joy it was to welcome it after that extraordinary 'arctic' winter - Gill and the children were able to join him in an idyllic rented home in Michaelston-le-Pit, only 10 minutes from the centre of Cardiff yet without a neighbour in sight. Delia and Peregrine went to school in nearby Dinas Powis, where they learned Welsh.

The family was joined in due course by Scorcher, Delia's first pony: " He was a gelding who had wintered out in that awful weather and on arrival was very subdued. The farmer assured us that he was ideal for a first pony, 'nice and quiet, see.' Well, three months later Scorcher had eaten enough oats to be able to put the terrible winter behind him and was virtually un- rideable!.

" So we sent for Tim Bucknall, an ex-Royal Marine friend of mine from Naval days, who was brilliant with horses and well known for standing absolutely no nonsense from them. One evening, we were having a barbeque in the orchard and Tim was busy lighting it when Scorcher , to whom he had just given a really strict and arduous workout, came across to see what he was doing. As the horse leaned over Tim's shoulder he turned and said 'Bugger off, you.' Quick as a flash, Scorcher spun round and kicked him clean over the bonfire. Roaring with laughter as he picked himself up, Tim declared: ' Game, set and match to the bloody horse!'

Cardiff proved a truly happy 'posting' for Christopher Pole-Carew and it was here that much of his management style took shape.

He says: " I enjoyed immensely learning from people in the so-called ' lower' levels of the organisation; seeing and sharing at first hand the great pride they took in the jobs they did and experiencing their generosity to me as an outsider who would one day be telling them how to do the work they were teaching me! "

Though he wouldn't have recognised it as such (he never has) those people would also have enjoyed and been moved and inspired by *his* tremendous ability to make *them* feel that they (not him) *really* mattered and that, no matter how mundane and low down in the pecking order of the business they might seem to others, *he* regarded and rated the jobs they did as being hugely important and genuinely appreciated.

It was a rare, natural and sincere quality, totally at odds with the national reputation which he was later to acquire.

As was also a foretaste of things to come, he was less at home here with the senior management:" Far too concerned with fighting their own corners; far too wrapped up in their own good rather than in the good of the company."

Fortunately, unlike later in his career, he was in those days able successfully to hide those feelings and so he completed his training to everyone's satisfaction.

Though not destined to stay there for long, the Pole-Carews found Great Chesterford very pleasant. Christopher recalls:" The population was just under 1000 ; it had six pubs, a country club, a general store and only four daily commuters to London... John Wrenbury, a lawyer, Anthony Twist, a stockbroker, Gilbert Stephenson, an ex- colonial vice consul in Nigeria and me.

"The store was run by Mrs Andrews, whose family dominated Great Chesterford just as the Lightning family dominated neighbouring Ickleton, just over the border in Cambridge. Each year the two villages competed in a football match of such passion and rivalry it would make your average cup final look like a vicarage tea party. Honours tended to be spread evenly over the years but some years after leaving Great Chesterford I read in a Canadian newspaper, of all places, an account of the latest Chesterford v Ickleton match in which Chesterford, the away team, was winning which was not acceptable to the majority of spectators, who lived in Ickleton, so they simply picked up the goalposts and took them away. Result: a draw."

It wasn't long before Pole-Carew's successful Thomson Management training resulted in a move to Lancashire & Cheshire County Newspapers, a stable of weekly papers based in Stockport and printed in Macclesfield, as understudy to the Managing Director, Len Harton, "an ex-editor who had proved to be an exception to the rule by being extremely competent, if not exactly lovable."

Six months later, Harton moved on to a bigger newspaper group thus giving Christopher Pole-Carew, in Naval parlance, his first command. He was 30 and became the youngest managing director in the Thomson empire. In the early 60s it was still the norm in the newspaper industry (indeed, in most industries) for top jobs rarely to be offered to people until they reached their 40s or 50s.

Pole-Carew says of his first big job: " It was a very happy set-up. The papers stretched from the Salford City Reporter, via Wilmslow and Wythenshawe, down to the Macclesfield Express. Thursday nights were for printing when the editor Norman Kelly, the accountant Phil Bowler and me joined Ernest Hackney, the works manager in the Conservative Club next door ,where we idled away the time between editions drinking pints, eating black pudding and mushy peas and undergoing detailed and comprehensive management training, otherwise known as making instant decisions on what characters to hold on the new electronic fruit machine.

"Ernest Hackney was a splendid man - small and cynical with a dry sense of humour. He said of Stan Braddock, his deputy:' Watch 'im -'e comes from Bollington (*a nearby village*). If you kick one of 'em there they all limp!'

"Many years later, after the World Trade Center disaster of 9/11, I was to send a message to an American friend to tell her that in England we were all limping.

"Ernest would stand and watch a Linotype operator (*men who sat at tall machines with typewriter keyboards producing the hot metal type with which newspapers were printed*) working and - turning away with scorn - would say: 'I could type quicker than him with both hands tied behind my back and only my bollocks to hit the keys with.' The men were constantly urging him to demonstrate but he always replied: ' Why should I show you how to do your job!'

Domestically, the Pole-Carews continued to indulge their taste for unsuitable old homes - this time buying Gadley House, a beautiful Derbyshire stone house in Buxton, with a corridor so long that you could roller skate down from the drawing room and dining room at one end to the kitchen at the other. And they did.

"We hardly ever used the dining room because we preferred our food to be at least luke warm. Buxton was cold. Very cold. And the 1,000 feet contour line went in through the front door and out through the back. Runner beans grew to three feet, flowered but never fruited. If you looked south there was nothing at the same height or higher, except the Cat and Fiddle Inn, until you reached South America. And it always snowed in May and October. The house was another wreck that had to be done up and we had two brilliant local builders. They were like two wizened little gnomes and what they lacked in sophistication (*Gill wanted a bidet and when he'd put it in one of these chaps told me it was the first time he had ever fitted two toilets in one bathroom!*) they more than made up for in hard work."

Gill recalls: " Gadley House was 1000 feet up on the moor. It was a bit lonely, not many kindred spirits, and very, very cold. The first snowfall was always in September and the last at the end of May. It was a bit bleak."

Meanwhile, Thomson Newspapers was expanding and changing beyond recognition from the Kemsley days. For example, the Research and Promotions Department, which had numbered just four people when Pole-

Carew joined Kemsley, was now a Marketing Division with a manning level of 120 and rising.

These were heady days in regional newspapers, witnessing the early dawn of what was to become massive growth in new advertisement revenues, particularly classified advertising, over the next 10 to 15 years.

Gentlemanly but slothful and, under-employed advertisement representatives, who had been there merely to help advertisers who traditionally came to the newspapers for the privilege to do so, were replaced by well-trained, thrusting young sales people skilled in the art of chasing advertising business.

Regional newspapers were now beginning to be marketed professionally like never before in their long history and Thomson became the recognised industry trailblazer in the new business techniques.

What was occurring in the regional newspaper industry during this exciting period was little short of a revolution and the giant, avaricious publishing groups like Thomson, Northcliffe and Westminster Press were acquiring titles by the dozen from local owners, in whose families they had been for a hundred years or more.

With this huge development came an equally vast increase in management bureaucracy and centralised control of the businesses and it was the intense irritation of all that rather than the potential for career advancement that, with his inherent desire for quality of life, contempt for the pursuit of personal wealth and absence of self ambition, most exercised Christopher Pole-Carew.

Add to that his steadfast refusal ever to suffer fools and it becomes obvious why to say that this man was never cut out for big corporate environments would be an under-statement of gargantuan proportions.

Pole-Carew became a grand master at dealing " with the inevitable mass of paperwork on every irrelevance under the sun."

With willing and able allies among *all* the Thomson provincial newspaper managing directors, he instigated a method to mitigate the constant head office interference in how they ran their local business by working together to co-ordinate the returns they made on issues like profit forecasts so that no office could be shown up as being better or worse than any other.

He also employed a tactic he had learned in the Navy: Select a head office return at random and tell his accountant to stop sending it but to keep it on file. If, after three months, its non-arrival hadn't been noticed he would scrap it altogether. This proved to be a remarkably effective way of keeping the tide of paperwork under control and its efficacy was bolstered by his apparently justified conclusion that those who actually read the returns wouldn't understand them anyway so there was no point in wasting people's time collecting the information when it could be done so much better and quicker by simply making it up.

In any event, the devoutly independent Pole-Carew had concluded that the future in the Thomson empire had an inevitability about it that had little appeal for him. For an ambitious, upwardly mobile executive, the mouth watering career path was to go from a weekly newspaper to an evening, on to a bigger evening, then on to a centre with a combined morning and evening newspaper operation before finally landing the Holy Grail of promotion to Head Office in London. The incomparable Pole-Carew, however, had a typically different slant on it: " Start with running a weekly newspaper. Then move to an evening newspaper (*Blackburn, Middlesbrough?*) ; then on to a bigger evening newspaper (*Belfast?*) ; then go on to a combined morning/evening newspaper office (*Newcastle, Sheffield?*). None of these were, for me, natural choices as places to live and bring up my family, I would not be able to put down roots, nor would moving every few years do my children's education any good. Finally, one would finish up in London - my least favourite place of all in which to live and work."

Viewing this prospect with so little enthusiasm, Pole-Carew was pleased to receive, one fine day in 1966, a phone call from Sid Batrick, an old friend with whom he had sold advertising space in London…

" Chris, there's a job being advertised that's right up your street. You've **got** to go for it! "

Pole-Carew sought out the advertisement:

"A privately owned newspaper company with both a morning and an evening paper is seeking applications for the job of Managing Director Designate to take over as Managing Director on the retirement of the present incumbent in four years' time. Those interested should write to *Management Selection Ltd* **enclosing CVs and other relevant details."**

Now, this appealed a bit…" Jumping several rungs up the promotion ladder in one relatively easy go; a job that wouldn't require having to move house every few years; a chance to put down roots and no chance of ending one's days in London. I like it! "

So, Pole-Carew rang **MSL**:

"**About this job with the Nottingham Evening Post and Guardian Journal…**"

"How do you know it's Nottingham? The advertisement specifically doesn't mention where the company is."

"**Oh, for heaven's sake. There's only one privately owned newspaper company in England with a morning and an evening title and it's in Nottingham.**"

"Well, you had better come and see us, but I should tell you that the list is nearly closed. When can you come to London for an interview? "

Pole-Carew's self-belief was such that he was not playing hard to get with his laid-back response: " I didn't see why I should put myself out so I gave a date ten days ahead when I had to be in London anyway for some Thomson meeting to do with the launch of some new marketing initiative or other. There was some tooth sucking at the other end but eventually the date was agreed. I went, did the interview and returned home. When I got there, my father-in-law, who was staying with us at the time, said he had received a phone message, only half an hour after my interview had finished, asking me to contact a certain Colonel Forman Hardy on a Nottingham number."

A meeting was arranged between Pole-Carew and Colonel Tom Forman Hardy, Chairman of T Bailey Forman Ltd, publishers of the Nottingham Evening Post and Guardian Journal, at the Mackworth Arms hotel, between Derby and Nottingham.

"I was offered the job (incidentally, it meant taking a drop in salary from £4,000 to £3,500 pa) and I accepted it. I didn't jump at the offer. But it made sense. It meant I could live in the country and Nottingham was a lovely city"

What was his impression of Colonel Forman Hardy?

"Neutral. Not a strong impression at all. He was a bit distant."

So the die was cast.

Christopher Pole-Carew was heading for the third chapter in his remarkable life story.

Nottingham. Computers.Unions. And **trouble.**

In that order.

And writ large!

4

A TIGER BY THE TAIL

'Daddy, there's a man on the phone who says he wants to kill you.'

THE 1960's were a time of great change and modernisation but somebody had forgotten to tell T.Bailey Forman Ltd.

When Christopher Pole-Carew arrived on the scene in 1966 the company was stuck in a Dickensian time-warp. Indeed, when the front office had been "re-organised" not many years before, in the back of a drawer on the public counter had been found a bunch of quill pens, neatly tied together with tape.

Pole-Carew remembers it as " a sleepy organisation, not noted for sudden changes and more concerned with paying proper respects to 'The Family', the Forman Hardys, than with business efficiency."

Nevertheless, in 1953 it had managed to buy the Nottingham Journal and the Nottingham Evening News from Westminster Press and thus merge the city's two evening and two morning newspapers into one of each.

Its morning title, the Guardian Journal, was an amalgam of the Nottingham Journal, one of England's oldest daily newspapers, which had been launched in the early 18th century and the lesser known Nottingham Guardian, which had been started by Colonel Tom Forman Hardy's grandfather - the first Thomas Forman. The Bailey Forman Evening Post, on the other hand, had vastly out-sold Westminster's Evening News.

The Evening News' managing director Frank Cragg, the man Pole-Carew had been hired to replace eventually, had become the combined company's managing director. Frank Cragg had joined the Evening News as an apprentice compositor at the age of 12 during the First World War, when the government gave dispensation for boys to start work so young if they had to support their mothers (Frank's father, a baker, had died and his elder brother was fighting in France).

"Take my word for it, Cragg," young Frank had been told by the Composing Room Overseer, "In 15 years' time, you'll be on this desk."

Such was the nature of the industry in those days that such progress would have been considered positively meteoric, but it was not to be. Though he showed plenty of talent in his trade, the boy Cragg was a sickly child and his doctor recommended that he be moved to a clerk's job because the accounting office was behind the counter of the front office, the door of which was almost permanently open, so he could get more fresh air. This primitive cure proved remarkably effective and the boy's health improved. So from that weakly beginning, the 1960's saw Frank Cragg firmly established as the elderly and very experienced Managing Director of T. Bailey Forman Ltd. Now, he was heading for retirement and able to instruct his new deputy, Christopher Pole- Carew, in the art of survival at the top of that company.

Pole-Carew recalls that the secret of this survival was simple:" Report constantly to the Colonel on what was happening, which was generally nothing in particular; make sure that the Colonel's parking space was **never** occupied by anyone else and **never** ask him to make a decision without first giving him a choice and telling him clearly which one **you** would prefer, thus ensuring that was the one you got! "

It has always been a bit of a mystery why Colonel Tom, as he was affectionately known throughout the company, would have wanted this tranquil, well ordered , unremarkable, distinctly and deliberately uncontroversial "pond" to be disturbed by a huge thrashing " fish " in the dramatically striking 6ft 5inch form of Christopher Pole-Carew.

Had he had any idea what he was taking on?

(*"Probably not,"* says Pole-Carew.)

Had he simply accepted the head hunters' choice.

(" *Quite likely."*)

Had he been beguiled by Pole-Carew's landed gentry status?

(" *Possibly. Frank Cragg confided that Col Tom had looked me up in Burke's Landed Gentry."*)

Had he been far more astute and forward looking than was apparent?

(" *Pass!"*)

Pole-Carew reminds us that, at that stage, his newspaper career had not been controversial. " There had been nothing controversial at Stockport. I was a Thomson management trainee who had made it to the top and Thomson was **the** newspaper company of that time. The agency would have recommended me very strongly on that basis. And then, of course, there was my natural charm!"

Whatever his reasons for choosing Frank Cragg's heir apparent, it can be safely assumed that had he known what was to come the quiet, shy, diffident and limelight hating Colonel Tom Forman Hardy would not have touched Christopher Pole- Carew with the proverbial barge pole!

Pole-Carew had learned, before he joined the company, that the Colonel was interested in computers, having been to the USA and heard a bit about them.

In the UK in 1965 they were still extremely rare to say the least and Pole-Carew confesses that the initial reaction of the man who was to become one of Britain's new technology pioneers had been one of ignorance and fear of the unknown. He admits to hoping that it might have been possible for him to get through his entire newspaper career without having anything to do with computers.

Typically, however, he became a convert, took a diametrically opposite view and set out to learn as much as he possibly could about computerisation, including enlisting with ICT (later ICL) for an introduction course. Consequently, when he arrived in Nottingham he was more than adequately prepared to serve the embryonic interest of his new employer.

Not surprisingly. Frank Cragg was more than content to leave such developments to his new deputy while T. Bailey Forman, along with the rest of the British newspaper industry, continued to operate much as it had for the previous 100 years. It was an unchanging, labour intensive, noisy, dirty world of Linotype machines, hot metal type, chases, zinc engravings, formes and stereo plates; A smooth-running, old fashioned industry which suited both its union dominated workforce and its generally elderly management in equal measure.

Christopher Pole-Carew, recent but now zealous convert to the revolutionary cause of industrial computerisation, was to turn that world on its head, not just in the fusty corridors of the Forman Street headquarters of T. Bailey Forman Ltd. but in the British newspaper industry as a whole.

The new Managing Director of T. Bailey Forman Ltd.

And the ripples he was already beginning to raise in Colonel Tom Forman Hardy's peaceful pond were to become a massive tidal wave which would wash away all traditional methods of newspaper production from Fleet Street to Falkirk and back.

It all began with two distinct and separate changes of direction introduced by Pole-Carew, still as *deputy* managing director, into T. Bailey Forman; changes which were seemingly independent of each other but proved to be totally entwined.

The **first** was a dramatic alteration to the entire payment and reward system of the company's heavily unionised production departments. The **second** was the introduction of an embryonic computer system.

From his old South Wales stamping ground in Cardiff he brought a new Works Manager who was instructed to improve " notoriously low efficiency " in the Composing Room but, according to Pole-Carew, his new appointment managed only to achieve a union 'go-slow' then, when it was settled, allowed unlimited overtime to correct the work imbalance that had been created. This had been done without Pole-Carew's authority and he was furious :

" *The idea that industrial action should end with the perpetrators actually benefiting financially was, to me, a perfect example of bad management , demonstrating clearly the sheer folly of entering into an industrial dispute that couldn't be won.*"

The unsatisfactory result of this skirmish had two outcomes:

(1) The new Works Manager's tenure was short!

(2) Pole-Carew became focussed on the whole payment and reward system at T.Bailey Forman.

The unequivocal and uncompromising nature of his recollection presents a glimpse into the attitudes which were to formulate his unique and hugely controversial management style and techniques: " The Forman Hardys believed in paying the minimum union rate. Fine. But people have their places in society and that includes their standards of living and their relationships with their friends and neighbours. Thus, a qualified tradesman, say a compositor, would expect to earn accordingly and therefore live in a different environment from an unskilled man, say a machine operative.

" If the payment for the skilled work was unreasonably low then steps would have to be taken to put the matter right and at T.Bailey Forman this had been achieved by the artificial creation of massive overtime which in the Composing Room amounted to 10 hours a week – ie. a 50 hour week for all every week - across a manning of around 200. To me, this made absolutely no sense at all.

"So, I concluded that if the money the men were getting was what they needed then why not pay it to them - but at least insist that they work properly and efficiently for it so the company got value for money. I put it to the print unions' Fathers of the Chapel (*shop stewards*) that in future they would be paid the same for a week's work, including the overtime element, but for their normal working week, without any overtime being worked. However, if they **did** go into overtime the first two hours per person would generate no pay at all - thus putting a barrier between normal hours and the new pay and the opportunity to slip in overtime to get even more. The universal consensus on the shop floor was that Pole-Carew was mad. If he thought they would work overtime for no pay, he had another think coming!

"Within a week overtime in the Composing Room ceased completely and all the work was done in normal working hours. Cost to the company in monetary terms: nil. Benefit to the staff, which they thoughtfully acknowledged to me after a few weeks: they got home each night before their children went to bed, so they discovered the pleasures of a proper home life, which they had been missing."

This was a defining moment in the relationship between Pole-Carew and his shop floor work force (" They suddenly thought that maybe this wasn't just some prat from the Navy and perhaps he wasn't stupid after all.") and the unqualified success of that clever manoeuvre meant that Pole-Carew's next move was accepted by the workforce with open and receptive minds.

" I decided that every time someone in a department left the company, usually through retirement, members of that department would share his wages equally between them for a month. At the end of that month a vote was taken on whether carrying the extra work load was sustainable. If it was, the department shared one third of the lost person's wage. One third would go to the company and one third to pay for the new equipment that would, as numbers dropped, make it possible for the policy to continue. No-one could fault this plan; in fact the attitude towards how people did their jobs throughout all the works departments changed dramatically and they started thinking seriously about how they could work more efficiently.

"Never once was a departing employee replaced.

"And thus the road to computerisation was created!"

Pole-Carew also used the opportunity to correct what he saw as two typical examples of bad standard newspaper industry practice.

The first was the ability of shop floor worker to earn more money than their overseers:" I became aware of this whilst having a pint in the Blue Bell Inn, just across the road from the newspaper's works entrance in Forman Street. A compositor 'accidentally' dropped his pay slip onto the bar in front of his overseer, who clearly showed his annoyance. I asked what this was all about and discovered that the compositor was taking the mickey by showing his overseer how much more than him he had earned that week. This had to be stopped since it carried the inevitable implication that the management rated overseers less than shop floor workers. It was bad for morale and bad for discipline. I put it right by increasing the pay of overseers so that no longer could anyone on the shop floor earn more than his overseer."

The second was the universal practice, facilitated by the sheer power of the unions, that any complaint from the shop floor almost invariably went to the union FoC and from him directly to the Managing Director, not via the Works Director: "This cut out all levels of management as if they did not exist and inevitably humiliated them in the process. I stopped this practice in its tracks and made it crystal clear that a man's immediate overseer was responsible for him, with complete rights to discipline him however he saw fit - up to and including sacking him. I made my point by the simple process of dealing with every case that came to me by settling always in favour of the overseer. The message eventually got through to all concerned."

Such delegation might not seem remarkable in the 2000s but back in the newspaper industry of 1973 it was a phenomenal Pole-Carew revolution and like all his innovations, years ahead of its time. The philosophy behind it did not end with the works departments. Pole-Carew argued that, as Managing Director, he had the ability to fire only **one** person in the company - his secretary. He maintained that *he* couldn't fire directors, department heads or anyone else in the chains of command that ran downwards. His policy, which he ensured became well known throughout the company, established that **all** managers , however junior, **were** managers.

This, in turn, led to discussions between the different levels of management whenever a possibly contentious disciplinary matter was coming up, thus improving communication and inter-departmental understanding and it brought a radical boost to management standards in general.

It was a very early example of the sort of industrial democracy which, having spread from other countries, notably Japan, became a Holy Grail of management objectives and achievement throughout British industry in the late 1980's and of Christopher Pole-Carew it illustrated two truisms...

He was never the personally power- crazed despot so often depicted by his many detractors and he was , albeit subconsciously, a genuine visionary in the business and industrial world of the 1970s. In 1966, Pole-Carew had prepared a plan for the computerisation of T. Bailey Forman Ltd. By today's standards it was primitive in its simplicity and limitations but it was the **first** time that **any** newspaper on this side of the Atlantic (and quite possibly on the other side as well) had **ever** done such a thing.

This was genuine innovation and serious pioneering. He was, quite simply, many years ahead of his time and on a different planet to his contemporaries in the rest of the newspaper industry. Plan prepared, he then put it out to tender to six computer companies (surprisingly, there **were** six companies in those days) to tell him how they would meet the challenges he was setting.

He wrote a booklet, *The Nottingham System Of Computer Typesetting* which told the full technical story of how the system was introduced - starting with the very simple technique of generating punched tape to run the Linotype machines and using what was for those days a powerful ICT computer that was 6ft long by 3ft wide and 5ft high with a capacity of 62k!

That booklet really should be in some museum of computer development.

And so, in 1967, T Bailey Forman Ltd., publishers of the Nottingham Evening Post and Guardian Journal, became the first newspaper company in Britain to install a general purpose computer for setting editorial text and advertisements. Revolution hit the composing room and the rows of clattering typesetting machines, with all their ancillary mechanical equipment. For almost 80 years the newspapers had been produced using Linotype machines. Then, as an interim measure between mechanical and computerised photoset composition, twelve Intertype Blue Flash machines and several Linotype equivalents were installed. These represented the ultimate in newspaper hot metal typesetting and, taking the text from perforated paper tape, they worked at speeds beyond the ability of human operators. The tapes were made by former compositors. Under a company training scheme these men had been retrained from the very different Linotype layout to a Querty keyboard similar to those on conventional typewriters. This also prepared them for the initial stages of a later switch to full computer production. A year later, the accounts department was computerised and in October, 1968 BBC Television shot sequences in the Forman Street offices for a programme on computer development called *Made In Britain*.

The gradual demise of the old Linotype machines was hugely symbolic. They had been synonymous with the traditional hot metal method of producing newspapers and - while it was impossible not to recognise the giant steps forward manifest in the emerging new technology - many mourned their passing for purely and unashamedly sentimental reasons. The sights, sounds and smells of hot metal newspaper printing were unique and evocative and were fondly and indelibly set in the minds of all who experienced them.

Emrys Bryson, revered Nottingham Evening Post journalist, now aged 82 and probably the best writer ever to grace its pages, describes it thus: " I entered into newspapers to the smell of printing ink and hot metal. I regarded it as a kind of aftershave and was proud, actually ***proud***, when people wrinkled their noses at the unfamiliar aroma that clung to my clothes. Fish and chips they could place, surgical spirit they understood, the tang of beer and tobacco, of course, but printing ink and molten lead was way out of their league for most. Not unpleasant. Not exactly pleasant. Just indefinable; at once acrid and strangely exotic. This was a smell that uniquely carried its own adventure. It virtually spoke to me, as if giving a running commentary; a raciness that somehow mingled the crash and tinkle of a Linotype with the magic of the mysterious profession I was in. I always knew it as a profession, despite the odd sneer from those who had no idea what journalists did and had absorbed the stereotypical bad press the Press gave itself in books, on the stage and on screen. The clatter of a Linotype, with its Emmett-like improbability and its overhead arm carrying along its oddly shaped brass matrices as if hurrying to hang on to some invisible Christmas tree, the delicate chinking of its flat keys and its bubbling crucible of silver liquid was, to me , pure alchemy. The noise rang in my ears every time I stepped from editorial into lino room on my way to an assignment. And when, as happened some days, I crept into the press room and stood watching the grey beasts of the Harrild or the Hoe swallow their league long paper bales and regurgitate them as neat parcels of finished newspapers, that was perfection. The feeling of my feet tingling on the quivering floor, my mouth agape at the animal thunder of the presses at speed while their blue-overalled minders swarmed over them, tending and taming, was to die for; When my time came, I felt, this was the way to go."

Christopher Pole-Carew realised that his trail blazing was going to succeed dramatically on the shop floor the night a compositor on the night shift told him that whereas he used to man one Linotype machine (the norm) he had just stepped up to running **five** of them as casters on his own and nobody, from the overseer down, had minded, or even commented. This was revolution in the true sense of the word.

Despite the ground breaking significance and massive potential of what was going on here, it was lost on the rest of the newspaper world and that scenario was merely the first of many to follow in which Christopher Pole-Carew - variously regarded by his peers in the industry, who never understood him, as a maverick, a nutter, an odd ball with an inclination to rock boats - was so far ahead of the rest that the importance and magnitude of his innovations were simply not grasped and consequently ignored or even ridiculed.

But the truth was that every one of his seemingly "mad cap" developments was eventually to become universal common practice.

That Pole-Carew was able to take his shop floor workforce of around 200 compositors with him on these incredible voyages of discovery was arguably his greatest achievement, particularly given the notorious obduracy and unshakeably unionised mindset of print workers in the 1960's.

This was helped considerably by the fact that he had set up new printing companies (*TBF Printers and Huthwaite Printing Company*) to create employment for staff rather than reduce numbers. He strove to ensure that the new technology would not destroy jobs.

He was by no means popular with *all* the staff of that newspaper company while he was treading his missionary path. Production journalist Ian Manning recalls :"Some of the workers saw him as a ruthless upper class twit playing at newspapers. Others saw him as a pioneering visionary."

As time passed and as each revolutionary new working method he introduced invariably proved itself, those of the latter persuasion grew in number and loyalty to this extraordinary man grew stronger.

No where was that loyalty more pronounced than on the shop floor, where you would have expected objection to this double-barrelled " toff " to have been strongest. And part of the explanation for that can be found in the way Pole-Carew went about his job in those very early days in the mid-60's. At least once a week, every week without fail, he would spend at least three hours, from 9pm until midnight, on the night shift with the print workers - not standing around like some visiting dignitary but getting involved, getting his hands dirty, learning and thoroughly understanding every detail of every job which made up the complex ritual of producing newspapers. This continued for 18 years, right up until the day he left the Company. The presence of such an exalted executive on a regular basis and in such close contact with the work was unique and the Night Shift Overseer was not going to waste such an opportunity. Every week, week in and week out, he would complain about something that was preventing the men from doing their jobs as well as he (Pole-Carew) would have liked. Every week, week in and week out, Pole-Carew made sure that by his next visit it had been put right. This went on remorselessly until the Overseer had literally run out of things about which to complain.

The night shift workers were loners. They resented Pole-Carew poking his nose in at first, feeling that he didn't trust them. But after he had appeared so often that he had become just part of the normal scene they accepted him entirely - even ribbing him when he went on holiday (*"Don't make a habit of it...sir!"*).

Pole-Carew recalls: " My attitude was - and still is - that any shop floor is full of bloody good blokes who are a pleasure to see and compare notes with. I enjoyed their company."

This was not " management bullshit." Pole-Carew genuinely meant it and the print workers, a tough, cynical breed renowned for seeing through and seeing off any phoney, recognised his sincerity. Gradually, they really took to this "toff" and a genuine bond founded on mutual respect developed between them.

In the years that were to follow that relationship, which spread throughout all the Company's departments, was not only to be tested to the limit but would prove to be absolutely crucial. And it was founded on Pole-Carew's basic philosophy that *loyalty is a two way thing.*

He says: "I was driven by a sense of what was right. I believed absolutely in the principle that loyalty must be two ways and I was deeply contemptuous of the attitude of much of the rest of the industry's managements who did not have that principle. It seemed to me that they didn't care about people. They were there just to make money for them; nothing more and that was that. I considered that people who were loyal to you were there to be looked after and I had been trained in the Navy to subscribe to that belief. I don't believe the industry suffered one bit - and certainly not T Bailey Forman - for having that attitude of mind taken into it."

The Pole-Carew family, meanwhile, had resolved to move down from the frozen wastes of the cold hills of Buxton to the flat, warmer plains of Nottinghamshire. Colonel Tom Forman Hardy provided them with High Westings, a house on his estate, while they looked around and a year or so later they moved into New Field, a farm house just off the Fosse Way (A46) at Flintham, just one village away from Car Colston - where the Colonel lived. This was precisely the antithesis of London commuting that Christopher Pole-Carew had craved; a pleasant 12 mile drive to work, mainly through open countryside, dropping the children off at school on the way.

New Field was a traditional Nottinghamshire farm house built at the time of the Enclosures Acts, around 1700 when, as the name tells, a new field was created out of common land. Unlike the Pole-Carew's earlier houses, New Field was not a wreck but it did require a lot of work. Not for the first or last time, Christopher had cause to be grateful for the wartime teaching of the eccentric RJ Mowll which meant that he was a competent joiner and able to make all the kitchen furniture himself: "A good thing because what with school fees, etc, money was tight."

New Field was to be the happy home of the Pole-Carews for some 20 years and both daughters, Delia and Camilla, were married from there.

Says Gill: " Camilla went to school in Nottingham and the other two were away at boarding school. Camilla eventually went to St.Mary's Wantage and that meant I had more free time. I became secretary to the Distressed Gentlefolk Aid Association, now known under the better name of the Elizabeth Finn Charity. It runs several homes for people who are in financial trouble (mostly retired teachers and professional classes who possibly have no relatives) and also helps people in their own homes, eg. gives them washing machines and so on. After a time, I also joined the Red Cross as a fund raiser - eventually becoming President of the Nottingham Branch. I did this for seven years. At the same time, I was Patron of the YWCA, which was very interesting as it was with young people."

The revolutionary new pay structure for print workers and the first steps towards computerisation at T Bailey Forman had been achieved without involving the newspaper industry's mighty trade unions outside the company at all.

Pole-Carew could not see what worthwhile contributions could be made by the branch and head office officials of the print workers' unions - the NGA, the Stereotypers, NATSOPA, and SLADE - or the journalists'

'Somebody Had To Do It'

unions, the NUJ and IOJ *"….and I had not the slightest intention of encouraging them to think of something!"*

Word had inevitably spread, however, and Christopher Pole-Carew was asked to receive a delegation. His latter day description of what he describes as this "visitation" illustrates that time has not mellowed his contempt for them.

" Firstly, it was clear that most of the print union representatives were unlikely to be challenging for the Brain of Britain title. Secondly, it was clear that the quality of the lunch they received, especially the liquid refreshment, was of great importance to them. The business of the visit appeared to come next in line and it largely concerned who should man the computer system, of which none of them had the slightest knowledge nor any apparent interest in learning. I made the point that the computer would be used for accounting and production purposes and so it seemed sensible that the manning should come from those two sources (which, of course, suited me perfectly) and they agreed. Without a precedent to refer back to the unions were unable to work out a solution of their own.

I also pointed out to them that according to Government statistics the amount of UK print work that went abroad, mainly to Holland, was so great that if every newspaper in the country computerised as we were doing and did commercial work to avoid redundancies, as we were doing, there would still be a substantial amount of printing going abroad. Trouble was, that seemed well beyond the ability of any union official of that time to get his head around and I reckon they didn't even try.

" Astonishingly, they all thought the expression ' journeyman' meant someone who travelled from place to place to find work, whereas anyone with a smattering of education about his own craft would have known that it originated from the French *une journee* - a day - because they were paid by the day rather than by the job or the hour, in fact the equivalent in medieval times of having an annual salary. The unions, in pressing for piece work and hourly rates, were condemning their members to labourers' pay when history was telling them they should have been pushing for professional remuneration and status.

"If ever a union missed an opportunity to look after its members' interests, that was it. But they lived in some out of touch world. They were happy for so many of their members to become almost mindless copy typists while surrendering the chance to take over the far more exciting, career challenging and better paid world of computers. The probable reason for this dearth of lateral thinking among the union leadership was that the unions had the printing industry, especially the newspapers, in an iron grip. Thus their natural and much practised negotiating tactic was simple bullying to extract improved deals for their members on a steady year-in-year-out basis. The newspaper managements, many of whom came from unionised backgrounds themselves, went along with this because by doing so they avoided confrontations which could result in strikes, which could cause questions to be raised about the competence of the management - and we wouldn't want that, would we! "

Pole-Carew's brutal assessment of 1960s industrial relations in the newspaper industry notwithstanding, the print unions' delegation to the pioneering powerhouse of T Bailey Forman had passed without problems. Another hurdle along the completely uncharted and exciting route to full computerisation of the company had been cleared effortlessly, the unwelcome national attention which union opposition would inevitably have focussed on Nottingham had been avoided.

In 1971, Frank Cragg, technically Pole-Carew's boss, retired but for all practical purposes, he had abdicated the running of the business to his deputy two years earlier as deafness impeded him more and more. Pole-Carew's influence on the company steadily increased and Allan Gale, the Company Secretary, noted that for the first time ever a member of the Board of Directors (*guess who*!) had attended a Board meeting in a **coloured** shirt!

Now officially Managing Director he decided profits in 1971 were unsatisfactory and streamlined a lot of the company's activities, including closing those branch offices that he considered no longer necessary.

In the Victorian atmosphere of the Forman Street headquarters of T. Bailey Forman this dashing, tall, slim, blond " whirlwind" literally running, as he always did, between departments, caused many a head to spin and many a staid or complacent attitude to change.

But they'd seen nothing yet!

Pole-Carew describes these as happy times at T.Bailey Forman: " Colonel Tom was a pleasant and friendly person to work for and his elder son, William, who was making his way through the business, was very much liked by all. William's involvement was welcomed by the work force, which tells you much about him, because human nature would normally dictate that the son of the owner of the business would inevitably be resented."

Young William Forman Hardy had a weakness - and it was nothing to do with his full grasp of the newspaper industry. It was speed.

Says Pole-Carew: " He drove much too fast and invariably in vehicles that encouraged this. On one occasion he picked me up at home for a journey we were making to Peterborough and I was so frightened by his driving that I was very nearly sick before we had even left the village."

(*William's love of speed, tragically but inevitably, killed him. In 1974 he died in an accident while riding a motor cycle just a couple of miles from his parents' home on the Fosse Way (A46). He was just 27. His death devastated all who knew him and Pole-Carew recalls :" There is no doubt that William's death was a serious loss to the Company; he was a natural to the business, he loved the world of newspapers. He and I worked closely together. We really liked and respected each other."*)

Dramatic though they were in their impact on T Bailey Forman and in their implications for the whole newspaper industry, Christopher Pole-Carew's pioneering technological innovations and revolutionary new business practice and culture did not happen overnight. The changes he introduced , though unremitting, were gradual and spread over a period of years making them, consequently, more easily assimilated.

Computerisation spread through all the Production departments and simultaneously through the Advertisement and Accounting departments. The Nottingham Evening Post became the first newspaper in the world with an integrated production and accounting system. Computer systems in those days were too primitive for direct input but by 1973, using a mixture of computer setting of type with etching on to zinc plates, production of all classified advertisements and most display advertisements was computerised.

Nottingham was leading the world and a conflict with the print unions was becoming inevitable. Dramatically new systems were making customary, comfortable ones less and less relevant and production manpower was steadily reducing. Nationally, the unions were beginning to wake up to the huge implications of the Nottingham revolution and given their enormous power in the industry at that time, the crunch was bound to come.

All T. Bailey Forman's compositors had been taught typing and so their union, the NGA, insisted that **all** matter that went into the newspapers must be keyed in by NGA members. In effect, this meant duplicating work that was being done by the classified advertisement staff. Pole-Carew was fiercely opposed to this. To him, it was a ridiculous restrictive practice. So, sneeringly, he insisted on referring to the skilled compositors who were to do this work as " Corrective Typists." This, as no doubt he had intended, did not help relations with the union. Neither, and equally no doubt intended, did it endear his compositors to the idea of doing the work.

While that potential volcano bubbled away in the composing room, Pole-Carew also felt it was becoming obvious (at least, to **him**) that there was no longer a case for having two departments - the Process Department (members of the SLADE union) and the Plate Making Department (members of the Stereotypers' union) - involved in the making of the printing plates.

He wanted them merged. The unions didn't.

Christopher Pole-Carew's version of the impasse goes: " The unions obviously realised that the time had come to stop this steady march of progress in Nottingham. The Evening Post and the Guardian Journal had to be brought back into line with all the other newspapers throughout the United Kingdom and do as the unions told them."

Had he deliberately picked a fight with them ?

" Not a bit of it.I just wanted to carry on moving the Company forward which was going to be to the long term benefit of our hundreds of employees throughout all departments, many of whom believed in what we were doing even if their unions didn't want them to. The issue with plate making was that we took up a method of magnesium etching parts of pages and then full pages by photo composing methods. If we had had offset presses we would have been etching the actual printing plates, which is the norm everywhere now, but we hadn't so, by this intermediate step, we had the advantages of photo composition but having to go back to hot metal stereo plates. This was much better than all hot metal. With two types of processing printing plates from the Composing Room to the presses it became obvious that there was no sense in having two separate departments any longer. In addition to that, offset printing was going to eliminate stereotyping and the jobs of all the stereotypers. If the two were merged then the increase in process work that photocomposition was creating would take up the slack for the stereotypers. But with bloody minded union attitudes we were, with hindsight, heading for trouble."

In the summer of 1973 the crunch came: the newspaper unions (the NGA, NATSOPA, NUJ, SLADE,Stereotypers' Union) called a joint strike against T. Bailey Forman Ltd. Pole-Carew's assessment of their intent: " It was unambiguous. It was to bring the management of T.Bailey Forman to heel."

When the strike call came, the response from T. Bailey Forman workers was a massive blow for the unions. The workforce at that time was around 1500. More than half that number remained at work. Take away the non-unionised areas such as clerical and advertising and this was still a huge rejection for the unions. Given the closed shop stranglehold (no union card meant no job) in which they held all the production and editorial departments throughout the industry it was an absolutely extraordinary situation.

Christopher Pole-Carew saw this as a direct vote of confidence in his own leadership, vindication of his *two way loyalty* philosophy and an indication of the changes he had made in the attitudes of managers, all of whom were compulsory union members but, with one exception (the brother of an FoC) resolved not to strike. A few days into the strike, Pole-Carew was approached by one of these managers - Wilf Mabbutt, a composing room overseer - who had clearly been asked to raise the concerns of all the non-strikers with him. Wilf asked if Pole-Carew would meet all the non-striking works staff in the canteen and at that meeting he asked: "What will happen to us when we lose this strike?"

"I hadn't planned to lose, Wilf," replied Pole-Carew.

"No daily newspaper has **ever** won a strike," said Wilf.

He told Pole-Carew, on behalf of the non-strikers, that come the inevitable defeat, they felt it would be reasonable for them to be given one year's pay each as compensation for the loss of their union cards and consequently their jobs.

Such fears are hard to imagine nearly 40 years later but the fact that this stark , rock- and- a- hard- place choice between loyalty to your union or forfeit of your livelihood was common in the early 70s is proof of the manner in which the unions controlled the newspaper industry and dictated its affairs.

Pole-Carew told Wilf and the men that he would have to talk to the Colonel about such a gesture, which would amount to a great deal of money, but could promise nothing. However, his own mind was made up immediately. While the rest of the industry believed that defeat for Pole-Carew in this industrial battle of wills was just a matter of time, there was not even the slightest prospect of a negative outcome on his own radar screen but, nevertheless, he felt that the unprecedented support he was getting from these men *had* to be repaid by agreeing to their request.

He went to see Colonel Tom Forman Hardy.

Pole-Carew recalls: "It was a difficult discussion. He was not a man who liked parting with money and he certainly hated any commitment that was not precisely quantified."

Despite Pole-Carew's best efforts to convince the Chairman of the justice of the men's case, it was a hard battle but he got his way eventually and the Colonel gave him the commitment he had asked for : " I had a really tough job persuading him but in all fairness what I was asking for was *so* unusual that he had a real job getting his head around it."

Pole-Carew reconvened the session with the workers in the canteen and told them:

" I have seen the Colonel and I have to tell you that your request for a year's pay with notice should we lose this strike has been turned down."

Then, after a pause during which the men's disappointment was palpable, he added:

"This sum is considered inadequate reward for your loyalty. Should we lose this strike and you lose your jobs you will receive THREE YEARS' pay!"

The following day, some of the strikers decided their loyalty lay with Pole-Carew after all and went back in!

The episode was typical of the maverick manner in which Christopher Pole-Carew was to conduct himself as Managing Director of T. Bailey Forman Ltd. for the next decade and it raised his already high stock enormously with his workers at a time when they were having to endure intimidating hostile picketing from union supporters bussed into Nottingham from all over the UK and venomous abuse from their own striking workmates. There can be no doubt, either, that among that Forman Street workforce, the experience nurtured a growing culture of union defiance and Company loyalty which was truly remarkable for its time and, perhaps even more significantly, was to endure.

(*It is interesting to note, too, that Nottinghamshire has a record for disobeying union orders, including two famous examples: The 1927 General Strike was broken by the Notts miners returning to work and in 1984 the county's miners defied NUM leader Arthur Scargill's national pits strike call, carried on working through intense and often violent intimidation and formed their own breakaway union, the Union of Democratic Mineworkers.*)

Pole-Carew not only formalised that three year deal but extended it beyond the shop floor to include, also, the non-striking journalists and more than 20 years later three years' pay was still having to be given to 1973 loyalists who lost their jobs through redundancy. To Pole-Carew that was simply fair and just.

Two way loyalty.

Today he insists that he did not have a deliberate game plan of looking after his staff as an insurance policy against the fierce union opposition which was an inevitable by- product of his technological march of progress.

" No," he says firmly. " I looked after them because you DO. I knew no other way and would never even countenance any other way. It was then taken for granted by me that they would return that loyalty."

This was well illustrated by the example of a compositor who, just before the strike, had needed a hip replacement operation. Pole-Carew had arranged the operation for him and ensured that the Company paid for it.

" In those days these operations were very, very new and you sure as hell didn't get them on the National Health, so the company paid for him to have one because of the principle of looking after our people. Now, when the strike came, he went into work **every** day, through the picket lines, on crutches. That was an incredibly brave thing to do because one kick from a picket could have left him in a wheelchair for life, but he said :' The company looked after me. Why should I let them down now?' "

The conflict of loyalties which characterised this fight was, to say the least, uncommon to industrial disputes in the newspaper industry. When the unions called the strike, they would have anticipated 100 per cent support from their members because that was customary in those days of supreme union power but, says Pole-Carew, those that did go on strike did so very reluctantly: " They did not go on strike because they had a quarrel with the management. They went on strike because their union told them to go on strike. **No quarrel with the management...**That was the fundamental point. In all the change that I had brought about there had been nothing which did not benefit the staff as well as the management. The only people it didn't benefit were the union bosses."

As the strike progressed, Pole-Carew's resolve not to give in grew even stronger. One of his first moves was to stop publication of the Guardian Journal in order, he said, to concentrate his reduced staffing resources on the Nottingham Evening Post. There were those who were to claim later that he had, in fact, craftily identified a way in which to close an historic but unprofitable newspaper.

Again, Pole-Carew denies any such deliberate game plan.

" The driving force was that the idea of giving in to union pressures and demands simply did not occur to me. The Evening Post was the big selling, successful newspaper with a daily circulation of around 150,000 copies. The Guardian Journal was selling less than a third of that. With reduced manpower I simply had to concentrate the company's resources on the production of the Evening Post."

Three weeks into the strike, while baying mobs of pickets laid daily siege to Forman Street, inside the imposing Victorian building Pole-Carew was very pleased with the way things were going.

"Production, with limited manpower, was going better than anybody could have expected. It had been difficult, of course, but gradually, those difficulties were being overcome. We had managed to clear 100.000 copies a day of the Evening Post and we were quite rapidly returning to normal print figures. The new equipment - computer operated paper tape punches to drive the Linotype casters and the automatic newspaper packing lines - was functioning better than it had ever functioned before, mainly due to it being untouched by interfering union hands."

So, ably assisted by the Works Manager Charlie Wright and his deputy Peter Mould, the Managing Director was relishing the continuation of the fight. But the Chairman was apparently not. Colonel Tom Forman Hardy was, according to Pole-Carew, " feeling the strain."

One evening at 9 pm, Pole-Carew received a telephone call asking him to go to Car Colston Hall, the Colonel's home. There, he was welcomed in to the Hall by the Colonel and they were joined in his study by Paul Granger, an accountant, who was a Director of T Bailey Forman Ltd.

(Pole-Carew remembers Paul Granger thus:" *Paul was an accountant from Mellors, Basden and Mellors, one of the components of what became Price Waterhouse. His involvement in newspapers stemmed from the advice he had given to the Colonel leading to the break-up of the family trust, set up by Tom's mother, which controlled the company. Under the trust, Tom received most, if not all, of the company's profits but had no say in the running of it. As a result of Paul's advice he had become the Colonel's financial 'eminence grise.'"*)

It was clear that Colonel Forman Hardy and Paul Granger were very worried that the strike was going to damage T. Bailey Forman.

What followed was a long meeting, with protracted argument, which is indelibly etched on Pole-Carew's memory: " Their logic was that the dispute was un-winnable and therefore any delay in settlement would lead to an ever heavier price to pay for a settlement. It should be said that they had very good reason for taking this attitude - it was the accepted opinion of the **entire** UK newspaper industry and it was summed up by Gordon Linacre (*Managing Director of the Yorkshire Post and a leading light in the Newspaper Society, the proprietors' organisation*) who had said when the strike started: ' It looks like Christopher Pole-Carew has got his come uppance at last.' My reaction to that had been: ' We will see.'

"I told the Colonel that it was *his* company and that if *he* wished to settle with the unions then that was that but I had one stipulation to make: **I would not, under any circumstances, be a party to a settlement that meant victimisation of those who had been loyal to the company by refusing to go on strike.**

" Tom pointed out that this would be inevitable and unavoidable, being the custom and practice of strikes in the newspaper business, but I made it clear that on a deeply held principle I would not even consider being disloyal to anyone who had taken such risks by being loyal to me. I told him that I believed my honour and integrity were at stake.

"The argument went on interminably until eventually I said I would accept the Colonel's decision to settle but only on condition that prominent space was given on the front page of the Evening Post to a statement that Christopher Pole-Carew had refused to accept the sacrifice of any employee who had been loyal to the company - that part of the settlement having been agreed by the Colonel alone, despite my objections.

"Paul Granger argued that since I had insisted on three years' wages for employees who lost their jobs through not striking I had, in fact, accepted the possibility that the sum would have to be paid and therefore had no good reason to disassociate myself from dismissals now. I told him that I had not thought along those lines at all. My attitude was that the strike did not end until the unions admitted defeat so the three years' wages issue was irrelevant.

"The meeting ended at midnight, after three very trying hours of argument on what I believed was a matter of integrity and reputation and a board meeting was called the following day to resolve whether the company should sue for peace with the unions."

Before the crucial board meeting Pole-Carew discussed the issue with Works Manager Charlie Wright, whose response was unequivocal:

" **If a single one of my loyal blokes loses his job I will make sure that the Nottingham Evening Post never has a successful print run again!** "

He was preaching to the converted, of course, but Pole-Carew was delighted with Charlie's response and the two allies discussed how best to handle the meeting.

"At the board meeting**,** the Editor Bill Snaith, the Advertisement Director David Teague and the Finance Director Barrie Bailey expressed no opinion, other than this was a difficult matter and the security of the newspaper should be paramount. Charlie Wright and I both expressed vehemently our belief that loyalty should not - and surely *would* not - be betrayed. End of board meeting. Continuation of strike and continuation of T Bailey Forman making record profits which, with half the production staff off the payroll, wasn't difficult to achieve! "

Now, the attitude of the unions was bound to harden and the picketing sure to get more aggressive. It did. And not for the last time in industrial dispute situations, Pole-Carew occasionally fought fire with fire.

"As our delivery vans left the premises with their loads of newspapers the pickets would gather round and lift the back wheels off the ground. Their intention was that the driver, not realising his back wheels were airborne would rev up, at which the pickets would let go of the rear bumper and the van would career forward at speed. This would then be presented as ' provocative, deliberately dangerous driving determined to injure lawful pickets exercising their inalienable rights.' Fortunately, nobody had been hurt but that was pure luck and this could not be allowed to happen again. So, I had all our vans sent to the Company's garage and I instructed the Transport Manager to grind the underside of all the rear bumpers until they were razor sharp. The next attempt by the pickets to lift the vans off the ground was unsuccessful.

" The attitude of the police towards the mass picketing was interesting and it was easy to misunderstand exactly what their role was. Most people assumed that they were there to protect individuals from criminal attacks and to ensure that private citizens could go about their lawful business without let or hindrance but I discovered that this was not quite so. Their primary duty was to keep the Queen's peace in areas over which they had responsibility - ie *public* areas - but not on private premises unless called in for a specific purpose.

" That the Evening Post was being hindered in lawfully being printed was of no interest to them whatsoever so long as there were no riots or trouble on the streets of Nottingham. There was, of course, a high risk of that because the pickets were doing their utmost to create it. Therefore, so far as the police were concerned, the sooner this strike ended the sooner their potential problem went away. Who won or lost was of no interest to them.

" Consequently, the superintendent in charge of the situation attempted to browbeat me into settling the strike. I was goaded to such an extent that I told the superintendent that I could not guarantee the behaviour of the pickets but, as the managing director of the Evening Post, I was going to exercise my lawful right to get my newspapers out, come what may.

" I added that if he didn't like it then he had better take his little boys in blue away before they got hurt. After that, relations between us improved enormously and there was no longer any muddled thinking on how events were to be conducted."

Inevitably, the strike affected the Pole-Carews' home life and Gill Pole-Carew recalls: " Christopher worked appalling hours, just coming home to eat, sleep and recover for the next day. It was a bit lonely for me and not much fun and I worried for Christopher. But he was generally in a euphoric state about the way things were going. Clearly, the possibility of losing never once occurred to him. It simply wasn't an option. I got the impression that he thought the unions were trying, rather feebly, to interfere with his running of the newspaper but that they hadn't got the intelligence to be treated as a real threat!

" What *did* annoy him and worried me were the telephoned threats we received. We got some very odd calls, some frightening. One day, someone pushed faeces in an envelope through our letter box. That was a bit pointless, I thought, since the sender could not have the satisfaction of seeing my face when I opened it!

" The telephone calls were, generally, stupid ones, like : ' *Tell your husband not to drive down any dark lanes if he doesn't want to get hurt.*' There were at least a dozen like that, but the one that sticks in my mind most was a telephone call that my youngest child Camilla took. We heard her say '*Yes*' several times, followed by '*…yes, I'll tell Daddy.*'

" Christopher asked her what it was about and Camilla said: '*A man said he would like to kill you, Daddy. Is he a friend of yours?* '

" Daddy didn't think he was! "

These calls had to be taken seriously and Christopher Pole-Carew always made sure that he travelled on main roads. He was on a police emergency list for protection and one day the police received a telephone call to say that a bomb had been planted in the Pole-Carews' house. The family were evacuated and had to stand outside for two hours while the police searched every nook and cranny before declaring it safe for them to return.

As the increasingly bitter strike continued, the unlikely bond between the " toff " and the blokes on the shop floor at the Nottingham Evening Post strengthened. A day never passed without Pole-Carew spending serious time in the works areas, talking to the workers, listening to their concerns, sorting out their problems. His theory is that there is a natural affinity between the upper class and the working class and that neither have much time for the middle class mass in between.

"I knew the people on the shop floor well but the more up the social scale you went, the less I knew them personally. For example, I didn't neglect middle management but I didn't spend much time with them, whereas I knew all the van drivers by their Christian names and I could tell you lots about their families."

During the course of the strike, two local Labour MPs offered to mediate but Pole-Carew was having none of it: "As a Labour politician each saw himself as a perfect representative in dealing with the unions, who would naturally trust him. I was of the opinion that someone who knew and liked union leaders was the very last person I would want on my team at that particular time. Newspaper sales were thoroughly healthy, only about 10,000 a day below full normal levels; profits were better than I could ever have hoped for. So who wanted the strike to end? Cerainly not me!"

Next to offer to help bring about a solution was the Newspaper Society, the newspaper proprietors' organisation. They were not high on Pole-Carew's popularity list because he felt they were disinclined to recognise and support his controversial but demonstrably successful innovations at the Nottingham Evening Post: "The Newspaper Society thought they should get involved but I just wasn't interested."

But a man whose advice and wisdom Pole-Carew *did* respect was Frank Barlow, a prominent regional newspaper managing director and a good friend.

"Frank made the point that you never knew what the future had in store which could give the unions an advantage, so why not cash in my winnings while I was so far ahead in the game. Sound advice, which I took."

The strike was now into its fifth week and the Newspaper Society provided the names of two representatives to act as mediators between the company and the unions. Pole-Carew turned them down and put forward instead two people of his own choice: Frank Barlow and Barlow's Works Director who Pole-Carew judged to be very much of the same temperament as his own works boss, Charlie Wright. These two were accepted and negotiations to end the strike began, but if the unions thought this was going to be an easy process of confirming a settlement they had reckoned without Pole- Carew, whose account of the meetings offers some explanation for the hostility which was to prevail between him and the print unions for the next 20 years and festers on in union minds to this day:

" Union officials, who in those days had total control over the newspaper industry, had a tendency to treat company managements in a patronising manner and those who came to Nottingham were typical. The NGA led the pack with their national representative. His Number Two in the process was the Area Secretary, one George (aka Terry) Brady, a member of the Evening Post's Composing Room staff.

" I didn't take kindly to the unions' attitude. They seemed to be under the impression that *they* were the winners in this battle and were there simply to tie up the loose ends, which didn't match *my* interpretation of the situation at all. So, the meetings were not conducted in the usual way – ie. with nervous, worried members of management hoping to win their union masters over with sweet talk and comforts!

" Meetings were held in a room which I made sure was bare except for a table and chairs. No refreshments of any sort were provided - no tea, no coffee, no water. When the management team felt it was time for a cup of coffee we would announce that we needed a break for a private discussion on the matter in hand. We would return, after enjoying our coffee, to the union representatives still sitting there un-refreshed . Should a union official wish to go to the lavatory he would be escorted there and back to make sure he had no meetings with any member of the company's staff.

" Charlie Wright made most of the running in the discussions and he was brilliant. His ability to waste time was formidable. Every evening, every single day, as each day's meeting drew to a close, Charlie would keep the discussions going until the union officials had missed their trains or any chance of driving back in time for their evening meals.

" The atmosphere was evil. On one occasion Terry Brady said to me: ' I would like to string you up from a lamp post, Mr Pole-Carew.'

" I said: 'Make it a high one, Terry.'

He said :'Why?'

" I said: ' So that I can kick your teeth in while you're doing it! '

" On another occasion, I told them: ' As long as these meetings last I shall have three ambitions. With luck, I shall achieve all three, but I'll settle for two or maybe one of them.'

" They asked :' What are they? '

" I said: ' To ruin your health, your career and your home life.' "

Pole-Carew describes these tactics as subjecting the union officials to " an effective war of nerves."

He says: " Eventually they had to face reality. For the first time in their experience they had lost and the pill was a bitter one to swallow. True, they took union membership off all those who had supported the company through the strike but not one of those people lost their jobs. I had made sure of that. The day arrived for the return to work and astonishingly the strikers came back into the building as if they were the conquerors. That didn't accord with the management's view at all. They had lost. And they were not going to be allowed to forget it.

" In the Machine Room, which was filthy through sheer lack of opportunity to clean it, the manager started by making the returned press crews clean the place out until it was spotless; all the steel handrails properly emeried with an alternating pattern. When they had finished, he took a bucket of rubbish and strewed it all over the floor and said: 'Right. This place is a mess. Now do it properly.' Then he added: 'All these years I've been like a father to you lot and you betrayed me. Don't expect any favours from me from now on.'

" The settlement eliminated every restrictive practice (including a paging limitation on the Nottingham Evening Post of 24 pages) on manning in any department; allowed interchangeability of employees from one department to another; the use of whatever equipment the company decided upon - you name it. The victory was total."

It is perhaps difficult to read Pole-Carew's triumphal account of that victory without feeling uncomfortable, but had it not been for his fierce and single minded determination the march of progress at the Nottingham Evening Post, from which a growing number of employees would benefit immensely in the years to come, would have been halted, possibly never to regain its momentum, and although his ruthless stance against the unions and contempt for the industry's management had made him hugely unpopular with the Newspaper Society it is worth recording that none of its members' newspapers declined to accept the wind of change on traditional restrictive practices which then blew in from Nottingham.

And the many contradictions in this complex man's character are epitomised by the way he describes his encounter with a picket standing at the front entrance to the Evening Post during the strike: " He was standing in the pouring rain looking so terribly forlorn. I said to him:' For goodness sake, come on in and stand in the lobby, you'll get absolutely soaked if you stay out there.' He was an inoffensive clerk in the Circulation

Department who would never have hurt anyone. He came inside and he said :' Thank you. I am sorry to be on strike. I really don't want to be.' I could have wept. This decent, harmless person was having his life made a misery just so his union bosses could prove how much power they had. It's always the foot soldiers who man the trenches and have to take the bullets, not the generals."

Strike over, Christopher Pole-Carew took his family on holiday to the lovely Scottish island of Mull " where a friend who lived there let me and Peregrine lie up in the dusk and shoot rabbits,which every father should teach his son. We also hired a sailing dinghy, to learn that art in the glorious Tobermory harbour. It was a wonderful holiday and when we returned to Nottingham my batteries were fully charged."

He needed those fully-charged batteries, because he walked back in to an embarrassing and potentially damaging scenario at T. Bailey Forman.

In his absence, discussion had taken place about the potential redundancies caused by the closure, during the strike, of the morning paper, the Guardian Journal. Pole-Carew had made it clear that he was opposed to any compulsory redundancies, although he knew these were going to be very difficult to avoid. While he was away, the unions had discussed the issue with his Assistant General Manager, Theo Kearton.

Pole-Carew had a firm rule that no-one talked to the Press about company policy but himself - or, by prior agreement on what was to be said, the Editor-in-Chief, Ken Burnett. Although it ran counter to his normal philosophy of allowing as much autonomy as possible for executives, he believed this control to be essential because of the risk of contradictory statements being made by people with differing understandings of how events were to be handled and because " neither the unions nor the Press could be relied upon to favour the company's point of view! "

Theo Kearton had slipped up on the golden rule and under questioning he had stated that the company's policy was to accept only voluntary redundancies. He went on to say that whoever volunteered would be accepted and at a rate of redundancy pay that was twice the legal limit (a condition previously insisted upon by Pole-Carew).

The unions, still smarting over the outcome of the dispute, figured that if every union member who had been out on strike applied for this generous package, along with some of those who had refused to go on strike but would still find the redundancy terms very attractive, they would **all** leave and the Evening Post would be unable to return to proper production because there would be only a handful of staff left. They were right. And Charlie Wright was inundated with applications for redundancy.

Pole-Carew returned to find panic in his upper ranks…

" Charlie - don't tell me your loyal troops have applied too!"

" *They have!*"

" Can't they be persuaded to think again? "

" *Could be.*"

" Do it."

So, throughout the weekend that followed and in great secrecy, Charlie Wright and Peter Mould visited all those they didn't want to lose to suggest that they should ask the company if they might , on second thoughts, withdraw their applications for redundancy, upon which all would be sweetness and light and they would be well cared for. On the following Monday morning, all the specially selected members of the production department formally applied to Charlie Wright to withdraw their redundancy applications. Charlie Wright told them that after giving the matter some careful thought, he felt it would be unreasonable not to allow them to do so.

" What a result! " recalls Pole-Carew with relish." All the good loyal production workers stayed with the company; all the trouble makers, idlers and bloody minded FoCs in the works departments had applied for redundancy which had been accepted by the company. Thanks to a slip by Theo Kearton, combined with the unions' inability to think things through, T.Bailey Forman Ltd finished up with a brilliantly cleaned out work force, ready to face any challenges that the future might present and a reputation for making only volunteers redundant. How whiter than white can you get!"

It was the final sequel to the strike of 1973 and thereafter, *every* Christmas until he left the company more than 10 years later *every* member of staff who had been a union member but defied the call and stayed in during the strike received a bottle of expensive whisky and a Christmas card signed by Christopher Pole-Carew with the inscription **" Lest We Forget"**

5
BLOODY BATTLES

' A hero to his employees; the envy of his gutless contemporaries and a hate figure to the unions.'

IN Nottingham, Christopher Pole-Carew acquired such a huge reputation for taking on the print unions and consequently attracted so much publicity, nationally and internationally, as a "union buster" that it is easy to form the impression that he spent every working day plotting and scheming against them.

In fact, nothing could be further from the truth.

To him, trade unions were an irrelevance that occasionally became an irritant; a gratuitous barrier to the bond of two way loyalty which was the cornerstone of his attitude towards industrial relations. When unions stood in the way of his relationship with his own workforce or obstructed the path to the progress which he believed to be in the best interests of the entire company, from cleaner to chairman, they had to be opposed. His methods of so doing were often distasteful to his contemporaries but, when battle was over, he would bear his enemies no grudges and for the rest of the time, unions really didn't matter one jot to him.

Thus, the picture so often painted of him as some demented crusader against the trade union movement and the working classes is as hopelessly inaccurate as it is, to this day, prevalent.

Throughout that dramatic period in and around the strike of 1973 there were many other innovative things happening which were to him (and it must be said, to the vast majority of people in the T.Bailey Forman empire) infinitely more important than heavily publicised punch-ups with the unions.

Among these were exciting new techniques in the commercial operations of the Nottingham Evening Post - not confined to that newspaper but nowhere pursued with more energy and imagination.

Barrie Williams

Crucial to that piece of Pole-Carew's revolution jig-saw was the appointment of David Teague as Advertisement Manager in 1972. One of a new breed of commercial executives in the newspaper industry, David came from Fleet Street, where he was Classified Advertisement Director of The Times and Sunday Times. He succeeded Sydney Morgan, a traditional TBF employee who had started as a clerk in the advertisement department, became a rep (there was no sophisticated " selling " of advertising space in those days) and eventually got the top job of Advertisement Manager. Pole-Carew didn't think this traditional background equipped Syd Morgan for the modern role, new methods, extra demands and heavy pressures of a burgeoning newspaper advertisement market and wanted him out.

He achieved this by telling Syd that he was going to create a new position of Advertisement Director and that he was not in the running for it. Syd duly resigned and Pole-Carew, typically, then ' saw him right' by way of severance pay. Syd's reported reaction was " Christopher is a real bastard - but at least he's a generous one." (" *I wouldn't mind that on my gravestone!* " *says Pole-Carew*) Then in came David Teague, who recalls: " For some time I had been looking for an opportunity to get away from London and return to the regional newspaper industry. One of the things which made this difficult were the ' golden handcuffs' of a Fleet Street salary well in excess of anything being offered by the regional press. A colleague had heard that Nottingham were looking for an Advertisement Manager and suggested that I call Christopher Pole-Carew on the basis that " you've got nothing to lose."

"I knew of Christopher. We had been contemporaries in Thomson Regional Newspapers, but we hadn't met. Similarly, I knew almost nothing about the publishers of the Nottingham papers, except that they were notorious as being the most backward of backwoodsmen and lousy payers to boot!

" Still, I was so eager to get away from London that I rang Christopher. My subsequent interview was typical of the man. After meeting him and the chairman, he arranged for me to be taken to lunch by the then Editor, Bill Snaith, the Promotions Manager, Bob Britten and the recently appointed Market Research Manager, Jacquie Hickman. The logic was that these were the three people with whom I would be most closely involved. If I didn't click with them, it was unlikely that I would be able to fit in. Very sensible. This was my first experience of the common sense Christopher often displayed in such matters. This was not a man who forced his personal choice on other people. Or, put another way, he ensured that he had their tacit approval in advance so they couldn't turn around afterwards and complain about the appointment he had made.

"Apparently I got the green light and the next step was an offer of employment. 'Well.' I said ' the idea appeals to me - but I don't think you can afford me.' Christopher asked what I was getting in London. It was £8,000 a year, a lot of money in 1972, well above what Thomson paid in the regions and, I suspected, light years away from what Nottingham had in mind. Christopher thought for a moment. ' I can't beat it,' he said, ' but I'll match it.' Trying not to look too pleased, I signed!

" Afterwards I discovered that the other senior people - Editor, Chief Accountant, Production Manager and so on - were on about 60% of that offer. No wonder they were pleased to see me. They soon joined me on the new salary scale. Oh, and I brought my smart company car with me as part of the deal."

David Teague says all this illustrated how serious and determined Pole-Carew was about uplifting Nottingham into the 20th Century and that he had the full support of Colonel Tom Forman Hardy in that resolve.

Hardly had the new Advertisement Manager had time to locate his desk, however, before the '73 strike erupted : " In my area, advertisers were under pressure to support the management stance or sympathise with the union point of view. Fortunately, the majority stuck with the company. The early casualty of the dispute, the Guardian Journal, was a sickly publication with a ridiculously small sale. Commercially, I could not have saved it in a hundred years and secretly I was glad to see it go, even though it halved my small empire overnight.

" The human cost of that strike was dramatic but as a relatively minor player I escaped the worst excesses of threats to life and family, obscene telephone calls and mail, etc. We all mucked in. A twenty four hour guard was mounted to patrol the newspaper building and discourage attempts at sabotage. We all had to brave the picket lines and this was particularly difficult for the likes of the girls on my tele-ad sales team. You had to ask yourself :' Why should youngsters like that, who have no part in this fight, be subjected to such vicious intimidation? ' In a few sad cases families were split, with some working on and others demonstrating outside.

" My personal loyalties were never in any doubt. One of the things that had driven me out of Fleet Street was the way in which unions on the national newspapers totally controlled what happened in all departments and routinely abused their power. Nottingham was a breath of fresh air. It was good to be fighting back and to have a management with the courage to stand up to bullying.

" When it was all over, Nottingham had become the first newspaper company in the United Kingdom to use computers and we never looked back."

What neither David Teague nor anybody else involved , including Pole-Carew himself, knew then was that this was to be merely the start of more than a decade of relentless innovation and achievement at the Nottingham Evening Post which would permeate and transform *every* area of the business and establish scores of pioneering precedents, many of which would eventually be embraced and adopted by the rest of the newspaper industry.

The implications of the victory won by Christopher Pole-Carew in those six dramatic weeks in 1973 were immense on a number of fronts…

The sleepy old Nottingham Evening Post had gone from backwoods obscurity to national notoriety. Christopher Pole-Carew had become a hero to all the employees who had continued to work through the strike; the focus of vitriolic abuse as the bete noire of the trades union movement and the subject of the grudging envy of the leaders of the rest of the UK regional newspaper industry who lacked the guts to follow Nottingham and resented the turbulent impact on their placid waters of this arrogant maverick who missed no opportunity to rub it into them whenever he was provided with a public platform, which (since he was now in great demand as a speaker at international industry conferences) was to be far too frequently for their liking or comfort.

With one or two honourable exceptions, those captains of the regional newspaper industry licked their lips in joyful anticipation of his early downfall.

" **Well,**" says David Teague, *" they had to wait a long time! "*

Meanwhile, on the home front, life went on as normal for the Pole-Carew family: " Our children were growing up. Delia had gone to Ockbrook, a school sited between Derby and Nottingham and chosen because of its religious background, which mattered a lot to both Gill and I, but it was not a great success for us. Bluntly, it was too parochial for our tastes. Most of the girls were local, from the Derby area, so they all knew each other. Delia was a weekly boarder so she didn't mix with them at weekends. Sadly, in our move from Buxton to Nottinghamshire, we had not told Tudor Hall, near Banbury (our preferred choice) of our new address so she lost her place at that school. Peregrine went to Radley, after a time at West Downs in Winchester. Radley was a great success - a lovely, civilised school under the leadership of the incredibly successful Dennis Silk. Camilla went to St Mary's, Wantage, which was still, in those days, run by nuns and she loved it. St Mary's was one of the last schools in those days at which a young lady's education was about getting married and precious little else. Small wonder Camilla got married at 18!

" Naturally, all three of our children went to private boarding schools. The idea of state education was not even considered. The approach Gill and I took was…*you don't go to school just to learn the three Rs. You go to learn an attitude towards life, with music and art included and to mix with other children who will, like as not, be your friends for life.*"

Back at work, as the unique *Nottingham System* of computerisation grew, Pole-Carew tried to sell it to other newspapers but never succeeded. In most other British industries at that exciting time of great technological development, his contemporaries would have been queuing up to buy and benefit from a system for which **he** had taken all the risks, coped with all the pressures, won all the battles then established it firmly as a tried and tested, reliable, modern, cleaner, cheaper and infinitely less troublesome method of producing newspapers than the essentially Victorian techniques still employed by most companies. He contributed this failure to add *purveyors of state-of-the-art computer technology* to the growing portfolio of T. Bailey Forman Ltd to " a mixture of union hostility and senior newspaper men within the Newspaper Society clearly opposing any spreading of Nottingham's wings."

Sardonically, he adds: " Consider this. If you were the head of a newspaper that was a public company, or part of one, there would be little pleasure in having shareholders wondering why Nottingham was able to enjoy all this new technology, whilst you seemed unable to. This was not a time for me to be able to make friends in the newspaper industry."

Neither was the sheer hatred from the unions, which was to endure throughout Pole-Carew's career, ever likely to smooth the passage of the *Nottingham System* into other newspaper companies. On one occasion, when he visited a newspaper in the north of England, the entire production staff downed tools, walked out of the building and stayed outside until he left.

Typically undaunted and even more determined, he steamed full ahead with the development of new technology in Nottingham. The Evening Post kept on leading the way and now manufacturers were asking them to field trial their latest products before going into production.

Then, just as typically, he grew impatient at the pace of progress and resolved that the Nottingham Evening Post would have to go it alone and start developing its own systems.

He appointed the company's first in-house computer expert, Stan Dziuba. Stan joined the company straight from school and he gradually improved the systems they had, but it soon became clear to Pole-Carew that Stan's knowledge and experience were going to remain confined to one newspaper office, unless...

He sent for Stan and told him he wanted him to **leave** T Bailey Forman, go out into the wide world to get more experience then come back to take over running what would by then be TBF'S Computer Department. So off went Stan, working for other trail blazing companies and on major computer development projects, including massively complex systems for the Metropolitan Police.

Says Pole-Carew: " At the time, Stan had assumed, wrongly, that I was sacking him, but back he came and - as promised - I put him in charge of the Computer Department. And very good indeed he was too! "

It was time to complete the circle of ground breaking new technology at the Nottingham Evening Post with the introduction of an editorial system. This was to be a massive step. Direct computerised input of material by journalists (ie. no longer any processes between the journalist and the page) was hugely revolutionary and would eventually change the British newspaper industry beyond recognition. This giant step was the subject of pioneering experimentation in the United States of America but, apart from the Nottingham Evening Post, no newspaper in Europe, let alone the UK, was anywhere remotely near such an advanced stage of new technology development to be even considering it.

For Pole-Carew, vigorously pursuing this goal, there was one major snag: the only system obtainable was an American one (on IBM machines) tailored to the character of American newspapers (which, in those days, were mostly made up of solid, uniform slabs of reading matter) and as such wholly unsuitable for an English newspaper with a vastly greater variety of lay-outs and typographic techniques.

So, he told Stan Dziuba to write a bespoke Nottingham Evening Post editorial system, which this exceptionally talented young man did forthwith. But there was another problem. In pre-desktop days, the processing of any matter had to be done in large, main frame computers, right down to hyphenating and justifying copy and handling different shapes and type sizes. In laymen's terms, this was the equivalent of having a factory in London and running parts up to Birmingham to have them modified then sent back; non-stop toing and froing in vast quantities. It just didn't make sense.

After much head scratching and burning of midnight oil, Stan Dziuba and Christopher Pole-Carew between them eventually came up with a solution, which was to buy from ICL a mass of their small 7502 computers, which were housed in a specially constructed air conditioned room off the Nottingham Evening Post editorial floor. Each editorial desk then had its own screen (Visual Display Unit) which was connected to its own computer which handled all the early stages of turning editorial copy into newspaper type: thus it did not need to go near the main frame computer until it was in a shape that would fit onto a page for printing.

In effect, what these two men had done was to invent the desktop computer.

The result was a brilliant editorial system which was way ahead of its time, created years before anybody else in the newspaper industry in the UK , or indeed the whole of Europe, even considered such a process. In fact, a whole decade was to pass before the rest of the British regional newspaper industry (followed even later by the nationals) made that leap of faith and this sensational development was so far off the radar of everybody else that it went, largely unrecognised and unreported that...

In December, 1976, the Nottingham Evening Post made newspaper history in Britain by publishing the first story to be electronically typeset by journalists.

Another British regional newspaper industry " first " followed in 1977 when the Nottingham Evening Post introduced colour magazines given away free with the evening paper. This, in turn, was a product of another Pole-Carew innovation when he changed the basic structure of T Bailey Forman by turning various production departments into subsidiary companies, obliging them to become profit and cost centres in their own right rather than service departments to the newspaper.

There were two clear and separate reasons for the creation of profit making subsidiaries, both of which stood up in their own right: " Firstly, I wanted to introduce some kind of standard measurement of efficiency into the production area. The normal condition in a newspaper was for production and editorial to be totally interdependent departments; the production side existing solely to turn the editorial creation into the end newspaper product; the editorial side to provide the material to do this. Thus, whether the production areas were efficient or not was not a matter for discussion. Either the paper made a profit or it didn't. The unions determined the manning and therefore the costs of production and the appeal to readers of what was written determined profitability above that level.

" With new technology, the situation changed. Suddenly, the profitability of a paper could be increased by the reduction of its production costs - but how was one to determine whether or not a production system was truly as efficient as it could be? "

Pole-Carew took the view that the only way was to operate in a commercial environment; that the ability to produce and sell your output on the open market would determine your efficiency. So, he created TBF Printers (a company to run in parallel with the Nottingham Evening Post's Composing Room but doing commercial print work) and the Huthwaite Printing Company at Sutton-in-Ashfield (which would have its own printing press to complement the main Forman Street presses).

Huthwaite also gave the parent company experience in offset printing, which brought the advantages of superior print quality and full colour (but not, in those days, the speed required for a big evening newspaper) and natural suitability to the photo composing system which he was also developing.

" Secondly, I was following a policy of doing more work with less manpower in tandem with an unwritten but absolutely unshakeable understanding of no redundancy. To achieve both ends, it followed that I must create jobs by bringing more work in. Hence: TBF Printers and the Huthwaite Printing Company."

Nationally, it was the firm belief of the print unions at the time that the purpose of the new offset press at Huthwaite was to man it with non-union labour, thus keeping it clear of possible union activities at Forman Street – ie. a "*blackleg press.*"

That, says Pole-Carew, was ridiculous.

" The choice we made was purely because we got a nice green field site near to Sutton-in- Ashfield and our Sutton-based weekly newspaper, the Notts Free Press, which was to be printed there. Where else would we put it?

" Even a pea-brained ten-year-old could have worked out that there simply wasn't anything even remotely like enough space for it at Forman Street, but over the years we got used to this sort of fiction being trotted out as fact by the unions. And how typical of them at that time to attack a plan that was both safeguarding and creating jobs, just because it was my idea! "

When colour printing had been perfected at Huthwaite, it was a clever development of the commercial opportunities it presented to produce the magazines which gave advertisers a platform from which to ply their wares in glorious full colour via the 130,000 circulation of the Nottingham Evening Post and journalists the chance to indulge their creative flair in colour photography

Like other Pole-Carew initiatives, the magazines were both a commercial master stroke and another newspaper industry development way ahead of its time, as were many of the steps being taken by his recruit from Fleet Street, David Teague who was bringing a new degree of professionalism to the money-making areas of the business and doing so with the sort of free hand Pole-Carew always gave to executives he had appointed.

It was a freedom much appreciated by David Teague, who recalls:" I cannot think of a single occasion when he created problems for me on any serious issue. That's a great relationship to have with one's immediate superior; to be largely left alone to get on with it. I'm entitled to some of the credit for that because Christopher knew that I was well on top of the job but, then, other people in a similar position in other companies had been equally competent but still had to suffer the unwarranted intrusions of a managing director who needed to demonstrate his personal worth and input. Chris was never like that."

Senior journalist Ian Manning has similar memories of the man at that time: " I saw him as a visionary pioneer at a time of great change in the newspaper industry, but for me the greatest of his many qualities was his loyalty to his staff and the way he cared for us. He seemed not only to know the first names of all of his hundreds of employees but what was happening in their lives as well - and he was always generous. He was, quite simply, extraordinary."

Still working in a senior production role at the Nottingham Evening Post, Ian Manning offers the following insight into Pole-Carew's enormous contribution to the newspaper industry:

" Today, multimedia is sweeping into the newspaper industry at a rapid rate as companies try to come to terms with the internet age by developing and perfecting websites to run in conjunction with printed publications.

" It may prove to be the salvation of newspaper publishers if they can marry the internet with printed publications while at the same time bringing in extra advertising revenue online to compensate for that being lost as circulations sink and clients consider whether their newspaper ads are still cost-effective. Hits on the internet are all very well but they do not necessarily bring in the lolly.

" The man who has given the industry a fighting chance of surviving in the internet age is, in my opinion, Christopher Pole-Carew, because more than 30 years ago he laid the foundations for it all by introducing electronic editing to British newspapers.

"As newspaper journalists today struggle to master the complexities of the web, with audio and video becoming increasingly important, it is far less of a journey into the unknown than it was in 1976 when the Nottingham Evening Post made newspaper history in Great Britain by publishing the first story 'set' by journalists. Pole-Carew was pioneering a revolution which continues to race along to this day.

" It was comparatively easy for reporters to switch from typewriters or pens to computers but for sub-editors, brought up on editing with pencils and pens and with type set in metal, there were many two pairs of underpants days and some incredibly long hours as they wrestled with the new technology!

" To put a 14pt headline onto a small filler story and edit it was fiddly. To do the same with the front page splash meant having to input nearly a whole screen load of instructions first. One missed space or digit could scramble it all and in many cases corrupt the system, sometimes leading to breakdown…all with deadlines pressing, delivery vans waiting and thousands of pounds worth of circulation revenue at risk. Breakdowns were frequent because the unique, trail blazing system was in its infancy and software was notoriously unreliable. There was nothing to fall back on.

" Our Chief Sub Editor ,George Hunt, bore the brunt of the problems from the editorial point of view and he coped magnificently, despite pretending to know far more than he really did about the technicalities of it all. When asked by sub-editors about the cause of the frequent breakdowns, George had a stock answer: ' It's a mainframe problem, mate,' he would say. It was a tribute to his tenacity and man-management that not one edition was missed and the new system led rapidly to 10 main editions and up to 18 major changes a day, which would have been totally unachievable with conventional production methods.

" Throughout all those incredibly hectic and stressful early days, Pole-Carew was enormously supportive of the journalists who were battling to make it work. When he first introduced direct input and all that followed he listened very carefully to the journalists, making sure that he was not asking for the impossible.

" He treated us very well indeed. He believed in adequate staffing levels and top pay for top journalists. We all got a big rise when the new methods were brought in. And it wasn't only financially that he looked after us. There were fears at the time that working on screen could lead to eyesight problems. This proved to be largely unfounded but Pole-Carew was not prepared to take chances. He arranged eyesight tests for us all and when those proved that some sub-editors needed glasses to work on computers all day he made sure they were paid for by the firm. Then he arranged free eye tests for us all every year. In those days, that sort of care for your employees was extremely rare. To Pole-Carew it was just second nature.

" He was a man in a hurry as he set out to drag newspapers, screaming and kicking, into the 20th Century but he was also a realist who knew that if his troops were not happy, well cared for, fully appreciated and well-paid they would be unlikely to deliver the revolution for him. We did deliver his revolution, because we were with him one hundred and fifty per cent. Such was the loyalty that he inspired.

" In my view Pole-Carew was a far more influential figure in British newspaper history than, say Eddie Shah, who took on the might of Fleet Street with his launch of the Today newspaper nearly a decade later, using techniques and technology pioneered by Pole-Carew.

" Without Pole-Carew's genuinely ground-breaking lead all those years ago, the newspaper industry might well have been years behind today in its fight for survival, let alone prosperity, as readers switch to the internet."

Another senior editorial man, Ian Scott recalls Pole-Carew's inspirational qualities in those days :" There was nothing that would stand in the way of his progress. Bursting with enthusiasm, he gave a talk to the main editorial people and many queries were thrown at him. We didn't quite grasp this new concept of not having any stories written on paper and I recall saying to him, rather stupidly: ' We'll need filing cabinets up to the ceiling.' He gave a wave of his arm: ' So, we'll **get** filing cabinets up to the ceiling!' Of course, they were never needed."

Pole-Carew's reputation had, inevitably, spread outside the industry. In 1995 he had been asked by a close friend, Stephen Dobson, if he would like his name to be put forward to become High Sheriff of Nottinghamshire.

High Sheriff of Nottinghamshire

This appealed to Pole-Carew who recalls: " The office of High Sheriff is all that remains of an old and very powerful post under the Crown, going back to Saxon days. The period in office is limited to a year - and that limit dates from the days when, as law giver and tax collector for the county, it was deemed that this was quite long enough for one person to hold it and how about letting somebody else have a go!

" Nowadays, the position is purely honorary with a kind of responsibility for High Court judges when they are sitting in the courts of your locality.

"A list of names for the office in each county are submitted to the Queen each year and, by tradition, she chooses one at random by pricking the list with a gold bodkin. Interestingly enough, she invariably pricks the name at the top of the list!

" In those days, the Nottingham list was three long so I could expect to be High Sheriff in 1978. And I was. But not without some disruptive clouds appearing on the horizon. My choice was opposed by the then Lord Lieutenant of Nottinghamshire, Commander Phillip Franklyn who told me I was the sort of contentious person (what with strikes and things) who should not be involved in a position of appointment by the Monarch. This was all said in a bated breath sort of way. In fact, it was none of his business - Lord Lieutenants being comparatively new appointments, military in origin as distinct from legal, started by Henry V111 and quite unconnected with the Shrievalty, so I saw no reason whatsoever to take his advice. It was quite an honour to become High Sheriff and if I dropped out the chances of being asked again were nil. Anyway, I thought, what had a strike in 1973 got to do with it? Maybe I had committed the cardinal sin of winning it! Events, however, were to show that Phillip Franklyn was not entirely wrong.

" The role of High Sheriff was fascinating: I met the judges when they came to Nottingham and accompanied them to the Crown Court where I sat on the bench alongside the judge. It was also most interesting sitting in the judge's room before a case started listening to the judge and Counsel discussing it beforehand. It all seemed very pally, I thought, when they were about to go out to fight over a person's liberty."

Like everything else in life that he tackled, Pole-Carew threw himself into the role of High Sheriff with gusto, high energy, total commitment *and a determination to change things for the better.*

It is perfectly safe to assume that no previous occupant of this historic office had ever approached it in the manner of Pole-Carew.

After finding the time, while still attending to the rigorous demands of the 'day job,' to sit through ten cases he " ended up with a disappointingly lower opinion of the English legal system" than when he began:

" The system seemed to be run very much for the benefit of the lawyers and in the first case I saw - what you might call a 'happy families' case with lots of under age sex - there were 14 legal people in the court.

" Everything was conducted at the speed of the judge taking copious notes in a variety of coloured pencils. I got bored."

Typically, Pole-Carew thought the processes of Nottingham Crown Court could be improved radically by the application of some decent management and he asked his Computer Manager, Peter Stocks to sit in court to see how newspaper practices could be employed to make the place run better!

Pole-Carew had been told that if the judge wanted a detailed transcript of a case he would expect it to take up to a fortnight. Such 'sloth' was anathema to the new High Sheriff so he asked Peter Stocks to devise a quicker method and the computer man (using standard newspaper copy-taking techniques but doubled up and fully recorded for total accuracy) came up with a system by which the judge could have his full, detailed transcript, plus an audio copy to overcome the time wasting ritual of writing copious notes, within *one hour* of returning to his lodgings at the end of a day's hearing.

Not for the first time in his colourful career, Pole-Carew's unbridled enthusiasm for doing things better contained, at the same time, an element of naivety and it should not have come as a surprise to him when the judge was not only under-whelmed by the proffered improvements but not the least bit amused by this attempt at interference with the time honoured procedures of his court.

Not content with wanting to streamline the procedures, Pole-Carew also concluded that the courts were more concerned with the letter of the law and lawyers' practices than the pursuit of justice, quoting the following case as an example:

" The case was a nautical one. A seaman in a fishing vessel, whilst letting the trawl net run out, realised that it was shorter than usual so he let it go and ran aft, tripping over a hatch combing and breaking a knee cap. On that basis, he was suing the trawler company.

"There I sat ,with my great wealth of nautical experience, alongside the judge ready, willing and able to assist him with his understanding of the niceties of the case.

"In due course, the court rose and we went back to the judge's lodgings for a pleasant and leisurely lunch over which I explained that :

(a) From the model of the windlass in the court and a little commonsense thinking it was clear that the rope, when running free, could not possibly have put the seaman into any danger and,

(b) One of the first things that all seamen are taught on going to sea is *never, ever* to run for safety along the line of a free running rope; *always* run at a right angle to it to get clear.

" This seaman had run along the rope. It was, therefore, clearly his own fault that he has suffered his accident.

" Back in court for the summing up and judgement, the judge found in the seaman's favour. Afterwards I asked the judge how he could possibly have done that and he replied: 'Ah , well. What you explained to me, however true or accurate, was said *outside* the court room so I couldn't possibly take it into account.'

" 'Not even to ask some prompting questions?' I asked.

"And the judge just gave me a pitying look."

That was not the only judgement with which the new High Sheriff took issue. Of the ten cases he sat through his conclusion was that no less than five others (ie. six out of the ten) were miscarriages of justice - mostly through not being found guilty!

In the black or white spectrum of the Pole-Carew philosophy there's no recognition of subjective judgement and this experience left him reflecting: " Even though details were discussed in the judge's room beforehand, clearly guilty defendants were getting off. Maybe our obsession with being innocent until proven guilty has a tendency to be overplayed; maybe juries should be given relevant background details in order to judge sensibly."

While the judges may not have been too receptive to the High Sheriff of Nottinghamshire's ideas about changing the English legal system for the better there was no restraint on his equal enthusiasm for improving the efficiency of the ancient office. He carried out what was effectively a time and motion study then wrote an exhaustive book during his year in office. Titled *Notes On The Office and Duties of the High Sheriff of Nottinghamshire*, his book covered just about everything : who sat where on civic occasions; which Courts were which in the Shire Hall; an analysis of all the people to be entertained and why; charities, civic dignitaries, forms of address and so on.

Says Pole-Carew: " The book is still in existence and was copied and adapted by the Shrievalty Association for general use by High Sheriffs throughout the realm. With my permission, of course! "

The new broom sweeping through the High Sheriff's office did not stop there. He also resolved to " sharpen up" the Under Sheriff function. There were two Under Sheriffs, one for the city of Nottingham and one for the county of Nottinghamshire, " both apparently making a loss on their duties on behalf of the High Sheriff." Pole-Carew decided one was enough: " With the two offices combined the result would be one office making a profit and therefore concerned to serve the Sheriff properly."

So, in a move that was not without its acrimony, he merged the two.

One imagines that in the musty, dusty circles of the Nottinghamshire establishment the end of the revolutionary Christopher Pole-Carew's year of office as High Sheriff could not come soon enough, but not so for the man himself who recalls that: " Being High Sheriff involved many formal parties, with the immense enjoyment of being given red carpet treatment on all occasions; greeting Royalty; meeting the many county and district councillors, most of whom I found to be delightful and intensely hard working for their communities; making so many friends. When my year in office was over I went to a dinner at County Hall and it was frightful. I no longer had my driver so I had to park in the general car park and walk through the rain to get to the event, at which I was no longer in the VIP drinks room before dinner and - it got worse - no longer on the top table. Back to reality with a bump."

He had also made a point, on more occasions than had previous High Sheriffs, of wearing the traditional uniform of historic finery, frills and feathered frippery - gaiters, extravagant white silk cravat, long black dress coat and buckled shoes.

Though he, himself, dismisses the view as " pure codswallop" there are plenty of his contemporaries who recall that with such flamboyant attire adorning his 6ft 5 inch frame the handsome, blond Pole-Carew cut a real 'medieval' dash.

This provided much gleefully used 'ammunition' for his bitter opponents in his next high profile clash with the unions - this time over the NUJ (National Union Of Journalists) pay dispute in 1978, coincidentally the year he was in office as High Sheriff.

This was a national dispute, culminating in a national strike, over journalists pay - particularly on the smaller weekly newspapers, on which the salaries were disgracefully low.

In common with all those in the regional newspaper industry, the 120 journalists employed on Christopher Pole-Carew's Nottingham Evening Post were called out on strike - but there was one huge difference between the Nottingham journalists and the rest. They were being paid an average £1200 a year **more** than the figure their union was asking them to go out on strike for.

This was all part of Pole-Carew's industrial relations philosophy of paying the best to get the best and looking after them exceptionally well in return for his implicit expectation of unbreakable two-way loyalty.

Every year, the Newspaper Society (the employers organisation) and the NUJ would negotiate an annual increase in pay. Every year, Christopher Pole-Carew would wait until the agreed national figure was publicised before announcing the increase for Nottingham Evening Post journalists - always ensuring that *his* journalists stayed a minimum £1000 a year ahead of all those in the rest of the country.

In 1978, £1000 was a considerable sum of money. Compared with the rest of the regional industry, Nottingham Evening Post journalists were very well paid and the call for them to strike came **before** Pole-Carew had announced that year's Nottingham pay increase, which would have put them even further ahead.

Not surprisingly, the vast majority of NUJ members on the Nottingham Evening Post pay roll did not want to go on strike.

The union sent its Acorn House HQ officials up to tell them that they had no option. They **had** to support their comrades in the rest of the country or lose their union cards - a very serious threat for an ambitious journalist in the virtual closed shop of the newspaper industry in the 'seventies.

Pole-Carew's response was equally emphatic. So far as he was concerned, the 1973 strike was the last one the Nottingham Evening Post was going to endure and he was adamant that no union had any justification in calling his management to account over the way it treated employees.

He announced that any Nottingham Evening Post journalist who joined the strike would be sacked.

Objective observers could sympathise with both stances.

* What else was a trades union for but to fight for the less fortunate and exploited among its membership and how could that battle be won without total support, solidarity and absolute loyalty to your union?

Barrie Williams

* What on earth was the point in going on strike for £1200 a year **less** than you were already being paid and why would you repay the goodwill and generosity of the best employer in your industry by withdrawing your labour when you had no quarrel whatsoever with your own bosses?

But the NUJ was not going to free its Nottingham Evening Post members of the burden of supporting its national fight and Christopher Pole-Carew was not going to move one inch from his implacable commitment to two way loyalty in his own local business. Irresistible force was meeting immovable object and the outcome was inevitable.

Eventually, 28 of the Nottingham Evening Post's journalists went out on strike. They were told they were never to come back. They were sacked.

The national strike, which began in December, 1978 was over relatively quickly, early in 1979, after the Newspaper Society agreed a pay rise with the NUJ.

The sacked 28 Nottingham journalists expected to be re-instated once the dust had settled - indeed their union has assured them that they would *have* to be - but Christopher Pole-Carew was having none of it. They would **not** be allowed back. They had been fired. And they would stay fired.

For the second time in a decade the wrath of the entire British Labour and Trades Union movement then descended on the Forman Street headquarters of the Nottingham Evening Post. For the second time in a decade, the maverick Pole-Carew broke with the rest of the British newspaper industry and took the unions on.

It has to be recorded, here, that this was at a time of immense union power, particularly in the newspaper industry; of a Labour Government still very reliant on the trades union movement and of no legislative protection from viciously intimidating mass secondary picketing.

Thousands of pickets from all over Britain travelled to Nottingham to flood Forman Street with protest and try to prevent production of the Evening Post. Hundreds of police officers were employed to control them. The Nottingham Evening Post and its controversial managing director had , just as in 1973, become a focus of national media attention.

In the eyes of the Labour and trades union movement and millions of their supporters, the " evil " Pole-Carew had committed the cardinal sin of sacking workers for exercising their fundamental right to strike.

In the eyes of Pole-Carew, and plenty of people who felt it was high time somebody stood up to union power, 28 of his employees had chosen loyalty to their union over loyalty to him and the company which treated them very well, thus sacrificing their jobs of their own accord.

In the eyes of the few objective observers at the time, the 28 journalists had been caught in a dreadful dilemma: Strike and you lose your job. Don't and you lose your right ever to work on any other newspaper.

Pole-Carew recalls: " It was a sad business. The strikers had no chance of winning and had only gone out because they feared they would never be able to work on any other newspaper if they didn't. Nothing subtle about the way the unions ensured the grateful, heartfelt loyalty and support of their members! "

Just as in 1973 and much to the surprise of the rest of the newspaper industry (and the chagrin of the trades unions) the Nottingham Evening Post never lost so much as one day's publication of the Nottingham Evening Post during the lengthy period of mass picketing during 1979. The 28 striking journalists were a small proportion of the editorial workforce and the shake-out of 1973 had ensured that the production departments were trouble free. There were also the crucial factors of the genuine loyalty this man inspired throughout the company and the new technology he had pioneered - direct computer input of material by journalists being still unique to Nottingham in the UK and providing huge benefits in ease and speed of production.

Consequently, despite frequent mass picketing, intimidation and blacking (removal of all professional relationships, co-operation and reporting facilities and refusal to speak to journalists) of the Nottingham Evening Post by national and local Labour politicians and their supporters, including the hugely popular and influential manager of Nottingham Forest Football Club, Brian Clough, it remained pretty much business as usual at the besieged Forman Street offices of the newspaper.

Barrie Williams

A typical scene outside Forman Street

Only once was the relative peace and calm *inside* the building disturbed, when one Saturday in June 1979, Pole-Carew received a phone call while he was having lunch at home to tell him that Arthur Scargill, the firebrand National Union Of Mineworkers official, had been spotted talking to the pickets outside. He decided he should go into the office to see what was going on and was greeted with the news that pickets had rushed the Forman Street entrance and had occupied the editorial floor.

Rushing upstairs, he discovered that around 20 pickets were staging a sit-in while working journalists were trying to get the paper's lunchtime edition out. He didn't recognise any of the protesters as striking Evening Post journalists and concluded that they must be " imports." A police sergeant and two constables were on the scene.

Pole-Carew turned to the police sergeant and told him:

" Get these trespassers out of here."
" It's not my job to do that, sir."
" Well if you won't - I will! "

'Somebody Had To Do It'

Pole-Carew then went downstairs to the Composing Room to recruit volunteers to help him "clear the rabble." He added the bouncer from the pub across the road to his group of about a dozen men and he was told by the police: " You have every right to eject anyone who is on your premises without good reason but you may only use such force as is reasonably necessary - and no more."

Upstairs, Pole-Carew and his volunteers faced the pickets and told them to leave the premises immediately or, carefully repeating the words of the police advice, be ejected by ' such reasonable force as is necessary.'

He says the only reaction to that ultimatum was that the three police officers disappeared down the stairs!

After repeating the demand to leave and getting no response, Pole-Carew charged the pickets, hoping that his posse was close behind. They were.

Together they pushed the pickets to the stairwell where most of them walked away and out of the building but a few lay on the floor, clinging to the journalists' desks. They were lifted a couple of feet off the floor then dropped, upon which they released their grip on the desks and were dragged by their feet to the stairs.

That is Christopher Pole-Carew's version of the events.

Evening Post production journalist Ian Manning who was one of those non-strikers working that day, recalls: " We were told by the police that we could use reasonable force to evict them and after I had been dragged from my seat and put into a judo hold, my assailant was stretchered to hospital with a broken nose. Rumour has it that I had punched him and that his bodyguard lost some of his long black hair - and his will to fight - after grabbing me by the throat. The police later investigated the incidents and I know Pole-Carew stood up for us all. He never asked me what really happened and the police never asked me for a statement.

" Pole-Carew's loyalty to us shone through, as we knew it would, throughout the strike and its aftermath and all the NUJ members who refused to go on strike plus the non-NUJ members, like me, who carried on working were given three-year rolling contracts in case we could not get jobs elsewhere if we decided to leave in the future."

The vitriol to which those " blacklegs" were subjected by the unions, particularly during the mass picketing, was vicious and relentless.

To the trades union movement, Pole-Carew's Nottingham stance had become a huge national issue.

Before one mass picket, on September 1st 1979, the following rallying cry, written by Lynden Barber, vice-chairman of the NUJ London Suburban Area Council was published in the Socialist Worker:

" The High Priest of New Technology, Christopher Pole-Carew, is in for a shock on Saturday. Hundreds of trade unionists will be marching from the Forest Recreation Ground in Nottingham at 1pm to join a mass picket of the union-bashing Evening Post, of which Pole-Carew is managing director.

" They will have one aim - to stop the Post's sports edition. The 1000 strong picket in June managed to turn back scab vans and the police could only get the papers onto the streets by using decoy tactics. This time, with enough pickets, it should be possible to block all three entrances.

" The mass pickets are essential as a springboard to launch a major blacking campaign. Just as at Grunwicks,* they can be used as a focus to encourage other workers to take solidarity action.

" But the argument must be won that this is NOT just an isolated bad employer. The dispute should be used to make workers aware of the bosses' plans for new technology.

" The Nottingham Evening Post have used the technology solely as a means of breaking the unions. Our future message to other bosses should be loud and clear : **THEY DIDN'T GET AWAY WITH IT - AND NEITHER WILL YOU!** "

(* *In the late 1970's a dispute over trade union recognition at the Grunwick film processing laboratories in North London became an epic issue. It began when one third of the largely female and Asian workforce, unhappy about wages and conditions, joined the APEX union and went on strike. Their Anglo- Indian employer, George Ward, did not believe they had a legitimate grievance and sacked the strikers. This led to mass picketing of Grunwick on a huge scale and resulted in bloody clashes between police and pickets when protesters tried to prevent those still working from getting into the laboratories. The long- running dispute also became famous for the appearance on the picket lines of three Labour Government Ministers - Shirley Williams, Denis Howell and Fred Mulley.*)

That same week, the magazine Socialist Challenge published a full page article, similarly rousing support for the forthcoming mass picket. This is what appeared, under the headline:

FOR A TASTE OF TORY RULE, MEET THE SHERIFF OF NOTTINGHAM

Management of the Nottingham Evening Post has taken its approach to the unions straight out of the Tories' copybook, crushing journalists' and print workers' organisations alongside the introduction of new technology. The story of that defeat and of the Grunwick style mass pickets that are now seeking to re-instate the 28 sacked journalists - the next is on Saturday - is told here by ROBIN ANDERSON , a member of the journalists' chapel at the Evening Post and its former father…

" The dispute which has left 28 NUJ members at Nottingham out of work since December has been brewing since the late 1960s. The issues involved are so serious, attacking the foundations of trade union organisation, that it has taken the NUJ and the print unions almost a decade to get to grips with them.

" T. Bailey Forman Ltd (TBF) is one of the few surviving independent, family owned newspaper publishers in Britain. In the 1960s it began to replace outdated equipment with computer technology. But the company's steam-age industrial relations survived and in the hands of managing director Christopher Pole-Carew, the Forman Hardy family's hired hit man, they became considerably worse.

" In 1967, the Nottingham Evening Post became the first UK newspaper to install a general purpose computer for setting editorial text and adverts.

" The introduction of the computer, using a system known as optical character recognition, met opposition from the NGA because of its potential to replace skilled printers with unskilled typists. TBF took a conscious decision to take on the unions and break them, so that it could introduce new technology entirely on its own terms. The company converted fully to photo-composition in 1973 and in June of that year its chance came to confront the unions over a new process of making the plates from which the newspaper is printed.

" Six days before the NGA and SLADE were due to finalise an agreement on operating this process - and it was not being used anywhere else in Britain at that stage - the management sacked print workers in SLADE who refused to handle it in advance of national talks. Three hundred staff were eventually locked out - the first time in the industry's history that all five unions have taken united action.

" The NGA / SLADE agreement was made within the first week but the dispute lasted another five weeks because of the company's insistence that union members loyal to them should not be disciplined. The unions successfully insisted on their right to discipline members according to the respective rule books. One NUJ member was fined £25. He paid up and is still an active member elsewhere. The rest were expelled and did not bother to apply for readmission, which at that time carried a maximum fee of £30 - a small price for six weeks' strike breaking.

" Claiming that unions had victimised members, the company withdrew recognition. Since all unions had lost their 100 per cent membership they could not press the company to change its attitude.

" The dispute was used by TBF as an excuse for closing the morning paper, The Guardian Journal and resulted in 148 redundancies. It was the second round of job-axing in 18 months. The first, at the end of 1971, cost 95 jobs. The NUJ, NGA and SLADE have been in dispute with the company ever since, over recognition and persistent breaching of national agreements.

" Repeated management threats that employees who took industrial action would be sacked were a major factor in the NUJ chapel's disobedience of several national union instructions to take action. Meanwhile, TBF introduced its new technology unimpeded.

" In December 1976, the company made history by publishing Britain's first - ever story to be 'set' by journalists. Electronic editing , with staff using visual display units instead of typewriters and copy paper, was steadily introduced into most editorial departments.

" Many printers no longer needed on newspaper production were transferred to work for two commercial printing subsidiaries which operated in liaison with a non-union plant.

" The only official meeting between unions and management took place in Nottingham in September 1977 when Pole-Carew repeated his views that trade unions had no role to play in his company. The unions, NGA, SLADE and NUJ in particular, then drew up a common course of industrial action which included a boycott on all TBF commercial print work. This was introduced last year by the NGA and SLADE. Within a matter of weeks the company had lost business worth well over £1million a year and failed in its bid to obtain a High Court injunction to have the boycott lifted.

'Somebody Had To Do It'

" The following year, 1978, TBF closed down the commercial subsidiaries and made 52 printers redundant, including the last of the 1973 SLADE members.

" That December over 8,000 provincial journalists took part in the NUJ's first-ever indefinite national strike. Twenty eight members at the Evening Post defied management sacking threats and pledged their support to the profession and to the thousands of journalists paid scandalously low wages, by voting to take part in the strike.

" Despite being a member of the Newspaper Society, the employers' organisation, TBF took unilateral action and sacked the 28, alleging breach of contract. At the end of the national action, which won NUJ members a 14.5 per cent rise, the Nottingham 28 reported for work but were physically prevented from even entering the building. The company has consistently refused to meet union officials and has rejected all suggestions of mediation or conciliation.

" So intense is managing director Pole-Carew's opposition to us that when a TV programme was being made about the dispute he refused to be in the same studio as NUJ officials. When pickets held a sit-in in the paper's offices earlier this year to demand talks, Pole-Carew and a posse of thugs kicked and punched them out of the building.

" Pursuing their own recognition campaign, the NGA and SLADE began to boycott the Evening Post's major advertisers in February. The response was quick. Lord Denning granted an injunction suspending the boycott and when the NGA unsuccessfully appealed against this, it had to fork out costs estimated at £80,000.

" The Evening Post has published throughout the dispute, thanks mainly to journalists who have been expelled from the NUJ for strike breaking. The union has been pledged by its executive to the NUJ's biggest-ever campaign to secure reinstatement and union recognition.

" This is taking place on several fronts. There have been several mass pickets, with 1,000 attending on June 16, including a strong contingent of print workers, as well as some 30 young Nottinghamshire miners. To a triumphant chorus of ' The workers united will never be defeated' we managed to turn back one of the delivery vans, but others were moved by a heavy police contingent.

" Among those arrested on the picket line has been the NUJ president, who was fined £250 for obstruction. It is pure coincidence that Pole-Carew is the present High Sheriff of Nottinghamshire and most unlikely that he bought the police 20 gallons of beer for their efforts on the June 16 picket.

" The isolation of supplies, materials and spares is another objective, but this hasn't been easy because of the non-union lines of supply which management set up between 1973 - 78 , preparing themselves for the inevitable dispute.

" The 28 have launched their own weekly, the Nottingham News, which has built up a healthy circulation of around 14,000.

" At a seven hour debate on the dispute held by the NUJ executive two weeks ago, it was decided that all chapels should hold mandatory meetings to discuss financial support , work-to-rule, disruptive meetings and fixed-term and indefinite strikes to secure our reinstatement.

" The executive has also recommended that there should be no further negotiations with the Newspaper Society until it either makes TBF comply with the terms of the last settlement or expels it. This would mean local instead of national negotiations in the provincial newspaper field.

" The executive pledges support to the Nottingham News workers co-operative and said it would use its good offices to raise the capital to make the paper commercially viable. But there was much criticism of the paper's lack of industrial and political coverage, not least the fact that it had not mentioned the June 16 picket.

" Securing those 28 NUJ jobs at TBF will be a long, hard slog but it's a fight to preserve the right of workers to strike without fear of being sacked - the most fundamental of trade union principles. No union can afford to see T.Bailey Forman win. Be with us this Saturday.

*Assembly point for pickets on September 1st is Nottingham's Forest Recreation Ground off Mansfield Road at 1pm, for a march to the mass picket outside the Forman Street offices of the Evening Post, to 'greet' the Saturday editions. More than 50 coaches, organised by the NUJ, NGA, AUEW,SLADE and NUM branches, will be heading for Nottingham."

Head for Nottingham they did. In their hundreds. And the picket on September 1st was massive and noisy, with several clashes with the police. But, again, the demonstrators did not succeed in stopping the newspapers from getting out onto the streets of the city and beyond.

When the NUJ's pay dispute with the Newspaper Society had been settled, the Newspaper Society tried hard to pressurise Pole-Carew into taking back the sacked 28. But there was no point in trying to get him to 'comply with the terms of the last settlement' on pay because, national increase notwithstanding, the Evening Post journalists were still being paid more than the rates agreed by the Newspaper Society. When Pole-Carew made it clear that he would not budge on reinstatement of the 28 strikers, T. Bailey Forman Ltd. was expelled from the Newspaper Society. Pole-Carew who, with his customary enthusiasm and energy and very considerable help from David Teague, had contributed more than most to the Newspaper Society, was furious. He believed the way in which his company's expulsion was handled (" no discussion, nothing") was extremely ill-mannered. It has often been reported that Pole-Carew never forgave the Society. He says that's not quite the full story, adding: "TBF's expulsion drew my attention to the irrelevance and pointlessness of the Society."

In any event, when, in future years, the Society tried from time to time to persuade him to re-join the answer he gave to his TBF colleagues was always an unequivocal '**No** ' - or words of a rather more descriptive colour!

The Society itself didn't even get to hear that. He just never bothered to respond : " What was the point? " he asks. " To me, the Newspaper Society was now as irrelevant to the running of our newspapers as were the unions."

The NUJ conducted a high profile and costly campaign to " re-instate the twenty eight" for the next three years and the blacking of the Evening Post by the Labour and trades union movement remained in place for all of that time, but the NUJ must have known that it was only their pride that kept the issue alive. Well before the three years had passed, all the 28 journalists had got other good jobs, anyway and if the union thought Pole-Carew would relent they were crazy. He was oblivious to all the controversy and back to regarding the NUJ as a total irrelevance.

Barrie Williams

The NUJ's high profile campaign.

'Somebody Had To Do It'

In a book on the centenary history of the NUJ published in 2006, co-authors Tim Gopsill and Greg Neale, recorded the events thus…..

" There was a grim hangover from the NS dispute. The hardest of all provincial employers was a company called T. Bailey Forman (TBF) , publishers of the Nottingham Evening Post. TBF and its managing director Christopher Pole-Carew were pursuing a demented crusade against trade unions and all who were in them. In 1973 they had taken on the print unions, moving production to a non-union plant on a green field site; in the process they had locked out the NUJ after journalists refused to work with non-union print staff and there was a savage dispute. Twenty two NUJ members blacklegged and were expelled.

" Now, when the NS strike started they made it clear they would sack all who took part and this they duly did, leaving the NUJ with a terrible dilemma. The Nottingham members had been persuaded to join the strike with a promise they would be protected but the union found itself unable to do so. As chapel delegates gathered to vote on the final offer they agonised: should they stay out and risk their solidarity falling apart or leave Nottingham in the lurch? There was not much doubt which way they would go and for all the blood and sweat that was spilled in Nottingham all the rhetoric invoking unity, it was never a dispute that was going to be won.

" The fight to reinstate the Nottingham 28 was bitter, frustrating and violent. The Nottingham police had been heavy with the pickets during the strike but that seemed like a rehearsal for the extraordinary scenes in Forman Street in the spring and summer of 1979. Hundreds of police were turned out to meet the regular pickets and rallies outside the building. They formed into well-drilled ' flying wedge' formations and charged the crowds. Dozens were arrested and harshly treated by the magistrates, among them the NUJ Deputy General Secretary Jake Ecclestone who was fined the maximum £250 for obstructing the police, on a first offence.

" The magistrate said he would have jailed him if he could.

" It was as if the union was taking on the whole city. TBF and Pole-Carew were powerful in Nottingham. It was more than just having the street named after the company. Pole-Carew was the High Sheriff of Nottinghamshire and used to enjoy parading around in a white silk cravat, dress coat and gaiters at ceremonial occasions. Though he seemed a ludicrous figure, he was anything but. One morning in June 1979 the NUJ pickets took the company by surprise and got into the building.

The leading union official present was Mike Bower, the former leader of the Sheffield chapel ,who was now full time organiser for the north of England.

" Bower says: 'We arrived one day and there was only one cop on the door so we just went in. Pole-Carew came down and said *Get out of this office you scruffy little man* . He went into a pub across the road and came back with a posse and they got hold of me and pulled me from behind a desk. I fell to the floor and trapped my nose and split the gristle from the bone. There was blood all over the place. A TV film crew had arrived by this time and filmed us - but nothing was broadcast.'

" In 1980 The Journalist (*the NUJ's newspaper*) got a leak from a friendly boss of the record of a private seminar that Pole-Carew gave for newspaper managers on how to break the union. He told his apparently spellbound audience of how he set out to humiliate and discredit union officials and institute a 'reign of terror' against staff on strike. Company doctors carrying out medical tests on new staff should report those that might be 'security risks' and once in post they should be 'needled' to test their reactions. Potential strike breakers should be bribed to stay in work. Perhaps it was no surprise that five years later he turned up as a prominent adviser to Rupert Murdoch as he planned the move to Wapping.

" The 28 sacked Nottingham journalists took cases to an Employment Tribunal but it refused to hear them. With little prospect of winning back their jobs the members threw themselves into a new enterprise, publishing a weekly paper, the Nottingham News. They had a boost from the great football manager Brian Clough, whose club Nottingham Forest astounded the football world that year by winning the European Cup. Clough was at the peak of his fame and a well-known Labour Party supporter and right from the start he announced he would not speak to the Evening Post and took a column in the Nottingham News. Such was his authority that the rival club Notts County felt compelled to follow suit and boycotted the Evening Post as well. The union ploughed thousands into the News, launching a £250,000 appeal and it was a highly regarded paper. But it could never succeed commercially and folded before the dispute was settled, on terms of meagre compensation , in 1986. For the NUJ, Nottingham was a glorious defeat and sadly, too, there were more to come."

(*In fact, when the Nottingham Evening Post dispute was officially settled and the NUJ was able to restore membership at the newspaper, there was no compensation, only agreement by the company to 'reinstate the twenty eight' - a* token gesture since only one of them wanted to return. For its own part of the deal, the company secured a unique clause which ensured that Nottingham Evening Post journalists would never go on strike on issues over which the local management could have no influence or control. Pole-Carew, in his customary management style, left the decision on whether or not to make peace with the NUJ entirely to the Editor, Barrie Williams. To Pole-Carew, the events of 1978/79 were by then genuinely irrelevant. Pole-Carew denies to this day that he ever advised " a reign of terror" against staff on strike. And he says: " I honestly have no memory of medical tests at all - it really wasn't my style and if there was any reporting of security risks it was not instigated by me.")

Messrs Gopsill and Neale deserve much credit for their pragmatic and mostly objective account of what had, indeed, been a long, bitter and violent battle against Pole-Carew and the Nottingham Evening Post but they were wrong to state that the company had been " pursuing a demented crusade against trade unions and all who were in them." That attaches to the unions much more importance than Pole-Carew himself ever gave them. What drove him was not some anti-union crusade but something far more fundamental - a totally uncompromising resolve to run the company's affairs according to his own creed.

He ran the company in the way **he** considered a company **should** be run - with scrupulously proper regard and meticulously consistent care for its employees (*so long as they remained ' **loyal**'*) but a fierce determination never to allow outside influences to interfere with his concept of the company's well-being.

To him, interference from people with no stake whatsoever in the company - " *whether from unions, the Newspaper Society, or weasley MP s and similar hangers-on*" - had always to be met head on and eradicated.

It was an unequivocal approach to running a big business and though it was often controversial and more often than not, completely misunderstood outside T. Bailey Forman Ltd, it was demonstrably and unarguably successful.

It possibly owed something to the military mind-set Pole-Carew had acquired when he was just a boy of 13.

But it was **never** anti-working class and **never** even remotely politically motivated.

The single-minded, some said 'merciless', methods with which he stamped out organised industrial insurgence would have been the same, no matter what its origins. The unions, all powerful in the industry then, just happened to be the vehicle and his creed dictated that the vehicle simply had to be immobilised. No alternative. No argument. No messing.

He will tell you : " I was never anti-union. Honestly I wasn't. I had seen too many examples of badly run companies not to recognise the need for unions to protect the rights of employees where those rights were being ignored or abused by employers. But I **did** feel that the unions had become far too powerful for the good of their own members because, in too many instances, that power was not being used properly. It seemed to me that the genuine interests of union members were too often abandoned in the determination to maintain that power at all costs."

While Pole-Carew's upper class persona and military bearing (*not to mention his dandy High Sheriff's uniform*!) made him an easy target for caricature and propagandist point scoring, the reality was that, inside Forman Street, where it *really* mattered, he was an immensely difficult opponent for the unions because he was emphatically and demonstrably the very antithesis of a proprietor's lackey. In fact, many of the employees, particularly 'shop floor' workers, who stayed loyal to him would tell you: " He was the best shop steward we ever had! "

But, inevitably, the two high profile Nottingham disputes of 1973 and 1978 with their extensive publicity had given Pole-Carew a national reputation as a 'Union Buster' supreme and Tim Gopsill and Greg Neale were right in their assertion that it was no surprise that he was later to become very closely involved in Rupert Murdoch's much bigger, more far reaching and even more violent conflict with the print unions.

The indiscreet briefing described in Gopsill and Neale's book was not one of Pole-Carew's finest hours. Given to management at Portsmouth and Sunderland Newspapers (" on an undertaking, accepted by Sir Richard Storey, the papers' proprietor, that no notes or recordings of the talk would be taken ") it had gone over the top and when it was leaked, the unions had a field day with it…

"PORTRAIT OF AN EXTREMIST" screamed the headline over the dramatic front page splash in The Journalist. And the story also appeared in the business pages of the national broadsheet newspapers.

Typically, Pole-Carew was not the slightest bit concerned about all the publicity and he never once complained about the NUJ making full capital out of it ('all's fair in love and war') but he **was** furious over his hosts' failure to maintain the confidentiality of the occasion and after an angry exchange of correspondence with the Portsmouth proprietor, Sir Richard

Storey, he ripped Sir Richard's letter into pieces and, in the same envelope in which it had arrived, posted it back to him!

Some of the more colourful content of what Pole-Carew had delivered to his audience of newspaper executives in Portsmouth that day had been hypothetical, for instance: "We told the unions that when the first brick went through the window of the home of a loyal member of staff we would retaliate with a petrol bomb through the window of a union official's home."

Of course, he would never have done any such thing but in the febrile post-strike atmosphere the legitimate message of fighting fire with fire might just have been a tad more carefully phrased by the recent High Sheriff of Nottinghamshire!

And as for what the reports of the leaked meeting described as " the political vetting of all new staff " at the Nottingham Evening Post - yes, in the aftermath of the dispute, an interview process was introduced with the intention of spotting militant union activists attempting to infiltrate the company but it was conducted by Theo Kearton, an assistant to Pole-Carew, who was an amiable, jolly, typical ex-RAF officer, a very likeable and easy going fellow who was nick-named 'the Wingco' by staff and probably wouldn't have spotted Arthur Scargill if he had arrived for interview with NUM emblazoned on his baseball cap!

Certainly, most journalists who went through the vetting process, knowing full well what it was all about, regarded the experience not as some sinister scandal, but as a bit of a laugh.

In fact, in proper context, most of Pole-Carew's talk to the Portsmouth executives was just common sense advice for any newspaper management caught up in an industrial dispute. But much of his tone had been rather unpleasantly triumphal ; some of his delivery had been theatrically exaggerated and his text had been peppered with verbal indiscretions which were gleefully seized upon and exploited by the NUJ.

And who could blame them for that?

In short, in propaganda terms, the Portsmouth affair was a classic 'own goal.'

But, annoyance about being let down over confidentiality aside, Pole-Carew didn't give a damn and significantly, neither did the staff of the Nottingham Evening Post. Those of them who thought about it all (not a majority!) just reckoned the boss had got a bit carried away, " but so what, he does sometimes? "

Stinging from its humiliating defeat, the NUJ and its supporters continued to use every conceivable opportunity to portray the employees of the Nottingham Evening Post as hapless prisoners of a despotic Pole-Carew. Stories abounded. Many of them were totally untrue, some contained a grain of truth but were grossly exaggerated and some appeared in quality newspapers which might have been expected to be more concerned about balance.

An article in The Guardian alleged that Pole-Carew used closed circuit cameras to spy on his workers. It was absolute nonsense but there were plenty of people who were prepared to believe it and Pole-Carew never forgave the newspaper for " failing to give me a proper right of reply to these statements, which were patently untrue."

Journalists, who sometimes can be incredibly myopic and self-absorbed, only ever thought, talked and wrote about the **editorial** department implications of the dispute, thus overlooking the fact that journalists were only ever just a relatively small part of a huge mix of more than 1200 employees of T. Bailey Forman Ltd - production workers, technicians, maintenance staff, sales men and women, marketing and promotions people, telephonists, accountants, distributors and drivers - all of whom would have suffered if the Evening Post could not be published because its journalists had gone on strike (*this newspaper had pioneered direct input technology so it had no printers to break the strike and maintain publication ,which is what happened with all the others*) and that Christopher Pole-Carew, as managing director, had always had a responsibility to protect the sustained employment of each and every one of them, whether they belonged to a union or not - a question which was mostly one of complete indifference to him anyway.

If you believed some of the stories, Pole-Carew's Nottingham Evening Post was a de-humanised Orwellian sweat shop with frightened, downtrodden workers being exploited by a fascist management which deprived them of every conceivable human right and spied on them to ensure domination and compliance.

The reality was that inside the Forman Street fortress, a comfortably large workforce of predominately happy people were well treated, very well paid and thoroughly enjoying a succession of technological innovations to make their jobs easier. It was a company that took training very seriously indeed, spared no expense in ensuring that everybody was properly equipped for their role and had a very progressive policy of career advancement.

True, Pole-Carew's awe-inspiring style and physical presence contained an element of fear for some of the staff and there were those who froze rigid in that presence but most of them liked, respected, admired and appreciated their managing director. He was engaging in industrial democracy long before it became popular and fashionable, with very open regular briefings in the canteen keeping the workforce fully informed of the company's performance and he was often to be found in the pub across the road from the office after work having a pint and a chat with anybody who wanted to talk to him about any aspect of the business. And he liked nothing more than his frequent night shifts with the lads on the inky presses, getting his hands dirty and enjoying the irreverent 'crack.'

Derek Winters, a manager on the commercial side of the business (and a superb jazz musician) who went on to become a managing director himself, describes the Pole-Carew induced atmosphere of that time as " a highly motivated style of management from which we all learned so much and I know that later I tried to emulate the sense of fun, fair play and competitiveness that he installed in all of us."

But Pole-Carew had **twice** taken on and beaten the unions during a decade in which you just didn't do that because they dominated British industry, so none of the above was ever going to be recognised much outside of Forman Street, let alone reported by a self-serving media which had covered both strikes avidly but had no interest whatsoever in the genuine success story which followed.

Not that the injustice of that ever bothered Christopher Pole-Carew.

He could not have cared less.

Marketing Director David Teague recalls: " Christopher had become a hero to the employees and the subject of the grudging envy of the leaders of the rest of the industry who lacked the guts to follow Nottingham's path."

He had also become a figure of hate to the entire trades union movement for the rest of his life.

Did that worry him?

Not one little bit.

Nor did he give a damn about the opinions of his peers in the newspaper world. To him they were, almost to a man, a " total waste of space! "

The drama of 1978/79 behind him, Christopher Pole-Carew got on with the business of running his company.

The five years that followed were full of continued success and innovation on all fronts.

Barely a month passed by without the newspaper industry trade press - publications such as UK Press Gazette, Campaign and ADMAP Magazine (none of which shared the general media's antipathy towards the Nottingham Evening Post) recording yet another success story.

In marketing, in newspaper sales, in advertising and in editorial the trail blazing achievements, often accompanied by top awards, came thick and fast.

But, by the early 'eighties, Pole-Carew - the man who had made it all possible - was getting more bored and professionally frustrated by the day.

" Looking back," he says, " there was little, if anything left for me to do. I had put such a great team together - David Teague, the Marketing Director; Barrie Williams, the Editor; Don Gray, the Newspaper Sales Manager; Charlie Wright, the Works Director; Barrie Bailey, the Finance Director - that I had effectively made myself redundant!

" My style had always been to attract the best people to fill our top jobs, reward them with the best possible salaries and conditions then leave them alone to get on with it. There's nothing worse or more pathetic than managing directors interfering unnecessarily or trying to bask in the reflected glory of their more successful colleagues. My top team was performing brilliantly. What did that leave for me? "

Between 1966 and 1981, Pole-Carew had changed T Bailey Forman Ltd beyond recognition from musty, dusty " Victorian" nonentity to international trail blazer. Now its top trio of Pole-Carew, Marketing Director David Teague and Evening Post Editor Barrie Williams were in constant demand as speakers on the conference platforms of the newspaper industry all over the world - a demand they met with relish!

Vienna, Venice, Rome, Amsterdam, Paris, Seville, Las Vegas, Berlin were just a few of the venues at which they appeared, always travelling in the company's own private jet ... a sparkling and much envied symbol of its success.

The Nottingham Evening Post may have been reviled by the unions and resented by some of the other major players but there was no denying that it was now the clear leader of the British regional newspaper industry in production technology, in marketing achievement, in advertisement techniques and in editorial excellence.

Forman Hardy Holdings, the parent company of which Pole-Carew sat on the board , had grown to consist of 12 companies.

For proprietor and chairman, Colonel Tom Forman Hardy this was now enough.

Despite Pole-Carew's frequent attempts to interest him in substantial growth within the newspaper industry, the chairman would simply not countenance buying other publications. Thus, opportunities to capitalise on the company's huge success and standing in the industry were lost - and with them went a very great deal of Pole-Carew's zest for the business.

Having given the company his all for nearly 20 years, Pole-Carew could have sat back, relaxed, continued to draw his salary; spent more time with his beloved family and on his many outside interests, which included shooting, fishing, beekeeping and carpentry and carried on for another 20 years.

Not him!

Pole-Carew's increasing boredom and frustration led, by his own admission, to him becoming a more and more difficult subordinate to the Colonel:" In fairness," he says, " having to give constant reports on nothing new month in, month out; year in, year out to someone who never, ever gave any response, let alone comment, would wear most people down!"

Following the death of his brother, William,the Colonel's younger son Nicholas had come into the business as the heir apparent to his father and became vice-chairman. It was a reluctant move for this extremely pleasant and likeable young man. He was a farmer, a very good one. And he loved that life. Reserved and shy, he was never cut out for the boisterous newspaper business in the way that his brother had been. Says Pole-Carew: " Nicholas certainly did his utmost to become a newspaperman but it really wasn't a goer. By comparison, I had lived almost completely for the company, which had become very much my own creation, so it was not surprising that Nicholas and I became estranged. Much as I liked him - and I genuinely did because he is a thoroughly nice man - I could not treat him with the respect which, perhaps, I should have given him."

The distance between Nicholas Forman Hardy and Christopher Pole-Carew was very apparent to their fellow directors at T. Bailey Forman and there were those who believed that the managing director should have shown " the young master" more patience and tolerance as he strove to learn and struggled to enjoy a business for which he was never intended. After all, it wasn't *his* fault his brother had been killed in that awful accident; 'Nick' really belonged on his farms but he was trying his very best to adapt to the alien cut and thrust environment into which he had been forced by the demands of the family business and Pole-Carew's frequent and open exasperation with him was the last thing he needed.

It may well have been what Pole-Carew would have seen as a waste of a great opportunity that led to his transparent professional impatience with Nicholas Forman Hardy. While he had always steadfastly resisted releasing shares to his directors Colonel Tom had been content for his managing director to control the business for all those years and Pole-Carew, although still just an employee, had understandably come to think of T Bailey Forman Ltd almost as *his* company.

He had devoted the best part of 20 years of his own blood, sweat, tears, toil and talent to creating a hugely successful business.

But he now suffered the intense frustration of a situation in which even though the company had become very much his own creation, he had no influence whatsoever on really important strategic matters and had to watch " time after time " as "wonderful opportunities" went begging.

" There is a very real difference", he recalls, " between having day to day control over a company and being able to make strategic decisions."

The massive waves he had created in the industry by leading TBF to such success had almost certainly ruled out any chances of his moving to any other company in the regional newspaper industry.

"So, I could only look forward to a future of frustration and boredom, doing a job way below my capabilities."

That must have been very hard to take.

On the other hand, Pole-Carew sometimes failed to conceal his exasperation with the family proprietors. By his own admission, he frequently took liberties with his employers. They must have found that equally hard to swallow and it was most certainly not an attitude with which to endear himself to the young heir apparent who, while he might not have been comfortable in that role, was most certainly nobody's fool. All this was a toxic mix of emotions on both sides and relations at the top of the company steadily deteriorated.

In the absence of anything else to which to commit himself and his professional passion, Pole-Carew directed his insatiable energies into the pursuit of further computerisation, in which he was so far ahead of his time that very few of his colleagues could keep pace with his revolutionary thinking. One or two had the guts to tell him so but others went along with him, pretending to be fully aware of " where you're coming from, Chris " when, in truth, they didn't have a clue.

'Somebody Had To Do It'

A close friend, Commander Mick Saunders-Watson, was heading up the computerisation of the British Library and that led Pole-Carew to examine putting the Nottingham Evening Post completely onto computer, with access for the general public.

In other words, he was talking about a version of the internet…**in 1983!**

He also explored the possibility of having a paperless newspaper which readers would access on a pocket computer screen.

Again, this was extraordinarily forward thinking for the early 1980s.

He was turning his vision of fully computerising the newspaper's own extensive library (containing a wealth of unique local history) into reality while also identifying viable means of commercially exploiting its potentially money-spinning contents.

None of the above - which, with his proven track record for innovation which was years ahead of its time would probably have succeeded - came to fruition because **Colonel Tom Forman Hardy sacked him.**

Pole-Carew takes up the story:

" One day (*in January, 1985*) my secretary Nancy Harris said that the Colonel wished to see me at the end of the day. I remember being irritated because it was an evening on which I intended to go up to Huthwaite to see what the nightshift was up to so I wanted to get home in reasonably good time. So at 5.30pm I went in.

" 'Sit down, Christopher, ' said the chairman. ' I have something to say to you which I think it would be better if I read. It has been decided that our relations are no longer satisfactory; we have therefore decided that you must leave the company. I have decided that you shall receive £200,000 by way of compensation for loss of office, to be accepted now. If you do not accept it, it will be the worse for you.'

" It didn't take any time at all to work out that to refuse would have been pointless since if the Colonel wanted to fire me for whatever reason he was well within his rights to do so and could just as easily reduce the sum to the minimum amount for redundancy pay-off. So I accepted. He said that he was sorry that it had ended this way and that I had half an hour to clear my desk and leave. So off I went.

" Back in my office, my secretary Nancy was distraught. Ken Powell, the maintenance manager, had come in and chained and padlocked all my filing cabinets.

" My next stop was down to Charlie Wright's office on the floor below where I found him and the other directors looking suitably amazed, although I had a distinct feeling that this was largely for my benefit, certainly in the case of Charlie.

" It seemed that the new MD was to be Charlie Wright - not my personal first choice but bearing in mind that the Wrights had been the Forman Hardy's baby sitters in the long gone past and were therefore better and more experienced than most at jumping to the family's wishes, he was their most natural choice. Mine would have been, without question, David Teague who was clearly the most obvious choice if talent was required - but maybe they had had enough of that for a lifetime!

So that was that and home I went.

" Gill, like me, was mentally stunned by the suddenness and abruptness of it but by the next morning I had come to terms with the reality and must admit to a feeling of relief more than anything else: No more Monday morning meetings, no more having to think up boring monthly reports for board meetings, no more having to tolerate the chairman's total lack of response to them. After only two days, the quite severe indigestion that I suffered from at that time vanished, which tells one something! "

Pole-Carew was wrong about his fellow directors having had prior knowledge of his removal - at least in the cases of Barrie Williams and David Teague, to both of whom the news came as a complete shock and desperately bad news.

Barrie Bailey? Well, he might have known given that he sat on the parent board as well. Charlie Wright? There was talk that he had been involved in getting rid of Pole-Carew, but the man himself thinks not.

Another rumour was that the last straw for the Forman Hardys was that Pole-Carew had an involvement with a separate computer company but, again, the man himself says that was not the case.

Whatever that final straw had been, Christopher Pole-Carew is the first to concede that his attitude towards the family in those latter days meant that he got what he deserved.

" If I had been Nick Forman Hardy I would not have wanted me as my managing director! " he says candidly.

" Later I learned that Tom Forman Hardy had decided to retire early and turn the company over to Nicholas who did not want me as his MD. I thought then and I still do, that Nicholas was quite right.

" I liked Nicholas a great deal and still do. He is an extremely nice person, as was his father, but in the newspaper environment, rightly or wrongly, I had little time for him and that would have made for a very uncomfortable relationship.

" So Pole-Carew had to go."

Typically, any negative impact on him of being sacked from one of the top jobs in Nottinghamshire and arguably *the* best job in the regional newspaper industry was very short-lived for the ultra-resilient Christopher Pole-Carew and his early recovery was helped considerably by the reaction of friends.

" Only one of our friends cut us off his social list," he recalls. "All the others expressed their surprise and then continued with us just as before.

" On the Saturday following my departure, Gill and I went to a party at Flintham Hall, a mile down the Fosse Way from us, the home of Myles Hildyard, from whom we had bought our house, Newfield, all those years before. It was the first time we had ventured out in public since Tom Forman Hardy sacked me and naturally both of us were nervous about the kind of reception we would receive.

" As I walked past other guests, I came across Tom Forman Hardy talking in a group, one of whom was Geoff Neale who lived across the Fosse Way from us at Kneeton.

" As I passed, Geoff turned to me and said, for everyone to hear :' Chris, I gather that you won't have a lot to do on Monday?'

" 'Yes,' I said (with Tom looking nervously uncomfortable and obviously thinking: 'What on earth is he going to say?') 'I think that's about right.'

" 'Splendid,' Geoff replied…' that means you will be free to come and shoot with me, then.'

" What a lovely, kind thing to do.

" And so our social life went on. What to us had seemed cataclysmic was to them of only momentary interest. Well, well! "

(*Nicholas Forman Hardy eventually succeeded his father as Chairman of T.Bailey Forman Ltd. Colonel Tom Forman Hardy died, aged 70, in 1989. In 1994 Nicholas sold the Nottingham Evening Post to Northcliffe Newspapers, the regional wing of the Daily Mail, for £94.3 million and he now heads up a number of successful business interests, including property and farming.*)

So it was that in January, 1985 the Pole-Carew era at the Nottingham Evening Post came to an abrupt end after 19 extraordinary years. Looking back, he regrets never owning his own regional newspaper company:

"It is a tragedy to me that I never owned my own newspaper company. But the opportunities didn't come at the right time and when they did come, they turned out not to be the opportunities I thought they were, busted flushes. It just didn't work out.

" And with T.Bailey Forman I was saddled with a company that was myopic as far as the future was concerned. Tom Forman Hardy loved being a big frog in a little puddle ; he didn't want boats rocked; he couldn't see the opportunities for growth that were there for the taking. That led me to pure frustration and that was my undoing. I don't blame the Forman Hardy's for firing me. Never have done. I blame myself for my departure. But they were the cause of my becoming what I became. I had hopelessly outgrown T Bailey Forman and I was not allowed to expand and develop the company any further, so in effect, I felt I was left to rot.

" That's how I saw it. And naturally I became (... *bitter is a bad word*) difficult; awkward. I couldn't disguise my disappointment and the people I was disappointed with. The Forman Hardys were thoroughly nice people but that wasn't what it was all about and if they had let me, I could have gone on to change that company even more - out of all recognition. Oh, boy. The opportunities that were there. Colossal."

And would *he* have been tempted, ten years later, by the opportunity to *sell* the company for £90 million-plus?

" ***No way !***

" We would have continued to have proved everybody else wrong; We'd have held our sales, even increased them; we'd have harnessed free newspapers to get the best out of the opportunities for local advertisers with blanket distribution while working in harmony with the big paid for evening newspaper, particularly with regard to its need for sensible on-going investment."

Later still, how would he have coped with the huge growth of the internet?

" Even before I left Nottingham in 1985, I reckoned that one fine day, you would have screens that would fit into your pocket like a wallet and I was convinced that what newspapers like the Nottingham Evening Post needed to do was to adapt themselves so that for a nicely profitable subscription, people on their way home in a train or a bus could access that day's newspaper, getting it, story by story, up on their pocket sized screen. We'd have been working on that. In fact, we'd already started to."

That Christopher Pole-Carew was thinking along those lines more than 25 years ago will come as no surprise to those who witnessed how he introduced computerised newspaper production at least a decade before anybody else in his industry.

But he had, by his own admission, brought about his own downfall from the company with which he'd led the newspaper world.

This man had not only changed the face of T.Bailey Forman Ltd but of the whole British regional newspaper industry. And in no time at all, his missionary zeal was about to be unleashed again…this time on Fleet Street.

6

THE MAN FOR MURDOCH

*Q:'Would you mind if I put machine
guns on the roof?'
A:' I think you **would** too!'*

THOSE who did not experience it would today find it almost impossible to believe the extent to which the print unions controlled Britain's national daily and Sunday newspapers in the 1970s and 1980's.

They were all-powerful.

If the *union* decreed you could not have a job, you had no job; If the *union* said a piece of equipment should not be used, nobody used it; If the *union* didn't want a story or advertisement to appear in the newspaper - usually because it offended left wing political views - it did not appear; If the *union* decided the newspaper would not publish that night, millions of readers had to do without it the next morning. Strikes were absurdly frequent and were often called for reasons which were trivial in the extreme. One standing joke was that if somebody said the crocuses were out in the park, the print unions would strike in sympathy!

It was unbridled industrial anarchy.

The main print unions, the NGA, Sogat and NATSOPA had for years been an elite, enjoying - and often abusing - immense power. The union rituals and rules governing the print workers were centuries old. The union branches were called Chapels and Chapels were known as the Companionship. They were unique and more akin to Freemasonry than normal union organisations.

The union bosses, known as Fathers of the Chapels, operated like Mafia, wielding more power than the hapless managements which had for years capitulated or compromised to the extent that they had, at least in the production areas, virtually abdicated control of their own companies.

The print unions operated closed shops - no union card, no job - so they enjoyed 100 per cent membership. The strength this gave them meant that they could shut down the production of the newspapers at a whim. And they often did.

Fleet Street was a fiercely competitive, dog-eat-dog environment and whenever your newspaper failed to publish, your rivals gleefully gobbled up your lost sales. This continuous threat fed the unions' appetite for bullying, intimidating tactics and led to frequently unreasonable demands of managements which, in turn, gave in far too easily, far too often.

The Fleet Street production areas were ludicrously over-manned at levels maintained not by management but by the unions, with the help of farcical " Spanish customs " such as shifts put in by non-existent workers with fictitious names. A job " in the print " in London was " money for old rope." And exceptionally good money at that. By the mid-1980s NGA compositors in Fleet Street were earning £1000 a week, an incredible wage for those times. And for a 16 hour week. Whether you turned up or not!

Australian Press mogul Rupert Murdoch, whose burgeoning News International company owned the Times, the Sunday Times. The News Of The World and The Sun, had entered this bizarre world as a new breed of national newspaper publisher - much more businesslike, much more ruthless and much less tolerant than the benign old Press barons whose preference for power before profits had contributed significantly to this industrial relations nightmare over the years.

It had to be only a matter of time before Murdoch took on the unions and set about dragging Fleet Street screaming and kicking into the 20th Century of properly run, fully modernised businesses but he knew that when he did, it was going to be a battle of monumental proportions for which he had to be meticulously well prepared.

In the regional newspaper industry the print unions had once been just as powerful, relatively speaking, as their Fleet Street brethren - albeit without some of the worst excesses - until one man had the nerve to take them on.

That man was Christopher Pole-Carew.

Remarkably (astonishingly, even, given the rapid speed with which advances in business usually progress) no less than **12 years** had elapsed since Pole-Carew first smashed the iron grip of the print unions. When that battle had ceased in Nottingham there were 300 fewer printers employed by T Bailey Forman Ltd, though to this day, he insists: " *This was mainly because the unions did everything possible to prevent me from **creating** jobs in commercial printing. I had argued from the very first meeting with the unions that the UK sent abroad to be printed, largely to Holland, enough work to employ **all** the industry's compositors if every newspaper followed Nottingham's lead on new technology. **Never** did I destroy jobs; only changed them.*"

Nearly **10 years** had passed since, in that same city, he had introduced the pioneering computer technology which allowed direct input of stories by journalists, thus eliminating completely several traditional newspaper production processes.

It had taken a decade for the rest of the British regional newspaper industry to catch up with Pole-Carew - let alone Fleet Street, which was persisting with production methods which had hardly changed since the turn of the Century while Pole-Carew was able to boast (and frequently did!) that Nottingham Evening Post journalists now produced their Saturday evening football paper so quickly that Nottingham Forest fans could buy a copy containing a full match report and pictures on their way out of the ground after the match.

Murdoch knew that if our national newspapers were to survive and prosper in an increasingly and rapidly changing world, *somebody* in Fleet Street *had* to grasp the nettle, fight the unions and bring direct input computer technology into this intolerably backward environment.

Pole-Carew had done all that and more at the Nottingham Evening Post before becoming bored and frustrated and pushing the proprietors beyond the threshold of their very considerable patience.

He was now out of a job.

Rupert Murdoch and Christopher Pole-Carew?

It might not have been a match made in Heaven.

But, at the time, it was certainly convenient for both.

Pole-Carew describes how they came together:" There was a story in the Financial Times telling of my departure from the Nottingham Evening Post so the whole world knew about it. Bruce Matthews, Murdoch's top man in England, telephoned me for a meeting. I knew Bruce quite well from fishing trips to Canada organised by the newsprint companies for newspaper executives who bought their paper and so I went - and learned that Rupert wanted to move his newspapers out of Fleet Street to a plant he had built at Wapping, which the unions had categorically vetoed.

" Would Christopher Pole-Carew, champion scourge of the print unions, be interested in doing it for him? Well, yes. Why not? It seemed a fairly straightforward job to do."

In no time, things started to move.

Pole-Carew was supplied with a base in Wapping - " a delightful two bed roomed flat in a converted warehouse with a living room and kitchen overlooking the Thames. Gill was really pleased to take herself out of rural Nottinghamshire and back into the big City."

The mutual respect shared by Pole-Carew and his Nottingham computer 'ace' Stan Dziuba meant that it was to Stan that his first call was made. Still employed at the Nottingham Evening Post, Dziuba readily agreed to consider joining his recently departed boss in this exciting new venture.

A trip to New York was swiftly arranged to meet with Rupert Murdoch to discuss basic steps and issues.

Pole-Carew and Dziuba flew, on Concorde, with the top News International executives. Pole Carew recalls that on the journey across Murdoch's men sat at the front of the plane while he and Dziuba sat at the back: " We had not been asked to join them, even though the plane was only two thirds full."

Pole-Carew and Dziuba spent the journey studying thoroughly more than 30 copies of The Sun that Stan had taken with him, analysing exactly how the paper could be computerised : " On the face of it, this was going to be a tough one," says Pole-Carew, " because there seemed to be no rules of make-up and design; it was as if each edition produced was a one-off. However, gradually as we worked it through it became clear that this was simply not the case, nor - when one thinks about it deeply - could it possibly have been so, because any newspaper *must* have an underlying pattern to it. The Sun had seven basic lay-out patterns across all pages which, in fact, when carefully analysed, did not differ very much one from another.

" Computerise it? No problem! Not to Stan, anyway... but then, he ***was*** the only qualified computer man present.

" Our time spent on mid-air research turned out not to have been wasted. On the other hand, the News International contingent's cold shouldering of us was a mistake, as they were very soon to find out."

The crucial meeting with Rupert Murdoch was in the great mogul's New York apartment. For Stan Dziuba, for all his exceptional talent still very much just a provincial newspaper man, the prospect of meeting Rupert Murdoch on such a mission was the stuff of wildest dreams.

Stan, who went on to become Pole-Carew's second-in-command on the project, recalls: " We were taken by limo to Murdoch's apartment block and up by lift to the 14th floor of the building. Then the lift doors opened and there to greet us was Rupert himself. We went straight into his lounge.

" Murdoch's executives, Christopher and me went straight into a meeting which lasted for more than three hours in which we talked about a project to print all of his Fleet Street newspapers at Wapping. The meeting was split into two - with Murdoch's executives mostly dwelling on what couldn't be done and Christopher and I talking about what could be done.

" For example, the Murdoch men were convinced that The Sun could not be produced our way at Wapping because of the variation and uniqueness of the type faces."

Pole-Carew recalls:" We were also joined by some of Murdoch's American people. Stan and I sat at one end, on Rupert's right. The others stretched from his left around the table but not quite meeting. It looked like two camps - and it was.

"After the preliminaries, Rupert commented that computerising The Times seemed to him to present no problems; its lay-out was not so markedly different from the US papers that had installed computers. Everyone agreed.

" But Rupert went on :' *The Sun and the News Of The World, they're different. I'm not sure how we can manage them."* And he asked for views.

"He proceeded around the table from his left and the answer from every one of his top newspaper executives was much the same:

' *Every edition of The Sun is unique.*'

' *It simply doesn't lend itself to computerising.*'

'*The complications would mean more work - not less*'

'*The Sun is too big a money spinner to take such a risk with.*'

"And so on…"

Then it came to the turn of Stan Dziuba, never a man renowned for his tact: **" We can piss it!"** he said.

And Rupert Murdoch sat up.

Dziuba went on to describe how he and Pole-Carew had spent their time on the flight from the UK and concluded that there was really nothing complicated about The Sun. It was just another newspaper to them and he explained why.

Pole-Carew remembers: " Murdoch liked what he heard. No-one else seemed to." Stan Dziuba agrees:" I said *'that's a piece of piss'* because it **was**. Quite apart from anything else, we were already overcoming this problem in Nottingham."

Dziuba says that at that stage, the meeting changed in character, with Murdoch wanting to hear more from him and Pole- Carew and somewhat less from his own executives.

After a discussion, raised by Pole-Carew, about the technicality of which newspaper - The Times or The Sun - should change its "measure" (*page dimensions, column widths, type sizes and faces*) to achieve compatibility with the other because at Wapping they would have to share a Press line (*The Sun won*) the meeting moved on to the crucial and clearly contentious confirmation of Pole-Carew's position in charge of the Wapping operation. Pole-Carew says this was formally confirmed by Murdoch, with the rider than in his (*Murdoch's*) absence he was to work through Bruce Matthews.

" This", he says, " was to turn out to cause considerable problems. It seemed clear to me that Bruce Matthews and others did not take kindly to this provincial upstart, as I believe they saw me, muscling in on their territory. It was an attitude that they made no effort to hide."

The meeting then moved on to discuss a name for the project and Pole-Carew suggested The London Post. He explains: " Murdoch was deeply concerned about security for the project. If the unions were to learn of his intentions all hell would have let loose in his Fleet Street offices and the lives of his top executives would not have been worth living. So what should be done to disguise those intentions, bearing in mind that there were bound to be leaks?

" I suggested that it be spread around that Murdoch was planning to run a new London evening newspaper from his Wapping plant. The new evening paper could well be called The London Post - why not? There was, after all, a successful evening newspaper in Nottingham called the Post!

" This was incorporated into the plan as a well designed and highly effective smoke screen that stood its ground right to the end."

This " plan" for The London Post, to be printed at Wapping, went on to receive widespread publicity. Whether Murdoch ever intended to launch an evening paper or whether that was always merely a smokescreen to divert attention from the preparation of Wapping for his Fleet Street newspapers, remains officially an unresolved issue to this day. It was discussed in such detail publicly; privately within News International (*a high profile and very successful editor, Charles Wilson, was appointed to head it up*) ; with the unions and in general throughout the newspaper industry that it is hard not to conclude that it was, at least for a time, a serious proposition. Certainly, if it was a diversionary non-starter throughout, the ploy was executed absolutely brilliantly.

Pole- Carew and Dziuba both are unequivocal on the point.

" It **was** a smokescreen; of course it was," they say.

" The next step," says Dziuba, " was to work out a strategy, so there were then several meetings with Murdoch in London between Christopher Pole-Carew and Bruce Matthews."

Pole-Carew discovered that one of Murdoch's key concerns seemed to be how to distribute newspapers from the new plant after they had been printed. The time honoured practice was to send millions of papers out all over the country by trains. On the train journeys, union labour bundled them up into packs for the newspaper wholesalers who would then send them out in smaller packs to the newsagents. Inevitable " blacking " of Murdoch's Wapping-produced newspapers by the unions would mean this could no longer work.

But to Christopher Pole-Carew, this was "simply no problem." At the union-free and " blacked " Nottingham Evening Post he had researched the possibility of printing the Financial Times on contract and had come up with the following solution:

(1) Stop doing identifiable individual bundles for wholesalers and newsagents. What was the point? The Nottingham Evening Post had stopped doing so years before and instead simply sent out standard bundles of 26 copies each (*26 copies is a newspaper industry "quire" – ie. 24 plus two to cover any possible damage*) with loose ones added to round any delivery off. This was much quicker, more accurate, entailed less damage and was much cheaper because it no longer involved bespoke labelling and paper work.

(2) Why use heavily unionised rail transport and all that extra handling into vans ? Instead, why not use independent articulated lorries driven direct to the wholesalers, entailing one or two - at the very most, three - drops in any one town?

The next question for Murdoch's operation was: Who could do that for them? " Easy," Pole-Carew told Bruce Matthews, " There are six road delivery companies in the UK big enough to handle it, including TNT ."

'Somebody Had To Do It'

(*Rupert Murdoch apparently shared the ownership of Ansett, an Australian airline, with the owner of TNT.*)

At the start of his appointment to the Wapping project, Bruce Matthews had taken Christopher Pole-Carew to see the flat that was being provided for him and Gill, overlooking the Thames.

" Right, Chris," Matthews said, " There you are. And you can tie your submarine up just outside! "

Says Pole-Carew: " We looked out of the window and guess what? Passing us going downstream on the tide was one of Her Majesty's submarines, painted black and looking suitably sinister. What an omen!"

Given the conflicts which were to follow, a submarine might well have been useful because Pole-Carew was sailing headlong into the stormy waters and hostile territory of a totally different world. It was the start of what he describes today as " the most unpleasant time in my career."

He had stepped from the comparative comfort of T. Bailey Forman Ltd, a well-organised, disciplined and de-unionised company in which his word had been law, into the brutal jungle of Fleet Street in which unions were King and management had an appetite for professional 'cannibalism.'

He recalls: " Fleet Street was a morass of anarchy with the print unions totally controlling the way the newspaper companies were run. The over manning was incredible, as were the so-called 'Spanish Customs' which, for example, required a crew of 32 to man a black and white press, whereas at our Huthwaite Printing Company the same press, plus colour units, was manned by **four**..

" The manning lists contained some well-known names, such as Mickey Mouse and Pluto. It was said, for example, that if the entire staff of the Dispatch Room (*where the papers were bundled up after printing*) of the Daily Mirror actually turned up for work there wouldn't be nearly enough room to cram them all in whereas in Nottingham , where we had fully automated packing lines, it took less than one man per line. It was claimed that something like half of the taxi cabs of London were manned by Fleet Street NATSOPA members.Well, be fair, they had to do *something* to while their days away!

"A union boss was a man with *real* power - and wealth. If a press worker or a dispatch employee was required, he could only be recruited through an employment agency owned by the union leader. "

Pole-Carew has a personal take on how all this came about: " There were two major contributory factors," he says. " The first was significant, because it established an innate dislike of management which had a history of autocratic, political power-greedy owners. Before the War, it was customary to take on apprentices in the works jobs then, when they had completed their time and qualified for full rates of pay, they were sacked and replaced by fresh cheap apprentices.

" The second factor was an amalgam of the competition between similar newspapers, eg. Mirror v Sun; Mail v Express, which was, to put it mildly, cut throat - with the prizes for success sky high in increased sales - and the fact, unique to newspapers, that if you lost production your rivals would pick up your lost sales. You couldn't stockpile your orders and meet them later because yesterday's news had no value. Thus, the threat of a strike generally met with only one reaction from management and that was instant caving in. What was the choice? Especially if you had come from one of those unions yourself and virtually all Fleet Street management had started their careers as union members. Little wonder that they managed to live so easily in such an environment. Also, if you were a top manager of a Fleet Street newspaper, answerable to an autocratic owner, wasn't it something of a blessing to have permanently available a cast iron excuse for any failure of management:' *Well, I had no choice - you know what the unions are'* "

With such typically forthright views on the way Fleet Street was being run and no inclination to keep them to himself, Christopher Pole-Carew was on an inevitable collision course not just with the unions, by which he was already loathed, but with the Murdoch management, most of whom appeared to take an almost instant dislike to him.

In her book *End Of The Street* (published by Methuen London Ltd in 1986) former Sunday Times journalist Linda Melvern wrote that Pole-Carew " *was to become alienated from most of the Murdoch team.*"

That, says Pole-Carew, misses the point. " Because I was never anything **but** alienated. From the very beginning."

Stan Dziuba agrees:" I believe that Murdoch's London executives were less positive than Pole-Carew about the whole Wapping project because they probably didn't think it could ever be accomplished. Pole - Carew then comes in with his 'I'm in charge of all this' approach and that put their backs up. I reckon the poor relationship between him and Murdoch's people was down to a combination of those two factors."

In *End Of The Street* Linda Melvern wrote: " He (*Pole-Carew*) behaved with an air of superiority. He would look directly at people when making a point:' Do you see ?' he would say, as though it should be self-evident. His clipped tones would be imitated later by the Murdoch men. He was to tell everyone, once the project was under way, that he was in charge."

Executives who worked closely with Christopher Pole-Carew in Nottingham would recognise that description of his manner but they would argue that Murdoch's men misunderstood him and his demeanour. In Nottingham he had been the accepted Number One so his colleagues knew that his " to the manor born" style of leadership was in no way intended to belittle those around him. They realised that he knew no other way. It meant no offence. And in the small pond of Nottingham (in which, contrary to the stereotype, he would actively *encourage* the stimulation of *dissenting* views) none was taken. However, he had now jumped feet first into a vastly bigger pond in which bigger fish than him were swimming. These guys were not about to rationalise, understand, excuse and tolerate the impression he gave and that Fleet Street pond, by comparison with Nottingham, must have been a seething cauldron of ego and testosterone.

Says Pole-Carew: " It was obvious to me that Murdoch's top team resented me. To me, it was also doubtful whether they felt any real enthusiasm for the whole concept of the Wapping plan. If I was right about that, my theory was that behind it lay years of Fleet Street failure in dealing with the unions and that the price of failure this time was certain to be very high.

" I believe they did not like, nor could they understand, my inability to recognise failure as an option - but then they hardly knew anything about what had happened on the Nottingham Evening Post and anyway, that was just a provincial paper, hardly worth considering in the real world they knew as Fleet Street."

Typically, Pole-Carew marched on regardless.

Having accepted a year's contract from Rupert Murdoch he set up his own company, which he called Computer Print Consultants, to deliver the project and recruited from Nottingham an executive team consisting of Stan Dziuba; Derek Winters, who had been the managing director of T.Bailey Forman's free newspapers division (*Derek moved on a short time later*); Peter Crouch and John Hayden, two very accomplished newspaper sales and distribution managers and Tim Brighton, who specialised in advertisement computer systems. They were joined by a secretary, Linda Applegate, described by Pole-Carew as " brilliant, extremely competent but, above all, possessing an invaluable knowledge of the way Fleet Street worked."

Pole-Carew believes that having his own team around him made a crucial difference: " I was actually the *second* person that Rupert Murdoch had foisted upon his top executives in order to fulfil his great Wapping plan. The first was an Australian, Bill O'Neil. I met him later and discovered that his story was a pre-run of what was happening to me except that he had brought no team with him. No Stan, no Peter, no John, no Tim. He was on his own, totally dependent on ' support ' from the top News International people. He simply didn't stand a chance of succeeding - and he didn't."

The role of Pole-Carew's team was to guide Murdoch and his executives through the detailed process of preparing Wapping (or Tower Hamlets, as Murdoch always preferred to call it) as a state of the art, computerised printing plant - shorn of all the old hot metal methods, thousands of traditional print workers and all those Spanish customs - so that it was ready, come the day of judgement, to print and distribute all Murdoch's Fleet Street newspapers. There also had to be a strategy on the enormous issue of how the infamous Fleet Street unions should be handled… a massive undertaking because all-out war was inevitable and the immensely powerful unions had to be out-witted, out-flanked and out- fought.

The eventual strategic plan was detailed and meticulous. It had to be. There are no records of it because it had been decreed that no minutes of meetings should be kept, but in May 1985, one absolutely top secret Discussion Paper *was* circulated, by lawyer G.W.Richards, to a select group of eight people who had formed a discussion group. That group included Pole-Carew.

Titled **Tower Hamlets - Finding The Right Strategy**, the Discussion Paper provides a fascinating insight into the thinking and planning…and if it had fallen into the hands of the print unions at that time it would have been dynamite; a huge national news story with immense political implications.

Under Terms of Reference, it established that the aim was " the practical matter of getting Tower Hamlets and later Glasgow and their respective eventual staffs in a position where they can produce newspapers each day, with the reasonable certainty they can be produced and distributed on time and in sufficient numbers."

It continued: " The background to KRM's (*Murdoch's*) plan for Tower Hamlets is the over manning, inefficiency and inordinate waste in the production (and certain other) areas of national newspapers. Conduct which would not be tolerated in other industries has become the norm in Fleet Street. An example occurred at the Sunday Times on 13/14 April. In the Foundry, work stopped because there was ' an unpleasant smell.' The Chapel had created an entirely artificial health and safety issue which was only resolved after a slanging match between the Managing Director and the Chapel. 80,000 copies of the Sunday Times were lost.

" The Tower Hamlets plant, large, spacious and air-conditioned, includes modern printing equipment and ultra modern and efficient publishing equipment. The plant (originally intended for The Sun and the News Of The World) has been lying idle, but near completion, for some two to three years. If the existing staff of the Sun and the News Of The World were moved lock, stock and barrel to Tower Hamlets, News Group Newspapers would end up paying as much (or more) for less work. Talks have now been held with the print unions but have got nowhere in relation to most production and publishing areas and only so far in relation to others. No attempt has yet been made to move The Times or the Sunday Times to Tower Hamlets or to discuss such a move with the print unions. If it is made, it is unlikely to be any more successful.

" If Tower Hamlets is not being used for the production of News International's existing newspapers, why should News International not produce a London evening paper, or even a 24 hour paper - the London Post? This would be manned more realistically, there would be greater flexibility among operatives and (in consequence) no 'chapels.' The production costs would be lower, the cover price of the newspaper could be lower than that of its direct rival (s) and, inevitably, other papers might be put out of business. If the print unions would not agree to man the paper realistically and flexibly, either another union/ other unions or no union would be involved.

" If News International was producing a newspaper with manning levels at, say, 50 per cent of the rest of Fleet Street (and a fortiori if non-print union staff were involved) it was clear there could be repercussions at Gray's Inn Road or Bouverie Street. The conclusion was that News International might be forced to move the whole of its operation to Tower Hamlets. The London Post thus became only a small part of the plan or might be dropped altogether." *

(* *The plan for the London Post* **was** *dropped altogether but it appears to have been very useful to the eventual strategy for the print unions to continue to be led to believe that* **this** *was the purpose of preparing Wapping, rather than for moving any of Murdoch's national newspapers to the site.*)

Under Aims and Assumptions, the Discussion Paper went on to state that Murdoch had two principal aims in relation to the Wapping plant:

(a) To have either no - or ' friendly' unions;
(b) To reduce manning levels and introduce new technology at the lowest practicable cost.

Under Subsidiary Aims, it listed:

(a) So far as possible, avoiding litigation - in which KRM (*Murdoch*) and BRM (*Matthews*) amongst others would be witnesses - which would involve the public ventilation of all the planning which has gone into the Tower Hamlets project;
(b) Being able to present what is being done in the best possible PR light, and;
(c) Doing what is to be done as quickly as possible.

The Discussion Paper examined a number of union issues. including the extent to which the ' sweetheart ' electricians' union, the EETPU (Electrical, Electronic, Telecommunication and Plumbing Union) should be brought on board as an alternative to the print unions. This union, under the leadership of General Secretary Eric Hammond, had become renowned for its moderate policies of co-operation rather than the conflict which predominated in British industry. Hailed as a harbinger of the end of " dinosaur " unionism by its supporters; reviled as " a lackey, a crawling capitulator to the capitalist bosses " by its detractors, the EETPU had been making a lot of headlines and greatly upsetting traditionalists on the Left of the Labour and Trades Union movements.

The Discussion Paper asked to what extent News International could rely on the EETPU and wondered " how realistic it is:-

(a) to think the Union and its members will face extreme pressure in the short term (c.f. the violence and intimidation in some mining communities) in the way they say they will;
(b) despite a new kind of collective agreement to believe that the relationship with the new workforce will not (seriously) degenerate over a period, and
(c) to believe that the national leadership of the Union can control the individual workers on the Tower Hamlets site.

On those points, the Discussion Paper concluded: " These concerns may be overstated but, if this matter is of the critical long-term importance to the EETPU we believe it to be, there can be no harm in seeking further assurances from the Union at this stage."

On union issues generally, the Discussion Paper went on:

" A major concern of all of us, and one which is not easy to evaluate, is the so-called ' bear trap' mentality which the print unions may have developed in the last year or two in the changing economic and legal climate.

" The ' Pavlovian ' response of taking strike action on the smallest provocation may no longer apply. There is, in fact, no single opinion within the discussion group on the extent to which the print unions will react traditionally to provocation.

" In some areas, we see disruption as more likely than a strike. This leads to problems, not least in terms of legal action/remedies. Only those individual workers who can be proved to have taken disruptive action can be dismissed (or denied pay) with complete safety. Those who (say they) were ready, willing and able to work will, or may, have remedies if they are dismissed. The fact that a chapel has taken action is unlikely to be sufficient - it might be accepted by a count that each and every member had taken action in consequence, but equally it might not - and so the problem of identification if there is disruptive action is likely to be serious.

" One preliminary view of the discussion group is that, if there happens whether by accident or design to be a strike at Gray's Inn Road or Bouverie Street and Tower Hamlets is ready to start production, it would be a mistake to transfer the title(s) on strike to Tower Hamlets immediately; at least, it would be a mistake if it was fundamental that all four titles were to be transferred to Tower Hamlets. We believe that it would be safer to leave the title(s) originally on strike off the streets until strikes can be procured/provoked at the other titles, thus enabling all four titles to be transferred at the same time. We believe that, once some titles have been moved to Tower Hamlets, it would be more difficult to provoke a strike at the other(s)."

Going on to deal with **Straightforward redundancy and its costs**, the Discussion Paper stated:

" In view of the enormous savings in labour costs likely to result from the move to Tower Hamlets and Glasgow from Gray's Inn Road and Bouverie Street (perhaps £70 million in a full year) it has been suggested that an option would be openly to make all existing production/clerical employees redundant and pay them redundancy payments, if necessary on the ' industry ' basis rather than the ' statutory ' basis.

" We have seen a major function of the discussion group as being to discover what practicable means exist to dismiss existing employees more cheaply and to map out the strategy and tactics for that. We must say at the outset that we doubt whether there is one simple, effective and complete solution.

" If News International argued that the reasons for dismissal were redundancy or economic efficiency it would be open to a court or tribunal to consider the real reason and whether the evidence fitted the narrow technical definitions of redundancy.

" It is true that there would no longer be work of any kind (or certainly, of a particular kind) in the existing premises - one test of redundancy - but a dismissal by reason of redundancy (or apparently by reason of redundancy) can still be an unfair dismissal. A dismissal, even where there was a redundancy situation, can be unfair because:-

(a) there was an unreasonable selection of the employees made redundant, or

(b) there was lack of warning/consultation over the redundancies, or

(c) there was a failure to provide or offer suitable alternative employment.

" If an industrial tribunal held that the dismissal was unfair the damages could be substantial, up to £16,512 for an employee with long service. The real risk, however, is that the tribunal would find that the real reason was membership of a particular trade union, in which case the damages could be very substantial - in excess of three years' gross pay.

" The lawyers have already advised that the cheapest way of dismissing the existing employees is to dismiss them while on strike, because:-

* if (which is more likely than not) they are in breach of contract, they will have no entitlement to notice or pay in lieu of notice;

* they may well not be entitled to redundancy payments, and

* industrial tribunals will have no jurisdiction to hear unfair dismissal claims (although that does not mean there might not be lengthy preliminary hearings to determine whether there was a strike and whether the employees were dismissed while on strike).

" And, if need be, to provoke the strike by whatever means, provided Times Newspapers Ltd and News Group Newspapers do not, themselves,

'Somebody Had To Do It'

act in breach of the individual contracts of employment with their employees. If they do, the protection is lost."

The Discussion Paper went on to say that the key question was how to procure or provoke a strike…
" Various methods of engineering strike action have been suggested. Not all the methods are exclusive of one another, some are not sufficient in themselves and indeed, the best strategy may use a number of methods in conjunction.
They include:-
(a) Provoking (possibly by the introduction of new technology or non-union labour) a walk-out area by area, working either ' downwards ' from the composing room or ' upwards ' from the publishing area;
(b) Compulsory redundancies, either at a rate of no more than 33 per month (so as to minimise the consultation requirements) or in larger numbers at one time, whether with or without consultation;
(c) Taking calculated disciplinary action against a few employees - one or two in each department;
(d) Announcing that production of the titles will begin shortly, either at existing sites or at Tower Hamlets, with considerably reduced manning levels;
(e) Publishing, or announcing the publication of, the London Post with EETPU labour from Tower Hamlets;
(f) Locking out employees on some pretext, but then converting the lock out into a strike by inviting the employees back without pre-conditions;
(g) Announcing that future wage, etc, negotiations will be conducted at union, and not chapel, level and/or announcing that attendances will hereafter be a matter for management and not the chapels, and;
(h) Withdrawing recognition of the unions either in respect of employees, or ending the closed shop."

Having examined in fine detail the advantages and disadvantages of each of those methods, the Discussion Paper then moved on to The London Post…
" The London Post was designed partly as 'cover' for increased levels of activity at Tower Hamlets. How much longer we can continue in that fashion is difficult to see. If more is to be done, it is likely to include the recruitment of journalists and other staff. It is unlikely that journalists

will agree to join a new publication without considerable security of employment. Accordingly, the costs of first hiring and then firing journalists could be considerable and that must be weighed in the balance against the advantages to be gained by taking the London Post idea further.

" There is the further complication that it is part of any strategy not to alienate the journalists as a group. The cynical use of the Post as mere cover would be likely to alienate some journalists CW (*Charles Wilson*) and the editors would like to keep. It is probably also true that if journalists are recruited for a non-job they may work out what is happening. If they do, they will certainly talk." *

(* *This would appear to confirm the assertions of Pole- Carew and Stan Dziuba that the launch of a London Post* **was** *' just a smokescreen ' but equally it would seem that at some stage it had also evolved into a serious consideration.*)

Under the heading **A Times Crisis**, the Discussion Paper went on to say :-

" Part of KRM's original thinking was (having suspended negotiations over moving News Group Newspapers' printing to Tower Hamlets) to 'offer' Tower Hamlets to Times Newspapers Ltd. The Times was at risk, it would be said, and Tower Hamlets could be its salvation. The print unions would be intractable, the EETPU would step in and (informed) public opinion would be on KRM's side.

" The recent correspondence from News Group Newspapers' chapels, couched in unusually moderate language and betraying perhaps a hint of nervousness, suggests that this idea should not be forgotten. Against that, it must be said that Tower Hamlets was designed for printing The Sun and the News Of The World and it may not be politic to reveal too early the fact that the plant has been/is being modified in the way it is."

The Discussion Paper then dealt with **BRM's Strategy** - new proposals put forward by Bruce Matthews ' since the earlier parts of this note were prepared' which were a variant of the idea of provoking a strike area by area, working ' upwards.'

Matthews was now suggesting that there may be merit in moving two titles only at the outset and his proposed strategy was…

(a) Fix a date ('X') to start printing The Sun and the News Of The World at Tower Hamlets;

(b) Say one week before ' X' announce to News Group Newspapers' employees in the machine room and publishing area that, with effect from ' X', no casuals will be required and all those over the age of 60 will be retired;

(c) That will provoke a sufficient walk-out in the publishing area and, perhaps, in the machine room. Those on strike, etc will be dismissed;

(d) The process department will be told that, with effect from 'X', flongs (*papier mache moulds used to cast the metal printing plates*) will be sent to Tower Hamlets;

(e) Either before or on 'X' (ie. when it knows how Tower Hamlets will be staffed) the process department will refuse to prepare flongs. Its staff will be dismissed;

(f) The compositors will be asked to continue setting type, as before. If they refuse, they will be dismissed;

(g) The journalists will be told that, if they are prepared to undertake single key stroking, their jobs will be secure and their pay and benefits will be improved. (it is thought that many, or most, will agree)

(h) Meanwhile, nothing would be done at Times Newspapers Ltd. Its production staff (it is hoped) would not appreciate the full capacity of Tower Hamlets. If Times Newspapers Ltd staff went out on strike, they would be dismissed and production would transfer to Tower Hamlets. If not, Times Newspapers Ltd's management would still be in a stronger position, ways would be found of reducing costs over a period and as and when there was a major dispute production would be transferred."

These ideas, the Discussion Paper concluded, plainly merited further study. They clearly had some advantages (eg the possibility of full production of The Sunday Times and the News Of The World on Saturday nights, but some disadvantages as well, namely…

" Compulsory retirement is a dismissal at law, so the over-60s will be dismissed; there will be redundancy payments to those who are told their services are no longer required; will the new directions to staff, even if in fact they are never implemented, be breaches of individual employment contracts? ; there is an assumption, which needs to be considered, that those who have worked at Bouverie Street can be directed to work at Tower Hamlets; if The Sun and the News Of The World (including their journalists) move to Tower Hamlets it will be very little time before the full capacity of Tower Hamlets is discovered and made known; will TNT be prepared to distribute The Sun and the News Of The World, but not the other titles? "

If that Discussion Paper was dynamite had a copy been seen by the unions, a top secret document, which he described as a **master plan,** sent by Pole-Carew to Rupert Murdoch in June, 1985 might well have caused a national strike!

In it, Pole - Carew told Murdoch:

" We have had many meetings to discuss the method by which we will encourage the various print unions at Bouverie Street and Gray's Inn Road to break their contracts of employment at a time suitable to ourselves.

" The intention is, of course, to offload the current union manning of the Group's newspapers at minimum cost whilst we reman with more co-operative labour at the new factory.

" I feel it necessary to express some concern about the way the meetings and discussions on achieving this aim have gone as they tend to be of a tactical nature without necessarily being strategically sound. The pattern tends to take the form of a 'scenario' where it is assumed that we make announcements (eg the Sunday Times is to be enlarged and the extra sections or pages will be printed at Tower Hamlets and not on the present presses) which, with other statements and intentions of activities, will lead the various unions concerned to go on strike. Yet, as we go through these various exercises, we find ourselves constantly running either into brick walls because there are innumerable pitfalls barring our way in the form of legal restrictions or into having no certainty that the unions will act in way we wish.

" One has to remember all the time that, whereas it would be marvellous to offload a thoroughly unsatisfactory work force, at minimal cost, the penalties for bungling such a step are terrifying.

" Currently, the unions are in a stronger position than the management, partly because the law is on their side in the area of unfair dismissals and partly because the Group's records with regard to conditions of employment would appear to be patchy, to say the least, and in some parts, non-existent, with a heavy reliance on what is called 'custom and practice' : factors guaranteed to make the finding of an ideal path through these pitfalls nearly impossible.

" My belief is that we should pay considerable attention to seeing how we can eliminate some of these pitfalls, even at the risk of industrial trouble whilst so doing, in order to make it easier for us to create a situation where we would have the ability to force the unions out on strike or , alternatively, get rid of their members by paying the basic minimum redundancy. Is it possible, therefore, to remove the house agreement elements in their contracts of employment? For example, we know that the manning on the presses is unsatisfactory (as, indeed, it is elsewhere) ; we know that there is practically no discipline imposed regarding drinking during working hours or even attending for the full shifts.

" It should be possible to give notice to the unions of our intentions to stop these practices and effectively to establish a more satisfactory arrangement with regard to their terms of employment. Furthermore, there is the obvious need to regain the right to make people redundant compulsorily and not solely voluntarily, as a matter of sound, in-control management, in place of the usual pleas of poverty or whatever.

" The above are examples of the types of conditions which need to be removed in order that we can, if necessary, obtain a position where we can make all staff redundant at minimum rates, at an acceptable cost.

" It would suit our purpose if we could create the situation where the printing of the papers could be removed from those who do it at present and transferred to whomsoever we decided should do the work (say, Tower Hamlets Printers Ltd .) at our will. Thus, our decision to close down the two production plants in Gray's Inn Road and Bouverie Street would then depend on our ability to find another printer with one, of course, prepared and ready.

" If we were in a position to do this, it would not really matter whether the unions were aware of our intentions or not because we would be in control of events, regardless of what they did. Thus, we would have a fall back position of - not the risk of being subjected to penalties by a court, running into hundreds of millions of pounds - but of the minimum Government redundancy rates for those with whom we decide to part company.

" My brief, then, to a lawyer, would be not (as at present) to tell me whether any suggested actions would be acceptable in law, but the reverse, namely: these are the obstacles that need to be removed to enable me to be in a strong enough position to carry out my intentions. Please tell me what steps must be taken to remove them.

" It might be worth continuing this document to examine a tactical policy to complement the strategic one, but before doing so, maybe we should examine the preparations that need to be made.

" We have a prime need to install and make capable of successful and reliable running, all the equipment that the ' alternative printer' (Tower

Hamlets) would require. This is currently being done with some success and should be completed by the end of July, given reasonable luck.

" At the same time, since the object is to deliver newspapers and not merely to print them, there is the need to ensure a method of delivery, independent of the present system, which we could trust to carry out our requirements. This has not been done yet and cannot be done before the end of September in a proper manner, although a barely satisfactory temporary system could probably be cobbled together in a matter of, say, four weeks should it be necessary.

" In parallel is the need to man up with key personnel,

(a) to take over the equipment on commissioning, and

(b) to provide the nucleus around which to expand the staff to, eventually, a full operational complement.

"As a matter of interest, the steps that need to be taken are precisely those used when commissioning a ship: key technical personnel, gradually spreading across all equipment, followed by experienced and knowledgeable members of the crew in various states of training and competence just before acceptance trials and the commissioning date. This point is followed by a 'working up' period before the ship can be considered fully operational.

" We are now (5th June) in the position of having authorised the very first intake of key personnel of the operating team and must start to increase their numbers as gently as possible because of the security risks to a point where, by 1st August, we could be within ,say, two weeks of going ' live ' and within four weeks of hoping to print to full requirements. The two weeks into August are accounted for by deliberate delays in taking on too many staff too early, thus risking a security break before being completely certain that all equipment was ready."

After detailing departmental staff numbers and recruitment time schedules, Pole-Carew's master plan went on to describe the tactics to be followed, assuming that equipment and manning had reached the required state of readiness by 1st August...

" On this date, the Tower Hamlets project should be capable of withstanding an instant retaliation by any or all unions to whatever action the Company might take. Nevertheless, any delays in such retaliation will enable the project to continue to develop in readiness; that is, to go through a ' working up' period.

" Thus, with every passing week, the Company's control over events will become steadily greater and, assuming that the lawyers have managed to succeed in nullifying the various pitfalls, this will lead eventually to the day when such changes as are required in the production of the newspapers can be made at will.

" It should be appreciated that once we have changed the relationship between the Company and the unions, the need for subterfuge or even secrecy will have gone. For instance, it would be in our control to change the printing to another company and the fact that the staff were (or even were not) organised by an unorthodox union would be a matter of no more than general interest.

" Furthermore, with the ending of the need for secrecy and subterfuge, so would end the need for a 'front', namely the London Post, and with it, all the complications, both practical and legal, that its projected existence causes.

" Similarly, the print unions becoming aware of our intentions would not affect the outcome of our actions. To return to a much used analogy: if you fence your bear round so tightly that it cannot move without falling into your trap, then its intelligence or wariness become irrelevant - at which point it is likely to lash out at its constraints ie. 'all out on strike' and will fall into the bear trap, which is where strategy and tactics come together, in harmony."

Eventually, the final strategy was in place, though never put into writing. In stark contrast to the rather verbose lawyer-speak of that early Discussion Paper and seemingly owing much to his own master plan, Christopher Pole-Carew today describes it succinctly thus:.

(1) **Prepare Wapping to the point where all the computer equipment being developed and tested under the direction of Stan Dziuba in a secret bunker** (*Dziuba's bunker, a huge warehouse in Woolwich, well away from the plant, was an amazing sight - an exact replica of all the relevant areas of Wapping*) **can be moved in and ensure that the plant is sufficiently secure to repel the mass picketing which is sure to ensue.**

(2) **Start recruiting non-print union labour…members of the EETPU** (*Pole-Carew says he could see no reason for using union labour at all but it was Rupert Murdoch's insistence that to go non-union would be to invite trouble from all directions - not just printers but journalists, maintenance workers, ink and paper suppliers, etc*: " Murdoch was shrewd," he says, " and clearly right and since the EETPU was available and willing, why not use them? ")

(3) **THE most important. When the whole Wapping operation looks ready to roll, start toughening up the attitude towards the print unions leading to the " bear trap" - ie. lead the unions on by gradually becoming ever more belligerent in negotiations until they have no option but to call a strike. Let them go on strike. Then fire them, thus saving about £11 million in severance redundancy payments.**
(*Pole-Carew today sees a rich irony in this plot in that* : " *I was actually reflecting the views of those who seemed so opposed to all I was trying to achieve. The unions had been abusing the system for so long; their arrogance and greed were breathtaking. There was, within the Fleet Street management, a very strong desire to get their own back in a very personal way - just this one last time - for all those years of humiliation."*

Throughout the months that followed Pole-Carew and his team worked on the refined delivery of that strategy, to which security at the new plant was absolutely imperative. On this most crucial part of the plan Pole-Carew, as ever more than willing to get involved in the detail, worked closely with Bob O'Hagan, a security specialist who joined CPC Ltd to organise the security of the site and the employees. " Bob was a natural, with great flair for the job," says Pole-Carew. " He even organised identity cards for everyone, with certain individuals having *00* numbers. Rupert Murdoch was *001*. Guess who was *007*. And I've still got the card ! "

The two men were in total agreement, when discussing the defences for Wapping, that it was absolutely paramount to ensure that not so much as *one* striker - let alone protesters in any numbers - could possibly get on to the site.

Pole-Carew recalls: " That would have led to a sit-in, such as happened once during the dispute in Nottingham, except this time, the strikers would have been much more determined and in far greater numbers. A serious sit-in could have led to the eventual collapse of the whole project.

" Bob O'Hagan came up with a new invention called razor wire, which he had discovered in Germany. He showed it to me and I instantly agreed to it. I believe it was the first time it was used in England.

" Bob and I jointly planned the defences - power operated entrance gates, sliding together so that no-one could possibly hold them open and two lines of razor wire encircling the site. We envisaged the possibility of strikers bringing a lorry up to the perimeter and running planks down to make a path over the wire…then they were in! So, we had a second run of razor wire *inside* and clear of the first to prevent this happening.

" I explained the reasoning behind all this to Murdoch, who hammered me hard on whether I was certain that the defences would be good enough.

After explaining it all and having him ask *'Are you absolutely certain?'* for the umpteenth time, I eventually said *' Yes I am. But if you want me to be **absolutely** certain, would you mind if I put machine guns on the roof?'* He laughed and said *' I think you **would**, too!'*

" His final words on the defences were: *' OK, I'll accept them. '*

" And of course, they worked exactly as required."

Progress reports on the delivery of the strategic plan would be delivered by Pole-Carew to Murdoch's London executives, to visiting executives from Australia and the USA and occasionally to Murdoch himself. Although Pole-Carew's team (*particularly the very talented Stan Dziuba and Peter Crouch, whose work on the logistical nightmare of the complex and ground breaking distribution strategy was of crucial importance*) got on well enough with Murdoch's men the relationship between the executives (*especially Technical Director Ken Taylor*) and Pole-Carew himself went from bad to worse.

Pole-Carew says that he found the whole experience intensely frustrating:

" The fact that absolutely no minutes were to be taken of any meetings had a disastrous effect on my control of affairs. With no record of what had been said or agreed upon there was no way of enforcing any required actions and when one of them denied what had been said there was invariably at least one other with total recall to support that denial.

" Furthermore, Murdoch was spending most of his time in the United States, largely in California, extending his interests into film companies and he therefore required me to be answerable to Bruce Matthews in his absence, particularly with regard to day to day matters. Since Bruce was always in Grays Inn Road or Fleet Street the chances of my getting decisions on anything out of him were always very slim.

" Murdoch would come over at infrequent intervals and I would never be informed of this until late in the day before he was due to arrive the following morning which gave me almost no time to prepare a proper report, let alone brief him beforehand or ever discuss matters directly with him rather than publicly in the meeting that invariably took place soon after he arrived.

" I found all this seriously difficult. For years, I had been used to conducting meetings in my own way, which entailed hearing everyone's opinions before making any decisions. It seemed the Fleet Street way was quite different, the aim apparently being to throw the speaker off balance. With no experience of such tactics I found myself being constantly back-footed in meetings with Murdoch in the chair. Not pleasant."

The tension that had built up between the Murdoch men and the CPC team is evident in the following exchange of confidential memos between Times Editor Charles Wilson and Pole-Carew.

Charles Wilson wrote:

" For some time, I have been getting increasingly fearful about certain aspects of our operation which I have voiced over the weeks and your memo about distribution, dated 23 August, provokes me to put pen to paper.

" I believe that, as we get closer to go-day, we are, in some major areas, no nearer to solving the problem that has been clearly visible since day one - the difficulty of co-ordination between the CPC team and the resident senior staff of Bouverie St. and Gray's Inn Road. Security and personality clashes in some areas have heightened the task but, instead of encouraging alternative secure sources of contact and information, these factors have encouraged a ' bunker' state of mind that is time-wasting, costly and, in the end, may prove disastrous.

" Your memo is excellent. However, I suggest it would have been more valuable if it had been written after the Tower Hamlets meeting on 27 March and certainly before the meeting with TNT on 30 May. For months now, it appears, Peter Crouch has been working in isolation drawing up print and loading schedules based simply on raw print capacity, tonnage and mileage. We now have a frightening set of schedules that contain no News Group nor TNL staff input giving geographical edition and product quality control patterns.

" Juggling with train times and machine room output figures from night to night to get the right edition to the right place, particularly at the SUN, is an art form. So I have been perturbed to hear you say three times at meetings: ' These lorries are not like trains. They will leave on time… even if they aren't full.'

"Surely, controlling our own transport should be an enormous boon. If an edition with late area news or sports results is going to appear in three minutes, we should be able to hold up that delivery to take it. The same art form will be necessary to decide whether it is prudent to let that three minutes stretch to thirty. The basic precept that all supplies should be sent by huge and slowly loaded and slowly moving lorries should be questioned : are there not certain areas, certain nights, certain news breaks or night matches when smaller vehicles should be loaded quicker and later and travel faster; perhaps sent direct to areas without unloading and reloading at major dispersal points; consideration to the difference in character of the two daily products?

" It may not be too late to re-think Peter Crouch's plans and schedules. But a lot of his time - our time - has been wasted because we have not managed to co-ordinate current knowledge and planning expertise.

" You will recall that I expressed worries specifically about The Times distribution in June and that I was shown the printing schedule by Peter on 15 August. When I told him that it needed re-thinking, he told me he had handled it himself and wanted to wait until he returned from holiday before we tackled it. You may, then , appreciate how your memo fans the flames of my co-ordination worries.

" There are other areas where lack of co-ordination causes apprehension. I will mention three:

" 1. SYSTEMS MANAGER:

When Rod Hunt was appointed there was no doubt in anybody's mind that he was being brought in to be in charge of all the systems at Tower Hamlets in the future. But since then he has not been included in any discussion on the Siemen's System. If he is going to continue in his present job, surely he should be part of the team setting it up. And if he isn't going to be Systems Manager, who is?

" 2. MINUTES :

The minutes of our meetings should, I believe, be better used to aid co-ordination. First, as they are, they are at best selective. They tend to list only decisions and progress dates. Because many of the project team have other full-time jobs, they cannot attend all the meetings. The minutes should fill them in on background to decisions, dissent and views that might prove vital. The 'distribution' is also ludicrous and renders them practically useless. The minutes of the last meeting are presented at the start of the next meeting and are collected immediately afterwards. There is no time for anyone to read them. Miss one meeting and you are out of touch; miss two in a row and activities adjacent to your own are beyond recall. I am aware that originally these minutes were seen to pose a security/legal danger, but there is now so much paper in existence I suggest that reason has been overtaken.

" 3. INFORMATION ON MEETINGS:

Throughout the project, information from your office regarding times of meetings, and sometimes cancellations, has been intermittent. On the last THREE occasions timing or cancellations have reached my office with only three hours to spare. Subsequently, on each occasion, I have found the arrangements were made or cancelled one or two days before. I would be grateful if your office would bear in mind that those of us who are helping to run the newspapers currently have schedules, meetings, conferences, responsibilities, and require maximum notice."

Pole - Carew responded:

" Thank you for your long memo which you gave me on Friday 30th last. It is a difficult one to answer because most of the subjects should not really have been addressed to me, since I do not control them. However, let us deal with the work being done by Peter Crouch first:

" I have a strong suspicion that if you had given your memo to me after, rather than before, our meeting with John Hayden on Friday morning it would not have contained the bit about distribution. I think you are now fully informed of our plans and probably agree with our methods. It is easy to have hindsight; yes, I am well aware of the skill in juggling the different components of newspaper production to produce the best results. I ought to be: I have been at it for over twenty years; even if the scale has not necessarily been the size of the present project, the problems have been the same. Anyway, there is no need to rethink Peter Crouch's plans and schedules as you asked; his time has not been wasted. We now have a datum system to alter and adapt to give you the best results we can achieve. I look forward very much indeed to the full meeting we will have this week in the hopes of nailing this matter before we go to Zurich next week.

" Regarding the other points your raised:

"SYSTEMS MANAGER:

" You mean, in fact, Computer Manager; a Systems Manager handles a system within a computer organisation, eg. One for The Times/ Sunday Times, another for the Classified and so on. I am not sure, really, how I can answer your query here because this is a top appointment within

News International and is obviously not for me to make. At best, I can only advise. Furthermore, I would have thought that it was the particular prerogative of the commercial (ie. non - editorial) side of the company, but it might well be that if I gave some background information it could be of help in understanding the situation.

" Rod Hunt is required to organise and manage the largest Atex system in Europe and this is a formidable task, leave aside the commercial systems. In order not to overwhelm him, I arranged for Stan Dziuba to take charge and ensure that the PCS and the Siemen's system were knocked into shape in order to be ready for our ' Go-day.' Stan's job is a very big one and he is doing it because he is easily the most knowledgeable and experienced person on the project in both these subjects - including Ross Wood whose system from Australia is but one tenth of the size we require.

" In due course these systems will be knocked into good shape and Stan will then be able to bow out. Bruce Matthews will no doubt decide in due course who he wishes to appoint to overall charge oc computers. Rod Hunt has little or no experience in the two commercial areas but that does not mean to say that he cannot learn, nor that he should not have the top job. Nobody needs to make a rush decision because Stan has the non-Atex areas under control (provided he receives the necessary information and the appropriate co-operation) until your top management make their appointment.

" MINUTES:

" This is another of those difficult problems that have stemmed out of the past. The weekly meetings are, as you know, conducted by Bruce Matthews and in the early briefs it was clearly established by him, on advice from Geoffrey Richards, that only the lawyers should take records of our meetings. This ruling has never been rescinded nor has one seen any of the notes that the lawyers took. When I finally got a secretary, I started keeping notes to check on decisions, etc. These were finally translated into a sort of minutes - but on the proviso, you will remember , that all copies were destroyed immediately after the meeting at which they were issued. We could have proper and more useful minutes but this is for Bruce Matthews to decide; even so, it really ought to be cleared by the lawyers first.

"INFORMATION ON MEETINGS:

" Again I can only contend that the meeting is not mine: It is Bruce's. In general, the time of the meeting is established at a fixed time in the week but this was changed in the period you refer to. Furthermore, we did the week before last have a prior meeting of a number of the more senior people who attend and as a result decided that it was unnecessary to have the full meeting. The answer to your point is really, therefore, that whereas I sympathise with you, I can only assure you that you are informed as soon as I have received confirmation of what will happen. We are all bound to be messed about to a certain degree because so many people are being required to do a lot too much and this leads to sudden changes at short notice - but then that is an inherent factor in the project, is it not? "

Game, set and match to Pole-Carew.
No wonder he got up their noses!

In February, 1986, the New Statesman magazine published a major investigation on ' How Murdoch Beat The Unions' under the heading ' *A PLOT CONCEIVED AND PLANNED SIX YEARS AGO* ' and in it described a clash between Bruce Matthews and Pole-Carew *in front of union officials...*

The New Statesman reported:

" In August, the unions finally began to suspect something was going on. The Wapping site had an influx of electricians who aroused suspicion because they came not from London but Southampton. SOGAT and the NGA approached Bruce Matthews for talks - and were told by him in September that he wasn't in charge, but Pole-Carew was. SOGAT national newspaper official Bill Miles therefore rang Pole-Carew, only to be told that no, he reported only to Rupert Murdoch, Matthews was the man. Back again in Matthews' office, Miles pressed Matthews to confirm that Pole-Carew was in charge and again rang Pole-Carew, this time with Matthews present. To the astonishment of the union officials, Matthews and Pole-Carew then argued over the telephone over who was in theory, if not in practice, in charge of Wapping."

Such correspondence as there was between Pole-Carew and Matthews during the year reveals a distinctly cool relationship between the two and Pole-Carew tells of one meeting at which, he says, Matthews invited him to resign.

" Bruce suddenly turned to me and said :'Do you want to quit?'" I was completely taken aback. It was the kind of thought I just wasn't accustomed to. I said: ' I don't understand.'

" Bruce said : ' You know. Quit. Give up. Call it a day.'

" I said: ' I'm sorry Bruce. I don't know that word, Quit. It must be Australian. I'm English. I don't give up on anything .'

And he didn't.

He drove on, bringing the strategy to fruition, working closely with his hand-picked team and with Tom Rice, the electricians' National Secretary with whom he was identifying how EETPU members could staff Wapping.

Meanwhile, the print unions were making numerous attempts to get to the bottom of what was going on. They were extremely suspicious and had been particularly riled by the hiring of their provincial bete noire, Pole-Carew. They didn't trust anybody but seemed to be reasonably satisfied that the London Post was going to happen and that Wapping was being prepared for that purpose. Negotiations over their acceptance of an eventual move to Wapping continued but, despite their intense mis-trust, they did not appear to detect any immediate intention to impose direct input technology on their own domain.When the rumour that Murdoch was planning a London evening paper reached the unions, Bruce Matthews telephoned Pole-Carew to summon him to an immediate meeting.

Says Pole-Carew: " It appeared that the combined heads of the print unions had demanded to see Bruce to learn exactly what was going on at Wapping, no doubt including just *what* was that bastard Pole-Carew doing there!

" Bruce's instructions to me were clear and to the point: *'Tell them we are planning an evening newspaper which is supposed to be secret because we naturally don't want the opposition* (the London Evening Standard) *to know of our intentions.'*

"Anything special about it? ": ' *No, not really. Murdoch has a plant full of unused equipment costing money to house and maintain and he thinks it is time it was put to good use. With only one monopoly evening paper in a city the size of London* (where there used to be three) *the opportunity to successfully set up a second paper is not to be ignored, especially if you have the production capacity on site and waiting to be used. I* (Pole-Carew) *have considerable experience of running an evening newspaper, which is why he has employed me.'*

" How about computers? ": ' *Look at the plant. It's all basic hot metal equipment.'* (" Which it was, because all the computers were down in Stan Dziuba's bunker at Woolwich, well and truly out of sight.")

So, Pole-Carew met the union leaders (including SOGAT's formidable and charismatic General Secretary Brenda Dean, for whom he admits his admiration) and, he says, he told them exactly what he had been told to tell them. It was one of very few occasions in his newspaper career that he did something upon which he looks back with no pride. Despite having come up with the London Post smoke screen idea himself at the very outset, he says he " resented having to lie so openly and so specifically " at that meeting with the union leaders.

Stan Dziuba recalls:" Gradually, the Murdoch executives became more enthusiastic about the whole Wapping project. I think they were now realising that not only *could* it all happen but that it almost certainly *would*."

Then Christopher Pole-Carew found that he was being gradually air brushed out of the picture. So much so that on December 13th, 1985 he wrote a private note to Rupert Murdoch.

That note said:

" I feel a quick note might be in order just to update you on my rapidly dwindling areas of responsibility for the Tower Hamlets project. The interminable Report has now been in Geoffrey Richards' (*a lawyer*) hands for some ten days and will be checked through with him when the opportunity serves. Bill Gillespie (*Times Newspapers Managing Director*) has taken responsibility for security from me today, as he wishes to have direct control himself. I have turned over a substantial list of things that need attending to so he is fully informed. It leaves me wondering what I do now regarding this project. On the basis of pride and emotional involvement I very much want to see it through to its culmination, but not particularly as an interested but un-needed spectator."

By Christmas, the crucial element of the Wapping strategy, goading the print unions into a strike, was nearing completion. The strategy had worked perfectly. The final demands which had been made of the unions to accept a move to Wapping - not just for the proposed London Post but now, by open implication, for Murdoch's national newspapers as well - were deemed to be totally unacceptable, as, of course, they were intended to be.

In a rallying call of resistance to its members SOGAT said: " The demands by News International would be impossible for any genuine, democratic, free trade union to accept…

* No recognition of chapels or branches and no negotiations with them.

* No strikes or other industrial action for any reason whatsoever.

* Anyone taking part in a strike or industrial action will be subject to immediate dismissal with no right of appeal.

* No closed shop - employees who belong to a union can leave it at any time.

* Union representatives in the company will be elected by the members - but can be immediately removed from office by management if they are given a written warning for any disciplinary offence.

* No union recognition at all for supervisors and management grades.

* Complete flexibility of working with no demarcation lines.

*New technology may be adopted at any time, followed by job cuts.

* No minimum staffing levels - either by agreement or understanding. The employer will decide the number of people required for any job and fix their starting and finishing times.

* The management has "exclusive right to manage." Management will select people for jobs, classify and reclassify people, hire, promote, demote and transfer employees as required. They will also suspend, discipline, dismiss, lay off employees from work as they see fit.

(*The fact that the terms in that last paragraph were deemed to be* **"totally unacceptable"** *can surely be seen, in retrospect, as indicative of the grip the unions had on Fleet Street.*)

At the same time, SOGAT's Brenda Dean was telling her members: " We want to negotiate. But if negotiations have clearly failed and it has to come to a fight, then so be it. We must hope for the best but prepare for the worst - and prepare our members for what could possibly be the biggest industrial dispute this union has seen since the war."

Dean's General Officer Responsible for National Newspapers, Bill Miles, was more colourful in his own clarion call….

" We will never bow our heads to those who believe that profit is more important than people, or that they have the power to destroy the collective force of ordinary men and women.

" ' **Rise like lions after slumber.
In unvanquishable number,
Shake your chains to earth like dew
We are many - they are few!'** "

Barrie Williams

The rest of Fleet Street's union leaders were also preparing their members for conflict. And it duly came.

On January 24th, 1986 the Wapping Dispute, which was to rank alongside the 1984-85 miners' strike as a hugely significant turning point both in the history of the British trades union movement and for UK industrial relations in general, began when 6,000 workers employed by Rupert Murdoch went on strike.

Immediately, dismissal notices were served on all those taking part in the strike. **Six thousand** workers had effectively been sacked.

Immediately, the Wapping plant, manned by EETPU members, was activated and Murdoch's four national newspapers were rolling off the presses and into the lorries which were to get them safely to the newsagents.

With the exception of a minority who became known as " the refuseniks", Murdoch's journalists (members of the National Union Of Journalists) who were absolutely crucial, now, to the production of the newspapers, decided to carry on working and moved to Wapping - their typewriters replaced by computers, so unfamiliar to them that it is claimed that some were heard to ask : " How do we put the paper in? "

There had never been much love lost between the journalists and the printers - who now despised them.

In an unsuccessful attempt to stop them and the rest of the new workforce from getting in, the mass protest which had been anticipated duly occurred and at its peak there were 10,000 pickets outside what had become known as " Fortress Wapping" but Christopher Pole-Carew's meticulously planned security (epitomised by the now infamous razor wire) held firm.

The protest was often violent and a large police presence was used to repel the pickets. In bloody clashes, more than 400 police officers and many protesters were injured and more than 1,000 arrests were made. The police operation was mounted throughout London to ensure that Wapping operated efficiently. Movement of local residents was heavily restricted and workers were bussed in to the besieged plant in specially modified vehicles with wire mesh over the windows and firm locks on all doors. There were many complaints about the police being heavy handed and aggressive - including one from the BBC which said the police had physically prevented its team from doing its job.

Like the miners' strike, the Wapping dispute assumed massive political and public significance - the respective rights and wrongs of both sides of the battle provoking fierce debate and splitting families. At the heart of that debate were complaints about the " politicising" of the police who, it was claimed, were enforcing Prime Minister Margaret Thatcher's reforming trades union legislation with a zeal that went beyond reasonable crowd control.

As the dispute roared on, the House of Commons debated the issue, with Labour MP Michael Foot claiming that employment rights had been abused by Murdoch: " The worst unfairness will not fall upon the people with the highest salaries, said Mr Foot. " It will fall - and is falling - on several thousands of people who have lost their jobs. They have no prospects of anything being done for them. The unions are trying to solve the problem and they are doing their best. However, their funds have been sequestrated and they are threatened with further sequestrations.

" I urge the Government , in the interests of decent people in the country, in the interests of decent treatment for individuals and their families and in the interests of decent industrial relations, to take responsibility for the matter. The Government must not wash their hands."

Mr Foot's plea was soundly rejected by Mr Peter Thurman, Conservative MP for Bolton North East, who answered the veteran Labour man's reference to the previous Labour Government's comparative record on employment by arguing : " What were they doing, bearing in mind that 6,000 people were producing a newspaper that can be produced by 600? Such over-manning is the cause of the country's difficulties. Our unemployment is the legacy of years of such nonsense."

On Mr Foot's claim of a diminution in employment rights, Mr Thurman replied : " There has been no diminution in employment rights. People have been freed from the domination of trade unions."

In the ensuing exchanges, Mr Martin J O'Neil (*Labour, Clackmannan*) referred to the suspension of negotiations between the unions and Murdoch's Bill O'Neil " following the employment of Mr Christopher Pole-Carew as an adviser"....

" That," said Mr O'Neil MP , " is rather like inviting the Russian social democratic party - as it was before the Revolution - to cease its activities pending the promotion of Rasputin to a more responsible position in the Tsarist hierarchy! "

Pole-Carew's appointment, he argued "…is an example of the lack of goodwill on the part of News International."

It was widely believed that without Margaret Thatcher's legislation to control trades unions, the print workers would never have been taken on - *though a certain Christopher Pole-Carew would have told them that he had already done it twice in Nottingham - under a Labour Government which was almost as hostile to him as the unions were !*

Thanks to the year of planning and preparation, Murdoch's newspapers enjoyed full production and distribution throughout the strike and a call by the unions for the public to boycott them fell mostly on deaf ears.

Thanks to the year of planning and preparation, News International was content to let the dispute run its course.

Thanks to the year of planning and preparation, the strike eventually collapsed on February 5th 1987.

And to what extent was that total victory thanks to one Christopher Pole-Carew?

Opinions on that are mixed.

In *End Of The Street,* Linda Melvern appeared to see Pole-Carew's role as considerably less significant than those of Murdoch's executive team of Matthews, Gillespie, Taylor, etc.

And one former Times editorial executive, David Flynn, says: " By the time the move took place, he had been well and truly placed into a corner; I gathered the management view was that his proposals were too hard line, even for Murdoch."

But Derek Winters, who followed Pole-Carew from Nottingham to Wapping, says : " In *End Of The Street* his character, presence and contribution seemed somewhat overlooked to me."

Linda Applegate, Pole-Carew's PA for the Wapping project says: " His management style earned him the respect and admiration of everyone at Wapping."

And Stan Dziuba is in no doubt whatsoever: " I do not believe it would have happened without him. His role was crucial and his confidence in achieving the outcome was total. He was the strategic planner. I believe that Murdoch had confidence in Pole-Carew's strategy and that the Murdoch executives eventually came around to that way of thinking. Anybody in the know over Wapping from the very beginning would agree that he was absolutely central to the strategy and to its ultimate success and despite the high profile he's always had, his part in it has never been fully recognised. I don't think there was a conscious plan to prevent that recognition but it suited everybody's purpose not to do so."

The meeting Pole-Carew had requested with the mogul before Christmas, 1985 never materialised and after seeing the project through to day one of printing at Wapping he and his team parted company with the Murdoch empire when their contract expired.

Stan Dziuba remembers that first day of printing at Wapping very well: " The first paper to be printed was The Sunday Times. We were late going to press. There were all sorts of people in all sorts of areas and we all helped load the freshly printed papers onto the TNT lorries. When a batch of lorries were fully laden and the sliding covers were fastened down they were ready to leave the plant and they went out in convoy. We stood on the ramp and watched the convoy go out. Once we'd seen the gates open and the first few lorries race through we knew that we had at last succeeded in printing the papers and getting them out. They had police escorts from there. Christopher wanted to run after them to see if they were all right. I had to hold him back. I didn't want his face on the TV cameras and in the newspapers. It was 3.30 in the morning. Time for a beer."

Pole-Carew recalls:" My team were all with me when those presses rolled for the first time and the Taut Liners, huge articulated trucks, were loaded and moved out for the first time. These were truly magical moments for us. And then we went. The job was done. Nothing left to stay for."

Stan Dziuba reflects: " We were mercenaries. We went in, we did a job and we walked away. We were used and abused but very well paid. Classic mercenaries."

For Pole-Carew, there was one last episode to this remarkable story when Rupert Murdoch invited him to lunch at The Savoy : " It was just the two of us at a table together and he thanked me for what I had done. It was a kind and thoughtful gesture from an incredibly busy man who I had liked and greatly admired throughout my time working for him and with him and for me it made for a much appreciated ending to Rupert Murdoch's extraordinary Wapping saga."

More than 20 years later, the place of the Wapping Dispute in British history is a significant one. Not only did it break the power the print unions wielded over the national press (*by 1988 all the national newspapers had followed Murdoch's out of Fleet Street to the newly developed Docklands and into modern plants equipped with the new technology*) but, following Margaret Thatcher's defeat of the miners, it confirmed the breaking of trades union power in general and changed the face of industrial relations in the United Kingdom for ever.

There are inevitably mixed views on whether the outcome of the Wapping battle was ultimately for good or ill in the newspaper industry.

Clearly, the absurd abuse of power by the Fleet Street unions **had** to be tackled and Canute-like attempts to resist the waves of new technology were always going to be futile. Accepting the reality of that is to accept that thousands of jobs would have been lost sooner or later, anyway and the dramatic finale to Murdoch's attempts to modernise his business was, surely, due as much to the intransigence of the unions as it was to the implacable determination of the proprietor.

But there are those who believe that Murdoch's victory marked the beginning of a decline for British newspapers; People like Barry Fitzpatrick, a SOGAT official at the time of the dispute who later became national newspapers organiser of the National Union of Journalists. Barry told The Observer newspaper on the dispute's 20th anniversary:" Promises of a bright new future for journalism never materialised. Wages for journalists have slumped in real terms. Far too many are desk-bound and staffing levels are inadequate in many national titles as well as in the regional press. Instead of investing in quality journalism, companies are spending millions on promotional gimmicks and as a result we're awash with CDs that nobody wants to listen to.

" Newspaper bosses constantly hunt for ways to do things on the cheap - an attitude that smacks of disdain for the readers buying their papers - and the public is voting with its feet, Circulation continues to drop and today's newspaper owners find themselves managing a steady decline."

To which Christopher Pole-Carew replies:

" The national newspaper industry's woes probably did start at the time of the technological changes that Wapping brought about - but most certainly **not** as a result of them. If anything, the changes delayed the decline.

" In the regional newspaper industry, into which I had introduced the changes a decade earlier, new technology made the newspapers far more profitable but, wrongly, at the cost of jobs that could and should have been converted into commercial print work, which would have generated even more profitability while at the same time keeping faith with the employees.

" It saddened me when the managements of some of the regional newspapers made the most of their new powers following the defeat of the unions by squeezing everything they possibly could from their workforces. If ever good strong unions were needed to prevent exploitation, it was then, but the leaders of both managements and unions maybe deserved what both did to each other. But then, it's still the soldiers who get killed - not the generals.

" New technology could not be stopped in other areas; the near instant visual image was bound to replace the printed word, causing the swing from newspapers to television, although the market for informed written comment remains, to this day, very strong.

" The practice of some greedy regional newspaper managements squeezing every last possible penny out of the advertising milch cow was bound to end in devastating competition from free newspapers and free advertising sheets. Those managements seemed incapable of understanding that a paper which doesn't cherish its readership and live and work with it and for it cannot expect to receive its loyalty in return. So they lost both their readers and their advertisers.

" How fascinating that it should come about that the disregard of the very philosophy to which I held so strongly all my working life - that loyalty must be a two way virtue - should lead to the decline of an industry that I had worked so hard to improve!

Murdoch mission completed, Christopher Pole-Carew took a long overdue break, which included a fortnight's fishing on the River Carron in the east of Scotland. He hired a lodge and invited family and friends to join him for a fishing holiday which " was the greatest fun - and dissipated a healthy slice of my bonus for the Wapping success! "

But he needed to work.

And not just for money.

He was 55- years-old now but he was bursting with energy and vitality. He had worked hard all his life and simply could not imagine not doing so. Retirement was simply not an option.

Back home in Nottinghamshire, during the summer and autumn of 1986 he investigated a number of possible openings but none proved to be suitable for him.Then, he received a telephone call from Peter Jay of Mirror Group Newspapers to say that Robert Maxwell wished to see him in London.

" Not something to be turned down lightly," recalls Pole-Carew "…and curiosity was a powerful spur! "

Born in Czechoslovakia, the infamous " Captain Bob" Maxwell, also known as the " Bouncing Czech", was already a hugely controversial figure when he approached Pole-Carew in 1986.

By 1991, after his mysterious death ,when he vanished from his yacht in the Atlantic, he was disgraced and despised.

Maxwell had bought Mirror Group Newspapers from Reed International in 1984, taking the Daily Mirror downmarket in an unsuccessful battle with Rupert Murdoch's Sun. He was notorious for treating those around him with appalling rudeness and for sacking people at the drop of a paper clip.

No wonder Christopher Pole-Carew was *curious* !

On the appointed day at the appointed time, Pole-Carew sat outside Maxwell's office in the Mirror building suite he shared with his sons and Peter Jay, his chief of staff and waited…and waited…and waited. This was a discourtesy he came to know as normal from Maxwell.

Throughout the newspaper industry at this time stories, many of them probably apocryphal, abounded about Maxwell, who was a big, bullying, bellowing brute of a man. Journalists, in particular, would swap Maxwell tales in the pubs and a particularly popular one concerned the day Robert Maxwell got into a lift in the Mirror building to find he was sharing it with a man in overalls, who was smoking.

" Put that cigarette out." demanded Cap'n Bob.

" No," said the man.

" Put that cigarette out….**now!** " roared Maxwell.

" No, I won't," said the man.

" I'm going to tell you one last time," shouted the furious proprietor.

" **Put that bloody cigarette out!** "

"And I'm telling **you** one more time. **No I bloody won't !** "

By now the lift had stopped and both men got out.

" How much do you earn ? Maxwell asked the man.

"A hundred quid a week," he replied.

" Right, " said Maxwell, "come with me"

With that, he grabbed the man by the collar and marched him into the pay office. " This man earns a hundred pounds a week," Maxwell told the startled staff. " Give him three months' money and throw him out. He's fired."

Outside on the pavement, the man could not believe his luck.

" I work for British Telecom," he chortled as he counted the cash.

'Somebody Had To Do It'

" And I only came in to fix a phone! "

Still waiting outside Maxwell's office, Pole-Carew thought back to previous occasions upon which he had met 'Cap'n Bob' - such as international newspaper technical conferences at which the Nottingham trailblazer was always in demand " because I was the only one from the UK who could talk about computers!"

He remembered him as large - " *gross, really*" - and totally dominating any company he was in. He smiled to himself as he recalled how Maxwell had decided his name was **Paul Crewe** and wondered if that had changed now and if he would get it right. It hadn't. And he didn't.

When he had finally been summoned to the presence of Maxwell and David Montgomery, the Chief Executive of Mirror Group Newspapers, **Paul Crewe** was told by Maxwell that it was his intention to launch an all-day paper for London, to be called the Daily News. And he would like him to head up the project.

" I suppose I was always a sucker for a challenge!" says Pole-Carew.

" I had heard much that was bad about Maxwell but it had never amounted to much more than gossip, suspicions and dislikes; nothing so tangible as to keep one away from him.

" I said it seemed like a good idea and I hoped that I could help."

At that, Maxwell got to his feet and stretched his huge frame.

" Good," he said." When the unions learn that I am employing **Paul Crewe** they will think that I have kissed the crooked cross."

" Good Heavens," said Pole-Carew to David Montgomery, " I never knew that they read Kipling in Czech schools before the War. How extraordinary! "

Montgomery laughed. Maxwell looked puzzled. He said nothing.

But given this short-fused despot's well deserved reputation, **Paul Crewe** was very fortunate not to have been thrown out of the building there and then!

However, the meeting continued and Christopher Pole-Carew accepted another highly controversial job.

He says he can't remember what the terms and conditions of employment were "...except that Maxwell said he would make me a director of one of his companies, presumably so that I had some status within the organisation.

" I then asked that if I was to do this job could I have direct access to Maxwell and not, for example, through David Montgomery as had been the case through Bruce Matthews to Rupert Murdoch when he was not in England.

" He agreed to it.

" My reason for making that request was that I did not want to suffer the lack of direct control that I felt had been my lot in my dealings with Bruce. I reckoned I had learned a hard lesson at News International and I didn't want to go through that again. If I was to set up the London Daily News then let me be free to do my job properly."

In the event, Pole-Carew discovered that such reservations were misplaced: " I had found the top people in News International to be, in my opinion, not very helpful and almost permanently involved in political infighting. I had found out, very early on, that I did not like them and there was not one shred of evidence to suggest that they liked me!

" I had assumed that my experiences at News International were typical of Fleet Street and that the Mirror Group would be much the same, but as it turned out, they could hardly have been more different: lovely people, helpful and supportive without exception.

" I asked David Montgomery on one occasion how it was that News International had an outstanding boss (*Rupert Murdoch*) who was not only a brilliant newspaperman but also always ,to me, quite charming supported by a bunch of people who, in my opinion, were difficult to work with, whereas at the Mirror Group it was the reverse.

" He replied with a smile: ' *We always support each other here, regardless. If we didn't, Cap'n Bob would pick us off, one by one.*'

So, Christopher Pole-Carew set about strategically planning the London Daily News. He lived during the week at the Hotel Russell in Bloomsbury: " Not an ideal situation but then the hours Maxwell expected didn't include spare time so where I slept wasn't really relevant! "

He kept his company, Computer Print Consultants, going and worked through it for pay and expenses - or tried to.

" I quickly found out the other side of being a director of a company that had only members of the Maxwell family as its other directors. I was too senior in the company for the Mirror Group's Chief Accountant to handle either my expenses (and London hotels didn't come cheap) or my salary. I had to go to Maxwell for both.

" Maxwell ran the Mirror Group like some 19th Century Turkish Pasha. An average of two hours in every working day was spent sitting outside his office waiting to go in to his Presence for meetings he had called. He had a habit of always picking on one of those present to deliberately humiliate (fortunately, never me - though I don't know why) and this would run like a thread throughout the meeting. A 10pm finish was not unusual."

Pole-Carew was given Maxwell's son Kevin's office; he was away in France. This was just two doors from Cap'n Bob's own office - too close for comfort!

The London Daily News was to be an all-day paper, starting with a morning edition designed to exploit the commuter traffic and continuing through the afternoon and into the evening, to catch the commuter traffic again.

Pole-Carew found that little work had been done in preparation for the launch, mainly because Maxwell's way of doing things was to tell his various Mirror executives that they were to get the Daily News up and running " as if they hadn't got more than enough on their plates with their own jobs."

He quickly discovered that there was nobody on the team, apart from himself, with the essential evening newspaper experience; nor was there anyone with the technical knowledge, crucial to this sort of operation, of printing a paper in more than one place at a time; nor was there anyone with the requisite understanding of photo-composition and web offset printing techniques. They were all hot metal men through and through - perfectly understandable given their current jobs but hopelessly inadequate for what Maxwell expected from his new paper.

It took Pole-Carew just two days of working for Robert Maxwell to realise " that the London Daily News, as set up and planned, hadn't got the slightest chance of succeeding." And it took just two more days " to understand that there was no way anyone would be able to make Maxwell take this in because nobody could ever have accused him of being a good listener, except to views that agreed with his own.

" I had walked into a nightmare. There were two printing plants to be set up with different print sizes and both away from the editorial base; There were staff to be recruited, though fortunately, for me, by the relevant Mirror departmental heads. However, I remember the head of Circulation coming to me one day to ask for my help. It seemed that he had taken on a good number of van drivers for the new paper, as instructed by Maxwell, to get the delivery system organised ahead of production. This was, of course, sensible - but it was now three months since he had hired the drivers and not one of them had received one penny of payment. Unbelievable. But so typical.

" Interestingly, these were ex- News International men who had lost their jobs on the various Murdoch papers with the strike on the change to the new computer systems. Newspaper delivery men are a breed apart; they live for their newspapers, perpetually on a high from the buzz they get out of frantically delivering the news to the public, hot off the presses, day in, day out.

" The opportunity to get back into their beloved newspaper world was, to them, like being taken from limbo and being allowed to live again. At the time, no-one was aware of the appalling finance problems Maxwell was suffering and so I assumed the reason these men had not been paid was simply that he would not be concerned with such ' low life' creatures as van drivers.

" So, as requested, I went to see him at the end of the day to plead their case. He told me : 'It will happen in good time.' In the event I was not able to get them *all* they were owed but six weeks' worth, which was under half - but better than nothing."

(What Pole-Carew didn't know was that these were early signs of huge financial problems for Robert Maxwell, the full extent of which only became evident after he had vanished in mysterious circumstances from his yacht in the Atlantic in 1991. It transpired that his business empire was at least £1billion in debt and that his companies' pensions funds were short of £440million, leading to the discovery of the greatest scandal in the history of the pensions industry - 32,000 employees having been robbed of their savings. Maxwell died while cruising off the Canary Islands and was found floating in the sea. His death was variously attributed to suicide, natural causes and even covert action by assorted secret services. Says Pole-Carew: " In later years I was to learn, as everyone did, what Cap'n Bob had done to his employees' pensions but by then he was out of reach, via the waters of the Atlantic Ocean! Many have wondered whether he jumped or was pushed. Which do I believe? Well, for me, what is certain is that the bulwarks of the yacht were far too high for him to have fallen accidentally and I cannot believe that anyone so vain as Maxwell was would ever believe that he couldn't get himself out of whatever hole he had got himself into.")

Eventually, on February 24th, 1987 the London Daily News was published in a blaze of publicity. The UK's first 24 hour newspaper, with the slogan: *For the city that never sleeps, the paper that never stops* was intended to challenge the dominance of the Evening Standard.

The Standard's owners, Lord Rothermere's Associated Newspapers, responded by re-launching the defunct London Evening News at a lower price to squeeze Maxwell's newcomer out of the market. This led to a cover price war with the London Daily News eventually selling at 10p and the Evening News at 5p.

Maxwell was dismissive of the cut-price Evening News, declaring in a BBC interview :" The Evening Standard and Lord Rothermere are so worried about their monopoly, which the London Daily News is finally breaking and so scared by the huge demand for our paper that they've brought out a cheapo Evening News, which is

really a joke."

But the joke was on Maxwell. The London Daily News failed and published its last edition on July 23rd, 1987. Maxwell conceded defeat two days later after paying undisclosed damages to Associated Newspapers for accusing it of lying about the Evening Standard's circulation figures. Associated then re-absorbed the Evening News into the Standard. Job done.

Cap'n Bob had been well and truly walloped.

The London Daily News had reputedly cost him around £25million, having sold less than 100,000 copies a day against a minimum sales target of 200,000.

Christopher Pole-Carew had by that time (**" thank goodness!"**) left the employ of Robert Maxwell:" I had served Maxwell's purpose. I had never been in charge, as such, of the operation since his various Mirror executives had to run their respective parts of it from the beginning. Nevertheless, he had used me to his benefit. Now all I needed to do to wind things up was to get my pay for three months work out of him.This took another three months of hard legal grind but my lawyers, Lovell White, knew Maxwell well and so eventually triumphed."

So what now?

The extraordinary, trail blazing newspaper career of Christopher Pole-Carew was stuttering in a way that was totally alien to the man's character and philosophy.

He did a handful of consultancy jobs (" *with the inevitable mutterings of abuse from print unions in the background!* ") but they held little real interest and, worse, no challenge for him. " It simply was not my scene," he reflects, " I think it's fair to say that I had never developed the skill of telling people what they wanted to hear as distinct from what, in my opinion, they needed to know! "

And so, in 1988, far too young at 59, Christopher Pole-Carew retired from the industry which he had revolutionised.

" This was not intentional retirement," he says, " because the idea of not working was totally alien to me but I needed to be needed and clearly the newspaper industry did not want to know me or my ideas, except in situations such as Wapping and the London Daily News where there was only an outside chance of any success but maybe that maverick Pole-Carew might just manage to pull it off."

The end of the extraordinary career of a unique man who had shaped the future of the entire newspaper industry over two tumultuous decades of radical change went unreported and unrecorded - a fact which, in itself, reflected little credit on the British journalistic profession, the majority of which still regarded him as an unspeakable pariah because too many of its members had swallowed trades union propaganda without following their own fundamental discipline of getting both sides of the story.

One of the few journalists to recognise Pole-Carew's enormous importance to any history of the newspaper industry, Kate Macmillan, found him living in idyllic rural retirement with his beloved Gill in Devon in 1991.

Managing his historic family's ancestral home for the National Trust and indulging his passion for fishing and shooting, Pole-Carew was flanked by his amiable gundogs as he told Kate, for an article in the national magazine Newspaper Focus :" If I'm going to vegetate - you find me a better place to do it! "

But later in their conversation he admitted to her: " If I had the right offer, I would be back like a shot. I am very happy until a friend of mine in newspapers gets in touch.

"And then I miss it terribly."

7

THIS MAN POLE-CAREW

' Christopher Pole-Carew is not a man about whom either friends or enemies have ever harboured doubts.'

ONCE in a while, but rarely, life throws up a genuinely unique character; a truly exceptional one-off personality of whom it can properly be said, they broke the mould ; to whom the word genius can be applied without exaggeration; whose contribution to the field of their choice can be described, legitimately, as immense.

One such is Christopher Pole-Carew.

And the fair city of Nottingham accommodated *two* at the same time.

The other was the late and truly great Brian Clough.

These two giant personalities strode their respective domains with colossal impact. Pole-Carew on the Nottingham Evening Post and on the UK newspaper industry in general; Clough on Nottingham Forest FC and on British football in general.

To say that both these men could be difficult would be a masterpiece of understatement. Some who knew both mused that they would love to lock them in a room together, throw away the key, then watch the feathers fly. It would have been a verbal fight of gargantuan proportions for which, in Nottingham in the late 70s/early 80s you could have sold tickets and packed any local arena...

In the Red Corner, Brian Clough - the working class Socialist ,wearing his humble roots on his sleeve - with his strong Teesside accent, natural intelligence, withering wit, wind-up wizardry and fierce, inherent hatred of anyone even remotely 'posh.'

In the Blue Corner, Christopher Pole-Carew - the proud aristocrat, oozing good breeding - with his clipped upper class tones, superb intellect, scathing satire, mastery of the acerbic put-down and intense dislike of anyone prone to prejudice.

What a brilliant battle it would have been!

What an epic bout of verbal fisticuffs!

In the event, they never even met- which is a shame because Clough might have explained why, without ever bothering to consider the other side of the story, he had boycotted and 'blacked' the Nottingham Evening Post during the 1978/79 national strike by journalists, giving his high profile support to the breakaway newspaper launched by the Nottingham strikers sacked by Pole-Carew and never wasting numerous public opportunities to berate Pole-Carew and his company, while for his part, Pole-Carew would probably have left Clough in no doubt whatsoever what he thought of all that and delivered a barrage of home truths of his own!

I (*Barrie Williams*) was exceptionally fortunate to know *both* men well and I admired both enormously, so I like to think that at the end of their verbal punch-up they would have been left with a lot of respect for each other.

These two giants of Nottingham were poles apart on the surface but they actually shared more in common than either of them ever knew. Neither suffered fools and both liked people with strength of character. Both could be much more intimidating, positively ***frightening*** to some, than either of them realised but both had a high regard for those with the balls to answer back and stand their ground.

Pole-Carew would have respected Clough because he is emphatically ***not*** a snob and readily recognises talent and self-belief in others, enemies or not; Clough would have respected Pole-Carew because he admired a ***fighter*** and always appreciated skill and depth of character in others, opponents or not.

These two men, both enormously successful and charismatic, epitomised the vibrant, exciting, argumentative scene that was Nottingham in those days. Both, full of supreme self-confidence and self-esteem, could infuriate you with their arrogance, stubbornness and occasional rudeness; Both, renowned for shooting from the hip, could be dreadfully indiscreet; Both could belittle a verbal target (who *always* deserved it) with one blistering broadside; Both could appear to be callous.

Clough could confine a troublesome soccer star to life's scrapheap with the same apparent nonchalance with which Pole-Carew sacked strikers. Yet both were capable of great human kindness and deep compassion; Both could show care, thoughtfulness and consideration for others; Both, hard men on the surface, could be moved to tears by the plight of others and frequently performed spontaneous, selfless and private acts of charity. And both could charm the proverbial birds from the trees and have people proverbially eating from the palms of their hands.

Enigmas, both.

It is also interesting to observe that neither was given full reward for their tremendous respective achievements - both with previously dull, under performing, unfashionable Nottingham organisations. Clough ***should*** have been appointed manager of England after twice winning the European Cup with Forest and Pole-Carew ***should*** have been offered a comparable position at the pinnacle of the UK newspaper industry after leading Europe in pioneering progress with the Evening Post.

That neither gained their just rewards was, in both cases, almost certainly due to their blunt, outspoken manner; to their refusal to suffer fools; to their contempt for pompous authority and to the controversy that both attracted. In both cases, that controversy discomforted lesser men in higher places who preferred the quieter life that comes with mediocrity - that latter condition being anathema to Pole-Carew and Clough alike. They were so similar in so many ways - not least in the enormous respect that both commanded and that word **respect** recurs more than any other when people who know him properly discuss Christopher Pole-Carew.

Like all larger-than-life characters he provokes strong feelings; he's never occupied the middle ground and rarely do opinions of him. But love him or hate him, you'll be hard-pressed to find anybody who, having known him and/or worked with him, does not respect him.

I first encountered Pole-Carew when I worked as a young features sub-editor on the Nottingham Evening Post between 1969 and 1971.

At that time the paternal approach of the proprietors, the Forman Hardy family, was a throw back to a different age and that, allied to the chairman's military background and style, induced a deference, a respectful protocol and a culture that would not have seemed out of place in a Dickens' novel. It was an environment in which anybody even slightly senior to you was called 'Sir' or 'Mister' (*no women executives, of course*); in which nobody ever challenged anything nor ever rocked the boat, which sailed slowly along on placid waters, making no significant progress at all.

That all began to change with the emergence of one Christopher Pole-Carew, heir apparent to the managing director, Frank Cragg who was due to retire. Like the chairman, Mr Cragg was rarely, if ever, seen by the vast majority of employees but Mr Pole-Carew was already becoming a dramatic wave maker in this placid ' Victorian' pool. For one thing, he was amazingly striking physically - blond, handsome and so very tall, he brought with him all the charisma and drive of a dashing young naval officer. And *dash* he did. Everywhere. He would race from one department of the newspaper to another, determined to get to know every nook and cranny, every custom and practice of the place. In his wake would trail ' the Winco' - his assistant Wing Commander Theo Kearton, recently of the RAF (*who I was later to come to know as a really nice man*). This pair frightened the life out of everybody.

But rumours of what enormous change Pole-Carew was to bring to the Nottingham Evening Post, the Nottinghamshire Guardian Journal and assorted local weekly newspapers were as near as I would get to experiencing it because, early in 1971, I left to join the Kent Evening Post where I was later (in 1975) to become its editor.

In 1981, after Pole-Carew's revolution had turned that stagnant old company into the hugely controversial trailblazer known throughout the world wide newspaper industry for its technological and commercial innovations, the Nottingham Evening Post advertised for a new editor to replace Bill Snaith, whose retirement was imminent.

This was an absolute peach of a job; none bigger or better in the regional newspaper industry and Pole-Carew, as ever determined to leave every other newspaper company standing, had seen to it that it also offered a far bigger salary and a much better package (including a top of the range Daimler for a company car !) than could be found anywhere else in regional journalism.

I was surprised, as was every other regional editor, to see this job advertised because we had all assumed that when Bill Snaith retired his replacement would be an internal candidate, reflecting the paternalistic nature of T. Bailey Forman Ltd. That it wasn't ,was another Pole-Carew innovation.

When I applied for the job, it was with little anticipation of getting even so far as an interview. Everyone knew that this would attract a really strong field of applicants, including mature, experienced editors of some of the biggest regional papers in Britain. I had just five years' experience of editing a small evening paper and I was still in my early thirties. " No chance, really - but, hey, what's to lose? "

I considered myself such a rank outsider that when I received a letter from Pole-Carew inviting me for an interview it was a genuine surprise. And the interview itself was every bit as surprising.

Though, as a mere minion in 1970/71, I had seen Pole-Carew around the Evening Post building I had never spoken to him, indeed never even met him. Knowing of his upper class and Naval background and having read so much about his incredible achievements in the newspaper industry - not to mention his union busting battles - I expected to find a stern, straight-backed officer and gentleman, very conscious of his own rank and full of his own importance. I was a young man bursting with confidence and self-belief but I did find myself wondering what on earth, as the working class son of a factory worker, I would have in common with this aristocrat and how difficult that lack of common ground would make our interview.

That doubt was entirely mis-placed.

Within minutes of meeting Pole-Carew, he had put me entirely at ease and in no time at all, we were chatting away like old friends.

The interview was a unique and fascinating experience and enough to convince me that if, against the huge odds, I managed to land this job I would love to work with this most remarkable of men. It soon became evident that Christopher Pole-Carew was one of life's natural enthusiasts. This man couldn't sit still for a second!

It was easy to see why he was such a trailblazer; such a true innovator. And, boy, was he inspirational!

Having risen from trainee reporter to editor in a comparatively short time by identifying career opportunities and going for them, I had experienced many job interviews - but never one even remotely like this. This was something else. Mainly because, for most of the time, Pole-Carew danced around his office in a flurry of incredibly long legs and windmill-like arms, enthusing like nobody I had ever met before about everything we discussed.

Then he took me on a whistle-stop tour of his domain - dashing from one department to another with me literally running behind him, just like I'd seen 'the Winco' do back in 1970 and making me wonder, momentarily, if I now looked as daft as he used to trailing in the wake of the 'mad' Carew!

The people to whom PC (*as he was known to everyone in the Company*) introduced me responded to this gyrating giant with equally energetic and enthusiastic responses (*some of which seemed suspiciously exaggerated and rehearsed to me* !) and one or two of them, particularly among those I had known a decade earlier, wore the vacant terrified expressions of mesmerised rabbits caught in headlights.

The fabric of the old Victorian building hadn't changed a bit in the decade since I left but the atmosphere , once so staid and safe, now seemed exciting and different. The technology was mind-blowing and the buzz around the commercial departments was audible. It seemed a very strange culture - but one to which I was drawn immediately.

I left the interview with my own head in a whirl of excitement and anticipation. Working with this man would be one of a hell of an experience. But would I ever get the chance? Not according to the industry grapevine, which had the plum job going to Colin Brannigan - the editorial director of Essex County Newspapers; a man of 50-plus; a big name in regional journalism who counted the editorship of the Sheffield Star among his previous positions and was recently President of the august Guild of British Newspaper Editors. Barrie Who? - the youngster from the little Kent Evening Post - wasn't even an also ran. Forget it.

Then, one Monday morning, I was at work in Kent, with all thoughts of a dream move to Nottingham banished from my mind. when I received a telephone call…

" Hi, Barrie. Chris Pole-Carew. The chairman would like you and your wife to join us here in Nottingham for lunch."

" *When* ? "

" Today"

" *But it's half past nine and I'm a five hour drive away* !"

" No problem. We'll send the helicopter for you."

After lunch with Colonel Tom Forman Hardy and his wife Marjorie; Nicholas Forman Hardy and his wife Jane; Christopher Pole-Carew and Gill, my wife, Pauline and I were flown back to Kent where we sat over dinner wondering if I was really in which a chance.

Then came a letter from Pole-Carew informing me that the chairman was offering me the job.Unbelievable This was like the unknown manager of Little Piddlehampton Wanderers being offered the chance to manage Manchester United.

Needless to say, I accepted without hesitation.

Later I discovered that Christopher Pole-Carew had fought hard to get me on to the shortlist (out of 73 high-powered applicants) then used his very considerable powers of persuasion to convince Tom Forman Hardy

'Somebody Had To Do It'

(who had, indeed, wanted Colin Brannigan) that he should give youth a chance.

This was so typical of Pole-Carew.

And my anticipation of how exciting it would be to work with him was confirmed immediately when he announced that the chairman had decided that I should be sent on a three month world tour of newspapers (including Australia, the United States and Canada) to broaden my professional horizons.

That the chairman was given the credit for this was Pole-Carew's way of adhering to the unwritten rule prevailing in the industry at that time, that - apart from on departmental fiscal matters - editors traditionally answered not to managing directors (for fear that they would be tainted by commercialism!) but to proprietors. My world tour and all its arrangements, including its very considerable expense, were entirely Pole-Carew's decision - about which he would have *informed* the chairman, persuaded him to spend the money, then observed the protocol by telling me that it was the chairman who wanted me to go!

"And you must take your wife with you because you can't leave her alone after uprooting her from Kent; And, by the way, you will be travelling First Class because we are a First Class company; Oh and yes, I forgot to mention that we've arranged a holiday break for you both in the middle of your tour, staying at the Waikiki Hilton in Honolulu! "

I soon discovered that such style and class were synonymous with this man. He required 100 per cent commitment but he would always see to it that you were well rewarded (***incredibly*** well for the regional newspaper industry) and was always intent on ensuring that your loved ones were considered and never taken for granted.

There followed four years of working closely with a man whose reputation outside the Nottingham Evening Post was to prove to be almost totally undeserved. He could be very difficult at times; unpredictable; short fused, impatient and opinionated. And some of those around him were absolutely terrified of him. But, in equal measure, he was charming, funny, thoughtful, considerate and exceptionally generous.

Above all, he inspired great loyalty - that two way virtue to which so much of his personal creed is devoted.

To me, Christopher Pole-Carew's greatest professional asset was that he always led by example, an elusive quality in business which, though often claimed by bosses, is rarely demonstrated. There was not one of the very varied and quite complex component parts of the newspaper industry of which he did not have a knowledgeable understanding and when a new one came along, as it frequently did, he made sure he was up to speed with it in next to no time. He had an in-built bovine excreta detector as reliable as any radar system… and heaven help any manager who tried to spread that substance at his meetings!

Apart from editorial matters, upon which he adhered scrupulously (if occasionally with great difficulty!) to the conventional principle of the editor's independence, his knowledge of every aspect of the business made him a very challenging managing director and he would stubbornly defend a contested opinion with the infuriating advantage of being almost invariably right.

But that assertive self-belief never excluded gracious acknowledgement on the very rare occasions upon which he was wrong and after one protracted and vexatious exchange, his Computer Manager, David Williams, received a fulsome written apology…inside an expensive hamper full of scrumptious goodies from Burtons, Nottingham's equivalent of Fortum & Mason.

It will surprise many who have accepted the superficial public perception of the man to be told that Pole-Carew was never one for the ivory tower existence of many in top management. Yes, he wanted the world to know that T. Bailey Forman was a big, successful company but its managing director bore no ostentation whatsoever and personally, the symbols of status were irrelevant to him.

While he insisted that all his fellow directors' company cars had to be top of the range Jaguars which were replaced by sparkling new ones every 20,000 miles (" because when you're out and about in the local business community, it's important to demonstrate, especially to advertisers, that this is a top company ") his own car was a well-worn, understated beige Subaru which, several years earlier, had replaced the beloved old Mini into which he would squeeze his 6ft 5inch frame, thus defying both nature and belief. He was particularly fond of that mini - an Italian-made *Innocenti* - of which only six right hand drive models were produced.

' Posh' accent notwithstanding, Christopher Pole-Carew is certainly **not** a snob. He was just as naturally comfortable supping ale in the public bar of the local pub with the lads off the shop floor as he was sipping champagne in five star London hotels with the industry's top brass; just as content and genuinely enthusiastic playing darts and dominoes with blokes in overalls as out shooting and fishing with country gentlemen in tweeds.

His enemies in the newspaper business like to paint a picture of a filthy rich product of privilege; a typical upper class twit (or worse!) who had so much money he didn't really need to work but played at newspapers and with people's livelihoods, just to keep himself amused. All that is as inaccurate as it is unfair.

Christopher Pole-Carew succeeded in the tough world of newspapers because of his ability, his vision and his courage. The double-barrelled background was, if anything, a **dis**advantage.

He puts this best himself: " I am **not** to the manor born. Whatever I've achieved in life has been achieved by my own efforts. It didn't come about because I had money because I hadn't. It didn't come about because I had connections because in the newspaper industry I sure as hell hadn't. It's forgotten that I started as a rep selling advertising space. In fact, I would say that having a double-barrelled name and going into the fiercely cynical and unforgiving newspaper business was actually a hindrance rather than an advantage. I wasn't right. Never mind me - *anybody* called Pole-Carew couldn't possibly be right! "

At Nottingham, in his dealings with the proprietor, he always looked after the best interests of those around him and underneath him - no matter what their place in the company's pecking order.

He would tell his fellow T. Bailey Forman directors :" I'm your shop steward, you know. And if I leave here, this place will change completely."

How right that proved to be!

In the year before he was sacked, I had gone to Pole-Carew with news which, had the reality of the man matched the myth, would have had him spitting blood and feathers. The National Union Of Journalists had approached me with a view to ending the dispute with T.Bailey Forman Ltd. which had rumbled on since 1978.

Pole-Carew had nothing whatsoever to gain from a peace deal with the union.For me, it was different. The ' blacking' of the Nottingham Evening Post by the Labour and trades union movement had remained intact, nationally and locally, ever since the dispute started. In real terms - and particularly commercially - it made not a jot of difference to the newspaper but to me, as a journalist reared on the principles of political impartiality and balanced reporting of two sided stories, it was a serious irritant because, officially at least, no member of the Labour Party; no trades unionist was permitted to talk to my newspaper.

The NUJ's terms for a settlement were re-instatement of the 28 sacked journalists (which I knew was no problem at all because only one of them wanted to come back anyway) and the right to represent journalists on my staff (much more tricky after all that had gone on.)

I reckoned I could handle it and to me the editorial advantages of being able to have a normal Press relationship with Labour politicians and trades unionists in a city and county in which that party was hugely significant far outweighed any difficulties.

Ending the dispute wasn't going to sell any more papers; there was no gain other than restoration of journalistic normality on political reporting, which was a mere fraction of the whole editorial output, and the rest of T Bailey Forman's directors thought I was mad to be even considering letting the NUJ back in to this famously non-union environment.

But when I told Christopher Pole-Carew, his response was calm and considerate:" What do *you* want to do? " he asked.

" *On balance, I'd like to settle.*"

" Barrie, I was never anti-union, just anti-stupidity. You do what you think is right."

And so, a team of top national NUJ officials entered surreptitiously and very gingerly into the lion's den to talk to the editor of the reviled Nottingham Evening Post and its despised managing director, the dreaded Pole-Carew - who met them with a disarming smile and a warm handshake, immediately shattering their misconception of the sort of welcome they would receive from him.

After a general chat in his office he left me to carry on the talks which 18 months of intensely hard bargaining later (it took so long because I was determined to get an agreement which would never again see the Nottingham Evening Post sucked into a national strike over which it could have no local control or influence) led to the dispute being officially settled. The rest of the news media, which had shown no interest whatsoever in the Evening Post's remarkable post-strike successes, descended on Forman Street and TV cameras recorded the scene as I signed the deal with the NUJ's leader Harry Conroy. Pole-Carew, in stark contrast to the distorted unfairness of his reputation, stayed out of the limelight and left me to get on with it without interfering in any way.

When I thanked him for that, he told me: " Barrie. I trust you to do what you think is right. Why wouldn't I? "

It was just one of many episodes in which I was both surprised and delighted by Christopher Pole-Carew's approach to business and by his staunch, unflinching support for me as the Evening Post's editor and editorial director and I was devastated the day he was sacked.

That day is etched indelibly on the mind of Nancy Harris, who was Pole-Carew's secretary for 13 years.

" Christopher was fantastic to work with - they were the best 13 years of my working life," she says.

" The handling of his departure was farcical, with Ken Powell (T. Bailey Forman's maintenance manager) coming into my office and wrapping chains around my filing cabinets. It was awful.

" There were so many happy times working for Christopher. Even at the height of the union disputes he never lost his sense of humour and that would rub off on all of us. One day, when Christopher was away from Nottingham on business, hundreds of union demonstrators were marching round and round the block shouting **'Pole-Carew out'** Anna Frayne (another secretary) and I could hardly resist opening the window and shouting : ' He **IS** out!'

Pole-Carew's sense of humour and fun is remembered by many who worked with him. One of his training methods was to send teams, mixed from all departments, to spend two or three days together in a remote ivy-clad country house deep in the east midlands countryside.

At these sessions the ratio was about 40 per cent work to 60 per cent recreation. In the evenings, after a sumptuous dinner, the owner of the venue would open up his exceedingly well stocked bar then discreetly retreat, leaving Pole-Carew's delegates to help themselves, just writing down what they had to drink on a list which he left on the bar. The list was always honourably completed - but so was the total consumption of the entire contents of the bar!

Nobody went to bed until every last drop of booze had gone. This bacchanal would be repeated the following evening. And the next. And all paid for by Pole-Carew.

During these marathon revelries, which rarely finished before 4am, the delegates would play drinking games and perform endurance tests, all introduced by the 'mad' Pole-Carew. One such test involved lying flat on the floor on your stomach with a beer bottle in each hand. At the 'referee's' signal you would then move off using the beer bottles, like stilts under each hand, to propel yourself across the floor. As you moved along, only the bottles and the tips of your toes were allowed to touch the floor and if any other part of your anatomy did you were immediately disqualified. The winner was the one who covered the longest distance before collapsing - each attempt being carefully recorded on the floor with white chalk.

The jeers when the over-confident among the contestants failed to make it to the chalk line and the cheers every time the previous best attempt was beaten would raise the roof of the old mansion. It was daft (not to mention dangerous because, though they never did, the bottles could have shattered under the strain) but it was good fun.

Another game, introduced by Pole-Carew involved the very considerable challenge of doing a complete circuit of the large, imposing old room in which the revelries occurred without touching the floor. Curtain hangers, picture rails, light fittings, chandeliers, the tops of open doors , the heads of bronze busts - all were legitimate means of propulsion around the room. But if any part of your anatomy touched the floor you were disqualified. Watching the great man himself, at 6ft 5ins tall, perform this feat was an unforgettable sight, but nobody did it better!

Stories of drunken achievement at ' PC's Away Days' became legend. They were, just as he intended , absolutely brilliant bonding sessions and he was doing this many years before companies started paying thousands of pounds to business consultants to achieve the same benefits to teamwork without the hugely enjoyable Pole-Carew excesses which would have rendered today's ' elf n safety ' zealots apoplectic!

As Trevor Frecknall, a journalist who worked for a time as Pole-Carew's editorial advisor in Nottingham, recalls: " Fancy him having the nickname PC. Was there ever a man who was **less** politically correct? But then again, has there **ever** been another man (except Caxton) to so revolutionise newspaper production? "

The answer to both Trevor's questions is an emphatic " No."

Nancy Harris speaks fondly of Pole-Carew's thoughtfulness:" For example , Frank Cragg, the managing director he replaced, would often call in to the office to say ' hello' and I was always most impressed with how PC would make time, no matter how busy he was, to take him out for lunch and bring him up to date with all that was going on. PC realised what a drastic step it was from being in charge to being retired and he was most considerate. It was a lesson I absorbed myself; to always try to have time for people."

Nancy had great respect, too, for Pole-Carew's pride in good workmanship. In 1981 T Bailey Forman Ltd added a substantial extension to the Forman Street building, the new space being rented out to the Nottingham courts service in a typically astute piece of Pole-Carew revenue generation.

The Evening Post building was an impressive landmark in Nottingham city centre and in order to stay faithful to its early Victorian appearance, Pole-Carew insisted on employing the best stonemasons available and on using local Derbyshire stone which was specially traced to match the existing frontage.

Says Nancy :" One afternoon he came into the office and said I simply *must* go up and see the amazing quality of the work of the stonemasons. He took me right up high on the scaffolding to see the precision of the work up by the parapet (and me in skirt and heels – what would today's health and safety bods have made of that!) and explained, with knowledge and customary enthusiasm precisely what the stonemasons were doing. He was so proud of that work."

So meticulous was Pole-Carew in ensuring that the new extension would be a credit to the Forman Hardy family and to the city of Nottingham that, with painstaking attention to detail, he had researched the old Forman Street building, managed to track down the Derbyshire quarry from which the original stone had been taken and been delighted to discover that it was still functioning. Similarly, the supremely talented father and son stonemasons he hired to do the work were descendants of the original craftsmen.

The result was an aesthetic triumph, delighting architects and historians alike and providing Nottingham with a new building of superlative traditional craftsmanship in which Pole-Carew's pride was well founded.

Pole-Carew was also especially proud of the Latin motto which he had inscribed in beautifully scripted gold lettering on the new stone above the pristine gateway to the extension. It read: VERBA VOLANT, SCRIPTA MANET which, being translated, stated that **'Spoken words fly, the written word remains'**

This was a brilliantly apposite motto for a good newspaper - but it was more than that: The gateway it graced so splendidly was directly opposite Nottingham's Guildhall and it was Pole-Carew's way of sticking two fingers up to the Labour city councillors who had blacked the newspaper during the union disputes and done all they could to try to drive the Nottingham Evening Post out of business!

That Latin inscription, boldly visible to anyone entering or leaving the Guildhall was telling those politicians: *Despite all your venomous rhetoric, we're still here. So b------s!*

Regrettably, it is very unlikely that any of them were sufficiently scholarly to get the message.

How sad that Pole-Carew's clever Latin motto, which was in itself a piece of Nottingham history, was allowed , disgracefully, to disappear along with the fabulous stonework he had had so lovingly created when the whole of that wonderful old Forman Street building was demolished in an act of scandalous vandalism to make way for an ugly shopping mall after Nicholas Forman Hardy sold the company in 1995. And if it had survived, how relevant that motto would now have been in alerting people to the drastic decline , some would say imminent demise, of Britain's once great regional newspaper industry.

Those fortunate enough to have worked with Pole-Carew in the 1970s and early 1980s enjoyed a vibrant, successful, expansive regional newspaper industry at the peak of its performance; without question these were the industry's golden years in which, following an unprecedented boom in classified advertising, regional and local newspapers had become hugely profitable.

This led to most of the then locally owned newspaper companies being gobbled up by the big corporate groups who made the family owners massive offers which they were unable to resist. T. Bailey Forman, however, stood firm. No amount of money would persuade Colonel Tom Forman Hardy to sell the Nottingham Evening Post and his managing director contributed hugely to that determined mindset.

Like any good managing director, Christopher Pole-Carew strove to deliver annual profit growth and more often than not, he delivered on that objective.

But unlike the big national corporate companies, whose pursuit of 'greedy' profit margins has, it is argued, hastened the drastic decline of the industry in recent years, Pole-Carew was a passionate guardian of the quality of the newspaper throughout its operations - from editorial excellence to the highest possible production standards and to sales and marketing initiatives and innovations. Since such progress and standards can only ever be maintained by spending money, he was a devout disciple of continual investment back into the business of very large slices of those profits.

Consequently, Pole-Carew delivered for his bosses, the Forman Hardy family, margins which, though good and apparently perfectly acceptable to them, would be considered wholly inadequate in today's bottom line obsessed newspaper industry.

'Somebody Had To Do It'

He would joke with his fellow directors that the family's finances were some considerable distance short of the ' little sisters of the poor' anyway so, for as long as he was managing director, the newspaper would never want for progressive investment.

Nor did it and this led to a superb, modern, thoroughly well equipped, well manned and very well paid working environment at all levels of the Nottingham Evening Post and its associated business activities.

It remains a massive irony that a managing director with such a philosophy was so despised, reviled and ridiculed by the industry's unions, particularly the NUJ - whose journalists, with their pens mightier than swords, ensured that their own mainly misconceived impression of the man as no more than a vicious, upper-class ' union buster' endured.

If the leaders of those unions at that time could only have been more forward thinking; less ideologically motivated and emotively inclined, they might have realised that, far from being the pariah they made him, this powerful man with his national profile could have been their strongest ally in what was to become a losing battle against corporate greed and shrinking investment in the regional newspaper industry.

He believed passionately that failure to draw a strong line between grabbing massive, rather than just good, profits and the need for on-going investment in the newspapers, particularly in good journalism, would lead, eventually, to their demise. Tragically and ironically, events appear to be proving that Christopher Pole-Carew was, in this conviction as he was in most things, 25 years ahead of his time.

Is it reasonable to speculate that today's modern, generally more moderate, less politically motivated and class-obsessed unions would have taken an entirely different stance towards a man who was, if only they could have seen it, actually **on their side**?

Maybe. But what an opportunity they missed at the time.

Meanwhile, for his part, Pole-Carew bears the unions with which he engaged in such fierce combat absolutely no ill will and holds no grudges whatsoever.

"All in the past," he says with a shrug of his shoulders.

I put it to him that in today's regional newspaper industry (with drastic retrenchment, closures and mergers, lack of investment, savage cuts in journalistic resources, thousands of redundancies and bleak prospects for survival set against the corporate owners' continuing pursuit of huge profit margins) Christopher Pole-Carew might even have become **a union leader.**

Barrie Williams

He laughs: " Steady on! "

But he's deadly serious as he adds: " I **do** have to tell you that I find much sympathy with union complaints about today's managements in the regional newspaper industry. I despise their indefensible greed and I despair at what seems to be their lack of love and genuine feel for good local newspapers. It makes me very angry and I would certainly be doing things very differently."

Now, in 2010 there are plenty of people who will tell you how much Christopher Pole-Carew did for their careers during the industry's halcyon days.

People like Don Gray, who was the Nottingham Evening Post's successful and innovative Circulation Manager and went on to enjoy a long career in the national newspaper industry, as Circulation Director of Express Newspapers.

Don recalls with great affection: " In 1978, I was working as Circulation Manager of the Newcastle Journal and my boss was a famous regional newspaper man called Geoff Clark, who claimed to have taught Christopher Pole-Carew all he knew when he was a trainee at Celtic Press.

" Geoff told me they were looking for a Circulation Manager at the Nottingham Evening Post and it would be a good opportunity for me as it was a very progressive newspaper. I checked them out and discovered that they were blacked by the NUJ over a major dispute and had had a torrid time.

" I decided to make the call and was met by the then Circulation Director, Charles Scarff who took me to see PC, with whom the interview went like this :

' *We currently sell 135,000 copies and we **should** sell 150,000. Can you do it?*
'If anyone can - I can.'
'*Right. Let me show you around.*'

" We then almost ran through the building from department to department on a whistle stop tour before he dropped me off with Charles Scarff and said a swift goodbye.

" On the way back to my car Charles Scarff asked :' *What do you think?*'

" I said :' I couldn't work for him. He's a hire and fire merchant - and mad as well!' And off I went back to Newcastle.

" The next morning at 9 o'clock my phone rang. It was PC. He said: ' I gather you think that I'm a hire and fire merchant and mad as well.' To which all I could muster was ' Yes.'

"He said: ' Could you come back and see me? ' I did. And that proved to be the best day of my career.

" I loved Nottingham, as did my family. After just three months PC had **doubled** my salary and I spent the next nine years working for what was at that time the most progressive newspaper in the UK, with a brilliant team and a truly inspirational leader.

" PC had an unfailing knack of making you feel good; of convincing you that you and your opinion really mattered to him. For example, when our long serving editor Bill Snaith decided to retire the hunt was on for a replacement and PC decided that all applicants for his job should be interviewed by those on the team who would be working with the new editor. After a long process, I decided that the outstanding candidate was one Barrie Williams.

" PC called into my office and asked me what I thought. I told him: " I think Barrie is great." He smiled and said : ' I will see what I can do.' Of course, the fact that Barrie got the job was down to PC but it was typical of him to make me feel that I was an important part of the process.

" PC could also terrify people - particularly at his regular Monday morning management meetings - but you could never doubt the sheer quality of his leadership. He was immensely proud of the Nottingham Evening Post and all its staff. He was a man before his time. Few people will know that his battle with the unions to introduce essential new technology at the Nottingham Evening Post took place in the early 1970s - preceding Wapping and the national newspaper revolution by more than a decade. That's stunning."

Another member of that record setting Nottingham team, Stan Dziuba, the computer wizard who later followed Pole-Carew to Wapping, agrees: " I don't believe anybody who worked with PC did not respect him," says Stan. " There may have been some who hated him but even they would have respected him and the majority, like me, had the utmost admiration for him. I was 17 years old when I first met PC and 37 years old when I left him and in those 20 years he influenced my life enormously - mostly for the better.

" He mentored me and I tried to take several of his good points into my own working life. He taught me the crucial attributes of loyalty; of not letting people down; of being honourable; of treating people properly; of thinking outside the box - and of realising that you cannot be right *all* the time.

" He's also the most sociable person you can think of. He'd talk to me as an equal when I was just a teenager and that meant that I was never in awe of him. Even though his brain is so sharp and his wit is so quick he has the ability to make *anybody* feel comfortable in his presence. Mind you , I saw some who offended him made to feel very *uncomfortable* but on such occasions you never felt that they hadn't deserved it."

Like many others, Stan talks of Pole-Carew's extraordinary generosity : " My wife Maura had a miscarriage while we were at Nottingham and within a day of him hearing about it, he had booked us a luxury holiday in Malta."

In his book, *The Accidental Editor*, Richard Harris, who was News Editor and later Assistant Editor at the Nottingham Evening Post before moving on to edit the News and Star in Cumbria, recalls: " Barrie Williams had warned me that he would be a hard taskmaster as editor of the Evening Post and so he was. But Barrie was also quick to give credit for a job well done and I knew that there was a mutual respect and that he appreciated my efforts. Having been a News Editor himself, Barrie understood the pressure I was sometimes under and he encouraged me to deal with it in the most enlightened of manners: 'You need time to think - and you can't hope to do that on a busy news desk ,' he told me,' so I'll understand if you just bugger off somewhere for some peace and quiet.'

" The managing director, Christopher Pole-Carew (so much reviled by people who didn't know him) was even more understanding than Barrie. Pole-Carew demanded hard work and high standards from his middle managers and could be brutal with them if they failed him, but he balanced the equation by being unusually supportive when things got tough. Pole-Carew once told me :' I know what Barrie's like and how hard he makes you work and don't think I don't appreciate it. So if you get to feeling you need some extra time off, take it - a few days, a week, whatever you need and don't waste time feeling guilty about it.'

" I found that an extraordinarily encouraging thing for a managing director to say - and his saying it was enough. As far as I know, nobody ever took him up on the offer but you knew that his generosity in making it was absolutely sincere.

" The higher I got in the organisation, the more I was aware that it was Pole-Carew's example and management style that resulted in its employees feeling happy and secure in their work. There was never any doubt that Pole-Carew was the boss and that he would take whatever drastic action was needed to keep the firm successful, but equally there was no doubt that if you were loyal and worked hard he really appreciated your efforts and made sure you were rewarded accordingly. And despite the size of the workforce, he had an uncanny knack of knowing who did what in every department. He was phenomenal."

Production journalist Ian Manning tells how Pole-Carew once asked if he would stand in for him in delivering a presentation on direct inputting to an International Press Institute conference in Moderna, Italy because, at the last minute, something had cropped up and he could not go himself. Ian was, of course, delighted to accept and - entirely in jest - he told Pole-Carew :' It's a shame you didn't give me more notice, I could have taken the family!'

" The next morning there was an envelope on my desk with tickets for me, my wife and my son, with meals booked every day in the region's top restaurants."

Ian remembers Pole-Carew as a man who " always got the psychology right when dealing with the work force."

He recalls what happened when Pole-Carew was told by the supervisor of the Nottingham Evening Post Tele-ads department that most of her girls wanted to join a union:"The next morning, there was a note on her desk from Pole-Carew which confirmed what he had told her verbally…that he had no objection to them joining a union. She was pleased. But when she read on, he had listed the wages the girls in the department would be on in future. They were based on union rates. And they were substantially less than what they were earning!

" There was then a unanimous vote **not** to join a union! "

Ian describes Pole-Carew as " a clever man who seemed to know everything about everyone on the staff - even, some said, what they were thinking."

But it had been Ian Manning's own turn to worry about what Pole-Carew's might be thinking following one Christmas Eve when he had had to stay on long after all the other sub-editors had gone home because the advertisement department's estimate of the amount of advertising for the next issue of the Nottingham Evening Post had fallen short by three pages. At 7pm,with his plans for family festivities in tatters. Ian was half way through the daunting task of finding enough editorial material to fill the three pages then editing them, when a cheery voice from the corridor of the newsroom bellowed : " ***What are you doing here? Happy Christmas!***"

Without looking up from his work and not realising that he was addressing the formidable managing director, Ian grumpily shouted back to the cheery reveller : " ***Get ****** Stuffed !***"

When the voice then repeated the seasonal greeting, Ian looked up from his desk… and was absolutely horrified to discover just who he had invited to visit a taxidermist in such unequivocal terms!

" I feared the sack - but he never mentioned the incident. And needless to say, neither did I."

To Ian, Christopher Pole-Carew was " a *big* man; *big* in stature; *big* on loyalty; *big* on courage. "Mind you, he also had one *big* failing, says Ian."When he danced at the firm's dinner dances - at which he was always one of the boys and very generous at the bars - it was like watching your daftest uncle jiving at a wedding. His leggy gyrations made lanky footballer Peter Crouch's infamous victory jig look like a Michael Jackson masterpiece!"

However, the long frame and somewhat disobedient legs did not prove a problem the day Pole-Carew demonstrated great poise and dexterity in dealing with a tricky situation in Nottingham city centre one Saturday afternoon.

It all began when the Evening Post's News Editor Bill Ivory, a genial Welshman with a wicked sense of humour, told Pole-Carew he had just received a call on the news desk telling him that a swarm of bees had settled on the inside of an open window of an office at the Midland Bank in the city's bustling Market Square.

Quite reasonably, none of the staff at the bank would go near the bees and the manager could not lock up and go home, leaving the window on which the swarm had gathered open.

Typically, the mischievous Bill Ivory told the Managing Director : " Well, *you're* a beekeeper - why don't *you* go and deal with it for them. It would make a nice story for us!"

Pole-Carew takes up the story: " Without thinking, like a fool, I said 'OK' and off I went, initially just to inspect. I found that everything Bill had told me was true. It was a lovely big swarm. I had no bee kit with me - no gloves, no veil, no hat - but I did have an audience who assumed that I would immediately take away the bees and let their Saturday afternoon routine return to normal.

" There simply wasn't time to go home and get my kit so I had better manage without. I found a cardboard box about the size of a wine case. Ideal. I would shake the swarm into the box then turn it upside down with the open bottom propped up so that any stray bees could get in and join the others-they will always go to where the queen is. Bees always go up inside a box. I don't know why, but they do. So far so good - but there was a problem. You can't *shake* a solid bank window. However, I could use a lace curtain as protection over my head.

" Swarming bees don't sting, they say. True? I was about to find out!

" I would have to scrape the bees off the window with my bare hand, the other hand holding the box. So I fanned out my hand , fingers as wide as possible, so as to reduce the chance of squeezing and hurting a bee because if I did that it would sting me in self-defence and 10,000 others would promptly go to its aid and sting as well. Wow! Don't even *think* about it!

" So I scraped gently down and the bees fell into the box; I turned it over and the stray bees joined the others, which showed that the queen was inside. I didn't get *one* sting!

" My audience hadn't the faintest idea of the risk that had been involved and went happily home. Bill had his little story to put into the late edition and I came back down to earth - **having used up about a pint of adrenalin!** "

Bill Ivory, like all veteran newsmen, was as cynical and hard to impress as they come and as a former wartime bomber pilot himself, took some convincing of the bravery of others - but he dined off the tale for weeks in the Evening Post's staff canteen and in so doing, was unhesitant in his praise of the Managing Director's courage, claiming that Pole-Carew had done the daring deed ..." *just to get us a nice little story*! "

Former Nottingham Evening Post Marketing Director, David Teague worked alongside Pole-Carew for the best part of a decade and - contrary to the much peddled image of the managing director who was at best 'difficult' and at worst 'mad' - he cannot recall having so much as one serious argument with him.

Says David:" There were some disagreements on trivial matters but those were so inconsequential I can't even remember what they were. On every single major issue; on every major development in my department (and these were numerous because there was so much innovation at that time) he was one hundred per cent helpful, supportive and enthusiastic.

" That all makes Christopher sound perfect but, of course, nobody is and nor was he. He had one or two creepy people around him and he was too prepared, sometimes, to listen to the tittle-tattle they fed him.

" His great passion was the production department. I don't think he ever completely believed that all the people working in that area had shed the old trades union attitudes, though a good many of them had, and he was probably right. A few of them knew which side their bread was buttered, so they did much forelock tugging to his face while still giving him a two fingered salute behind his back. But his great strength was that he knew and understood every facet of their work and for their part, they knew that they could never pull the wool over his eyes in the way they almost certainly would have done with a lesser managing director. Every year saw another small but significant advance towards total computerisation of the production process - a massive undertaking completed at least ten years before any other company in our industry. That was an immense achievement, the sheer scale and national significance of which were huge. It needed a shoulder as powerful as his to keep the wheels rolling in the right direction and without him, it simply would not have happened.

" Christopher was fond of telling us that his family had been here before William the Conqueror. But there was *always* an element of tongue in cheek and self mockery when he told these stories. He was definitely not a snob, but he did believe firmly in the military hierarchy of officers, non-commissioned officers and other ranks. As a director of the company you were an officer, regardless of your personal background and as such you were entitled to privileges not made available to the rest.

" Christopher suffered fools most unwillingly. God help any waiter or door man who failed to snap to attention or provide the best of service. Once, on a visit to Marseilles, where he and I had been invited to give a joint presentation on two tier cover pricing for newspapers, he took Don Gray and I, together with his wife Gill, to a rather smart restaurant which specialised in the local bouillabaisse. Unfortunately, Christopher, who took great pride in his knowledge of good food and drink, decided we should round off the evening with a glass or two of ' the finest brandy in the world.' I say 'unfortunately' because the combined efforts of the waiter, then the head waiter and finally the restaurant proprietor failed either to understand or to produce the immortal brand. Christopher was outraged. He raced into the kitchen where, no doubt, he terrorised the chef and his staff before he emerged at last - triumphant with a bottle of brandy.

Trouble was, it was horrible! Absolutely foul! Undrinkable! Don and I nearly harmed ourselves trying to suppress our laughter.

" When Christopher left T. Bailey Forman Ltd so unexpectedly, it was a great shock to everybody from top to bottom of the company and to this day, people still ask me why he went. I don't know - but I **do** know that it was never the same again."

In June 1985, six months after Pole-Carew's sacking, a multi-page, in-depth article appeared in ADMAP magazine. Written by William Phillips and headed *The Nottingham Rebellion* it told the story of Pole-Carew's 20 years' of trail blazing in Nottingham and began:

" Something in the air of Nottingham seems to breed rebels: from Robin Hood, by way of Byron and D H Lawrence, to the miners who defied A J Cook and Arthur Scargill. Since 1973, the 1.1million who live in and around the East Midlands city have been served by a renegade among regional newspapers.

" The Nottingham Evening Post has put itself outside the establishment of the Newspaper Society, mortally antagonised every trade union and driven forward on all fronts.

" Technologically, commercially and editorially the Post stood among the most progressive newspapers in Europe when its managing director - an outsider in a family business and a maverick *par excellence* - was abruptly deposed in January.

" Christopher Pole-Carew is not a man about whom either friends or enemies have ever harboured doubts. To both, he has always figured as Captain Kinross, the hero of *In Which W e Serve ;* a commanding officer who believes a happy ship is an efficient ship, refusing resolutely to sacrifice either objective to mutineers or external assailants."

After running in detail through an exhaustive roll call of industry-leading innovations and successes achieved by the Nottingham Evening Post in the first half of the 1980's - in technological advances, in marketing, in advertising, in editorial and in profit building initiatives - William Phillips reported that Pole-Carew had managed to sustain substantial profits and ploughed them back, not only in holding down advertising rates and cover price but in promoting the newspaper.

" Meanwhile," wrote Phillips," the Newspaper Society's ' Project Breakthrough' for single-key stroking (*direct input by journalists, which was by then* **ten years old** *at the Nottingham Evening Post*) has failed to get past first base with the unions. This year, even the pacific pioneers of Portsmouth, Wolverhampton and Kent have encountered a hostility to technology which would only catch up with what the Nottingham Evening Post could do in 1976. Did these and more backward managements feel a touch of *Schadenfreude* when he was abruptly golden-handshaken out of T. Bailey Forman in January? "

Phillips' article concluded : " The hump in T. Bailey Forman's depreciation charge for technology investment was in the mid-1970s; the charge has been tailing off in real terms since then. The company's profitability may leave latecomers to computerisation way behind, if they have to invest and fight internal battles during the slump in advertisement volume and sales which is predicted.

" The great bloated monsters of Fleet Street have the same problem in spades, hearts and diamonds. Eddy Shah * has come forward as their saviour, if they will hear the word of new technology; Christopher Pole-Carew could fairly call himself Shah's John the Baptist. Like that surly saint, Pole-Carew fell out with a family and lost his head – but not before he had shown the way."

(* *In March, 1986 Eddy Shah, previously a local newspaper proprietor in Warrington, launched a full colour national tabloid daily,* **Today**, *using advanced printing technology and without traditional Fleet Street union agreements*)

For all his relative fame and notoriety, Pole-Carew rarely, if ever, stood on the dignity of his position within T. Bailey Forman but there was one among the other ranks who always had to know his place in the presence of the managing director...

Colin Bond was the company pilot. TBF had its own company jet and a helicopter and 'Captain Bond', as he was known affectionately to the top team, flew the directors around the world on business. Marketing Director David Teague and Editor Barrie Williams liked 'Captain Bond' a great deal and could not help holding him in very high esteem and treating him with great respect. After all, their lives were frequently in his hands - literally. Christopher Pole-Carew, however, felt the company pilot should be kept in his place. He didn't think he had enough to do and thought his job too cushy a number. " He's just a chauffer with wings," he would say - and he treated him as such.

Teague and Williams shared a theory that this situation wasn't helped by the fact that although there was very little in life which needed to be done that Christopher Pole-Carew could not only do himself but excel at, he could *not* fly the aircraft. The proprietor's son Nicholas Forman Hardy *could* - sometimes taking the controls on the directors' many flights abroad - and this, Teague and Williams reckoned, didn't help either. Whatever the reason, to Christopher Pole-Carew the affable, likeable, superbly accomplished and well qualified 'Captain Bond' was " just a bloody chauffer" and this attitude was epitomised, it was alleged, the day Colin Bond was very intently lifting the aircraft and its passengers up cautiously through the incredibly congested skies above Holland's Schipol Airport, said at the time to be among the most difficult in the world to navigate. The dials on the control panels were flashing like Blackpool illuminations; the conversation between pilot and air traffic controllers was worryingly animated and intense concentration was etched on Bond's face when Pole-Carew, hard-boiled egg from a packed lunch in his hand, leaned forward, tapped the pilot on the shoulder and asked him :" *Where's the salt* !"

To Derek Winters, now a jazz trumpeter and author, who worked in management for T. Bailey Forman from the late 1970's then followed Pole-Carew to Wapping, the man is ' an extraordinarily charismatic and remarkable leader.'

Says Derek: " I was introduced to Christopher Pole-Carew by David Teague, the Nottingham Evening Post's Advertisement Director. Chris was pioneering his new technology very successfully. I had spent some time in the Middle East and he felt that there might be some possible export interest. He arranged for me to visit Tehran but Iran was changing and that idea could not be pursued. However, as a result of my visit, I was offered a job and I joined the staff full time in Nottingham and was soon reporting directly to PC. Here, I was able to see his intuitive approach to management at close quarters and in various situations. He decided to set up a free weekly newspaper in Mansfield and called it The Recorder. It was a bold move and way ahead of its time. Printing in full colour, it was to be type set and printed at the company's stand alone print works at Huthwaite. The Recorder grew into The Recorder(s), several editions eventually being introduced, and I ended up as managing director of them, reporting to PC.

" His management style was unique but invariably innovative and sometimes startling. I was on a visit to Huthwaite with him one day and he was appalled at the rather untidy and dirty machine room. He hired a firm of industrial cleaners to valet the whole area over a weekend and told them that by Monday morning he wanted it to be so clean that he could literally eat his breakfast in there. And when they had finished on the Sunday night, it was. He then called a meeting of the machine room staff and told them the newly achieved sparkling cleanliness of their area presented a golden opportunity to save on waste. If this was achieved and the cleanliness maintained they would see results in their wage packets. And they did! How many other MDs would simply have given them all a bollocking and ordered them to clean it up themselves? His way was a hundred times more effective.

" On another occasion, a management colleague and I had given him wage increases for our staff for his approval and they had gone through - but he had made no mention of increases for ourselves. So, I went over to Nottingham one afternoon and asked his wonderful secretary, Nancy Harris, if she thought it was a good time for me to talk to PC about my salary. She was always a good indicator and she told me now was as good a time as any but he was preparing for a meeting so get straight to the point of my visit quickly. It was during his year as High Sheriff of Nottingham and on entering his office to deliver my well-rehearsed pay request I found him struggling into a pair of ladies tights!

" The tights were part of his 'medieval' High Sheriff's uniform which he was putting on with some difficulty. With no hint of self-consciousness, he had me make my case in full as he continued dressing. I got my rise.

" He had a way of getting us all to jump when necessary. A little dissatisfied with the way our company garage had serviced his car, he returned it and told the staff that there were *five* things wrong with this vehicle but he was only going to tell them about *two*. They had to find the other three faults themselves. That way, he would know that the car had been thoroughly checked and fully attended to. I'm sure he did not know the panic he caused but **the garage was closed to anybody else for a week!**

" He always knew how to get the best out of his managers - on one very hot summer's afternoon we were all having a rather tiresome time at a difficult meeting in his office when he suddenly jumped from his chair and announced that we would all go to his house and continue the meeting from the swimming pool. We did. And all the problems were solved. This sometimes overwhelming and authoritative ex- Naval officer, with his outstanding business prowess, was also fun to work with. Reporting to PC was often a roller coast ride. But it was *always* exciting.

" Later, I had the privilege of spending time with him at Wapping where Rupert Murdoch had so wisely hired him to direct some of the operations in the revolution which changed UK national newspapers and their practices for ever. We had all been recruited to work on what was then a top secret project. In the offices of News International it was easy to see the regard in which Rupert Murdoch held Christopher and his immense management skills came to the fore when dealing with so many people from varying disciplines, including Americans and Australians. He particularly had the respect of the senior secretaries. They loved this very tall, aristocratic man who on Monday mornings, coming up to London from a week-end at his home in the country, would bring them gifts of his home produced honey and organic eggs."

One of those secretaries was Pole-Carew's own, Linda Applegate whose ability and loyalty he was to appreciate so greatly.

Says Linda: " My first meeting with Christopher came about as a result of a telephone call I received from a recruitment agency in Bond Street, London. The agency had been charged with finding the right person for a new, top secret project."All I was told was that it was a twelve month contract of the utmost secrecy and would I please go to the Tower Hotel to meet the man who had requested the services of an experienced, discreet, confidential PA/Administrator to work with him and his project team.

" Needless to say, I was intrigued and duly arrived in the Reception of the hotel, not having been given the name of the man I was to meet, nor a description. I was told that *he* would find *me*. So, I sat waiting, slightly anxious as to whether I was doing the right thing, when a very tall figure bounded towards me, shook my hand and introduced himself to me…. Christopher Pole-Carew.

" At that first meeting, he explained that he could not be specific about the job but just wanted to meet to see if he thought we would get on. I was even more intrigued. We had a second meeting and I was duly offered *The Job*. I was still very much in the dark but being the type of person who enjoys a challenge and having been totally charmed by CPC I accepted.

" And the following twelve months were about to be the most exciting time in my working life, which I look back on with great fondness. Fortress Wapping, with its razor wire boundary fencing, was a shell of a building when we first arrived.

" We were a small team....Stan (*Dziuba*), Peter (*Crouch*), John (*Haydn*), Tim (*Brighton*) and me - led by Christopher - each with a specific role. There was no office furniture, no phones, no computers, not even a kettle to make coffee.

Everything was bought for cash in our own names; no accounts were set up and a cheque book did not exist. Every week or so, we indented for cash from Rupert Murdoch's Finance Director and one us would be despatched to collect it; or it would be delivered in a plain brown envelope.

" We had one small area at the end of the building and Christopher would literally run and then *slide* the rest of the way down the corridor towards us in a very John Cleese - like fashion!

" A telephone line was installed and every call was answered with just one word ,' *hello*' - no company name, no personal names, were ever given. The lengths to which everyone concerned with the project went in order to preserve secrecy and anonymity were truly amazing and probably could not be repeated today because of the advances made in communications.

" As the months went on, people were recruited to key positions at Fortress Wapping, all of whom had to pass one of CPC's stiff interviews. Among them was a security chief who advised me on the perils of driving through the anticipated picket lines in my Spitfire convertible…' *Just keep driving and don't make eye contact.*' However, when the time came for my first drive-through he was staggered at my response when someone in the crowd shouted '*Scum*' at me. He said he didn't think ladies used language like that!

" I told him that nobody was going to call me '*Scum*' without getting a strong response. Luckily, Christopher did not witness this incident.

" Meetings with Rupert Murdoch's executives usually took place off-site at one of the dockside flats which had been rented for the purpose and when the time came for several of his top-level managers to be seconded to Wapping from Australia, it was left to me to find their accommodation, arrange their cars and to generally take care of them during their time in the UK, earning me the title of '*Mrs Fixit at Wapping.*'

" Christopher's management style earned him the respect and admiration of everyone who was working at Wapping. From the lowest ranking member of staff upwards, he was universally liked and I cannot ever remember anyone ever questioning his authority with regard to the job in hand. His determination was absolute and the day that Wapping ' went live' was a bittersweet one for me… a huge sense of achievement that our historic and secret project had remained just that for the previous twelve months; fascination with the way such a massive operation had all come together, co-ordinated by Christopher and a degree of sadness that the hard work, excitement and fun had finally come to an end.

'Somebody Had To Do It'

" Personally, the thought of not working with Christopher and ' The Boys' anymore did not fill me with happiness but then, just a short while later, Christopher asked me to join him on the ill-fated venture with Robert Maxwell. A very different story!

" I feel privileged to have worked with Christopher, It was only for a year, I know, but with a man of such stature it is impossible for him not to have left his mark on all of us fortunate enough to have known him.

" And it is so typical of him, as a genuine 'people person' to have remained in touch with us ever since the days when Wapping hit the headlines."

Linda Applegate was by no means alone in recognising and admiring Pole-Carew's attributes as ' a genuine people person' and he offered an insight into his methods and principles when he addressed a national conference on his management techniques in 1990.

He told his audience:

" I have always been concerned with getting better results by trying to make my employees' time at work more interesting, more dignified, more worthwhile and more involved and these must, I believe, be essential ingredients in any improvement in the working place, regardless of the rate of change of ideas or equipment.

" In fact, I would go further: If the order of the day is constant change, then the trust and co-operation of all levels within a company towards one another simply must be of the highest.

" Let me first go through the training **I** received in management - or in some cases, *lack* of training - because this was where my views and experiences were gained…

" I started my managerial career when, at the age of 13, I joined the Royal Navy as an officer cadet. You can imagine my feelings at the time: there was a war going on and actually to be a genuine officer was too wonderful for words. As a matter of interest, history records that the Germans were, in actual fact, beaten without my direct assistance - a disappointment for me, if for no one else - but my experience convinced me that the Armed Services are the only organisations in this country that take management training really seriously. This is hardly surprising when you think that they have literally thousands of years more experience than almost any other walk of life.

" Before anyone holds up their hands in horror at this statement, please understand that I am not talking about the actual training the Services give; nor for one single moment am I advocating its application to civilian organisations. I am simply referring to their attitude towards ensuring that they have genuine leaders, properly trained in the specific way that they require, in the arts and skills of managing people.

" Small companies maybe can't, in all honesty, afford to become obsessive about managerial training, even though there is much they can do simply in the way they run their affairs. Large companies, in my experience, merely pay lip service to the idea of management training with a week's course here or there and maybe a long course (for example I did one of eighteen months in Thomson Newspapers) but with no proper **managing** content at all; Lots on how to manage the accounts, how to manage machines; how to manage this, that and the other but nothing of real value on how to manage **people**.

" Real management training is all about teaching managers to encourage people to do well what they may not actually want to do at all but to do it because they trust the guy who wants them to do it.(I think that makes sense. If it does, I think it's rather good. If it doesn't, forget it!)

" We started as cadets at Dartmouth Naval College by doing drill before breakfast in the pitch dark of a January morning. When you can't see where you are going you quickly learn to trust the person giving the orders. You haven't got any choice. But we learned many other interesting things - and not only how to tie fancy knots or how to find out where you are by peering at Saturn or Betelgeuse through a sextant.

" For example, I remember at the age of 16 being told that Naval Officers never, ever arrive on parade on time. To the ignorant, the assumption would be that they were too superior to conform to the customs of lesser mortals. The real reason was much more subtle: if a sailor arrived late and the officer was not there, he merely got cursed and told to get fell in by his Petty Officer. If the officer was there before him, then the Petty Officer would be obliged to report him for being late and then, oh dear, trouble and anguish and all so unnecessary. I think that's a good example of sound, considerate managerial thinking.

" Let's touch for a minute on the generally taboo subject of money.In the Army or Navy, you can find out exactly what anyone earns by looking up their seniority then working it out. It is so easy that no-one ever does it. This is why there is no bitchiness or envy about pay within the Services... however much they may gripe about better conditions in civilian life.

" In my experience, business and industry seem obsessed by what other people earn - to the point where the old adage *'If you do more for what you are paid to do you will find yourself being paid more for what you do.'* is really turned upside down. Maybe the trouble is that in the average firm, the likelihood of virtue being rewarded should not be counted on too much.

" To me, the sensible way to deal with this particular managerial problem is not to keep salaries secret. With an open salary policy, people know where they stand - and so does everyone else. If someone reckons he is being unfairly treated, whether or not compared to someone else, he need only see his senior manager to learn the truth - or possibly get a wrong righted.

" More to the point, the manager is obliged to justify his actions to a large extent publicly, which makes for much better managing - especially in the case of cowards or those inclined to favourites.

" Here's a rather way-out example from Army life that might, perhaps, illustrate another managerial point…If you are racing across open countryside in the Falklands and some misguided bunch of Argentines start shooting at you, would you like your manager to use his initiative or would you rather he waited for someone senior to tell him what to do whilst you and your friends get killed? The answer is obvious, isn't it - and it hasn't got much to do with regimentation. But please keep that little word initiative in mind…

" Business is a battlefield of a sort, but how regimented are junior managers and how often are they allowed to use their initiative to further the company's interests? In my experience, almost never. If they do and they are right, don't put any money on their getting the credit. If they do and they are wrong, God help them - because those above them most certainly won't.

" Let's move on and take a brief look at my 18 months as a senior management trainee in Unilever. It won't take long to summarise the management training I received because it was not one single day, or even part of one. But I did check that 20,000 files were in correct numerical order. It took days of mindless drudgery.

" The head filing clerk in the Purchasing Department where I spent my time was a mean and desiccated spinster of uncertain years. She disliked management trainees intensely but every now and again, the system was kind to her and let her have one to lighten her days. I bet you've met them!

" What a waste to use a potential manager as cheap clerical labour. Was that *really* the best that that great international company could manage in the way of management training? I'm afraid it was.

" My main career has been in newspapers and in that jungle (and believe me, it *really* is !) there are many horrific stories to be told of the nightmares to be experienced at all levels of management.

" Question : Is it sensible for a person on the shop floor to be able to earn comfortably more than his immediate boss?

" The answer must surely be 'no' yet it happens so often. The effect is to imply that the manager is worth less, especially as he gets no reward or even credit for the many gallons of midnight oil he burns on reports, etc on the company's behalf. How does one stop this? Well, basically by paying managers better and at the same time preventing the excessive proliferation of overtime which is more often than not caused by the working habits of those who gain by it.

" Next Question: How on earth can a junior manager keep his self respect and exercise proper authority if it is always possible (in fact very common) for people on the shop floor (generally via the union) to go upstairs to get his instructions reversed, quite often solely for the pleasure of undermining and humiliating him?

" Hands up all of you who have **not** seen this happen time and time again. Yet there is a simple solution: as a responsible senior manager, just don't let it happen. It's true that simple solutions can often be very hard, but weren't we taught that the straight and narrow is a better road to salvation than the slippery slope?

" What of the man or woman who believes that a strike is wrong and feels bound to support the management of the company that employs him or her?

" When the dust has settled, guess what happens to that loyal employee. During the strike, praised and feted; after it is all over, at best ostracised and probably noted by the management as a stirrer who ought to be watched and at worst, in a closed shop industry, out of work; sacrificed with virtually no hope of getting a job of the same sort.

" Some of you may be thinking that I keep on about industry, whereas in business or commerce it's different. But it's not. The unions might not be in there organising things but victimisation and in-fighting exist just as much as in a factory environment.

" Maybe I should spell out clearly what I am talking about: it's called **loyalty.**

Not the normal, every day form that we all know so well which simply expects you to be loyal to the firm that pays you. In my case, it's loyalty **from the management downwards** that I believe in absolutely. It is the natural right of any employee - especially when it is taken for granted that the same employee gives loyalty upwards.

" It is, I believe, a vital ingredient in the mix which makes up any worthwhile management philosophy yet , sadly, I believe it to be a rare if not endangered species in this country.

" I have witnessed the President of the Guild of British Newspaper Editors pleading to the Council of the Newspaper Society for its members, the owners of the provincial press, to give job protection to editors - **editors, note, not just ordinary journalists** - when they support management in industrial disputes and being turned down because well really, how can they expect such special treatment?

" But to me it is the absolute right of any loyal employee, however junior or senior, because it is the other side of this coin called loyalty.

" It will, I am sure, come as no surprise to you to learn that I have gathered much criticism and dislike for holding this view.

" There are a lot of overlaps in this art or science of management and before you have finished talking about loyalty you find that the subject has become self respect.

"**All** people are unique (I know the grammar isn't right there - but I hope you know what I mean). The point is that they must be made to feel that they are known and respected for their uniqueness and the more junior their position the more important this is. We all have names so that our uniqueness can be identified.

" To the person who has little or nothing, his self respect is vital. That is why the humbler the employee, the greater the courtesy and consideration top management should extend to him. The creeps at the top of the pile can take solace in their healthy bank balances when they are humiliated, but downstairs this doesn't apply.

" I raged at managers who reported that 'one of the clerks in the general office has gone sick.' Or ' one of our van drivers has given in his notice.' The important thing is **who** has gone sick or given in his notice. When you know that you are three quarters of the way to knowing **why** and maybe being able to do something about it.

" Management is all about communication. If employees give all those hours, days, weeks, months and years to a company doesn't it seem reasonable that they should be allowed to have some inkling of what on earth is going on in the organisation? After all, you have staked the well-being and happiness of your entire family on that company, so why should you not be told what's going on, or off?

" This, incidentally, is one of the biggest and most consistently voiced gripes that unions have against managements and I think the unions are absolutely right. Communicating effectively is a vital, essential skill of good management yet so many managers can't even communicate properly with their secretaries, let alone stand up and address all comers.

" So what makes a good manager ? An interesting way of finding out if someone has the natural basics of management in him, or her, is to take them across to the pub which members of the staff use and introduce them around. You can find out a lot about a person in half an hour in a pub, if you put your mind to it.

" A manager must be gregarious to be a good one; you must like people as people and find that what they say and do; hope for and fear is really and genuinely interesting to you because if you don't, you will always be out of touch and will have only one pillar of management to rely on …the fact that 'them upstairs' put you in charge.

" Generally speaking, accountants are not gregarious, which is why they don't often seem to make good managers and their departments are often depressing and underpaid. You might say they prefer numbers to figures! If you don't care for your people you are hardly likely to fight for them.

" It was my custom in Nottingham to give a talk once a year to anybody who cared to attend on the state of the company; how we were doing and where we were going. Generally, about three hundred out of three thousand would turn up which - allowing for shifts, distant branch offices, holidays, etc - was pretty good.

" Two of these occasions stick in my mind : the first when we weren't doing so well and I made the point that any wage increases would have to be nil or very low and that the same would have to apply, generally, with spending around the company. I gave, as an example, that if a manager hadn't got a carpet in his office it wasn't that he wasn't entitled to one, it was simply that he wasn't going to get it this year, so don't bother getting steamed up about it.

" Interestingly, this impressed a lot of the people because I had picked out bosses and carpets as a symbol of status as an example. It seemed they could accept a needs must scenario and therefore doing without - but not with injustice, however minor.

" On another occasion, I commented about the firing (or early retirement as we call it now) of a director. Frankly, he was hopeless and really had to go and I said so to the assembled hordes. I told them that on the shop floor and in the offices they weren't as well paid as managers and were expected to do as they were told and to do it well in exchange for pleasant and secure jobs. Managers, on the other hand, got high wages and fancy cars and in return were required to see that the people for whom they were responsible were properly paid and that their jobs were pleasant and genuinely secure. If they didn't achieve this, they had to go - and that included directors.

" This had a surprisingly good effect within the company, helping to close the gap between managers and staff and generating better relations with a bit more respect for their respective roles. All for a little communication. It also illustrated that you should never assume that what is blindingly obvious to you as the managing director is necessarily anywhere nearly so clear to your employees

" Moving to another issue, don't you think it would be a wonderful thing if there was *genuine* equality of opportunity based on merit? How many of you, I wonder, would have male secretaries.

" Even so, there is much more equality of opportunity today than there was twenty years ago. Thanks, I suppose, to having worked in newspapers (where, in the editorial departments at least, there has long been equality of pay and therefore a bias towards equality of opportunity) I have never had hang-ups on this subject.

" At the Nottingham Evening Post in the late 1960s we needed a new General Office Manager. There was no-one suitable within the firm, so we advertised. There were two serious contenders - one male, one female. To me, there was no contest: the woman was streets ahead of the man. So, as managing director, I said that she should have the job. No problem. Until the Chairman's secretary got to hear about it. Then all hell let loose. The Chairman sent for me and told me that his secretary was the senior female employee in the firm and that she could not accept a woman being employed in a position that could be construed as higher than hers. So I couldn't have her. I saw her and told her exactly why she hadn't got the job because it didn't seem fair to pretend that we had got someone better when she was so obviously outstanding. She was even more angry than I was and we finished up with a fat slob who was kicked out after a few months for persistently wandering hands, if you know what I mean.

" So, what - in this attempt to describe to you my philosophies of management - have we dealt with so far. Let's re-cap…

* The need for training and the sensible application of managerial power.
* The essential need for loyalty *downwards* as well as upwards.
* The vital need to communicate.
* The importance of a sane and fair wages structure.
* That junior managers must be supported to the hilt by those above them.
* That people are individually unique, so treat them as such.
* The distinction between modest pay but high security and high rewards but much less security.
* And the value of genuine sexual equality.

Not bad, eh?

" Now please will you do me the credit of accepting that everything I have just preached, I did in fact practice?

" If you do, then you will understand how it was that at the Nottingham Evening Post, we led by many years the introduction of new technology into our industry as well as pioneering any number of marketing and editorial innovations.

" You see, if people know where they stand; if they respect their managers; if they know what is happening and why (or, put another way, if they are treated as intelligent human beings) ; if they know that there is good security of their job (while accepting that nothing can be **totally** secure in this world, save the knowledge that one day, we shall leave it!) you will find that far from resisting essential change and progress, new ideas and new technology, they will actually welcome and encourage them.

" It is a fact that at the Nottingham Evening Post, in all departments, there was a constant push and pressure on the management from the bottom up for technological advancement. There was no holding us.

" If we are to conquer this world of constant change in which we live, there is a crucial need for proper human motivation and the creation of **genuine** team spirit - not just the lazy lip service to those qualities that you see in so many British companies.

" I asked you early on in this lecture to remember a small but hugely significant word, namely **initiative**. To that, I would like you to add another word : **enjoyment** " If we are to manage well, it should go without saying that people should like what they do and be fulfilled by their work so that they do not adopt the appalling attitude of a trade union official who once told me at a meeting:' Let's face it, we only come here to earn enough money to enjoy our free time.' How dreadful to consciously write off nearly 20 per cent of one's life to drudgery.

" I have always tried to follow the policy that any manager who cannot contact his boss when he needs advice or a decision should make the decision himself, as if he *were* the boss, in order to achieve the best that circumstances offer. To me, the worst managerial crime is the one that can be summarised as : ' Well, sir, I know what we should have done but I couldn't find you, so I thought it best to do nothing.' If a manager uses his initiative and gets it wrong then, to me, that is a fair managerial risk; nobody can get things right *all* the time. But the other type? Well, how can they be right except by default, because they have not influenced anything

" This is how bright managers, who are going places, are created: by giving them the opportunity to back their own judgement - and that is where the *enjoyment* comes in.

" Let them then encourage the same attitude down the line and you have sown the seeds of real enjoyment and a sense of purpose throughout your organisation."

Today's proponents of best management practice will find much that is familiar in that lecture by Christopher Pole-Carew. But consider that not only did he deliver it nearly **20 years ago** but was actually **doing** all that he preached in it **40 years ago** and you realise how enlightened and progressive he was in business.

The trouble was that he was **so** enlightened and progressive that he frightened the life out of the newspaper business establishment and the trade unions alike, thus becoming an enemy of both - a bizarre situation which contrived to drive him, ridiculously prematurely, out of the regional newspaper industry which should, instead, have been embracing him with all the enthusiasm and gratitude it could muster.

Pole-Carew's equally controversial Nottingham contemporary Brian Clough would have had a phrase to sum up the nonsense and waste of it: " There's nowt so queer as folk! "

But then, Christopher Pole-Carew is, himself, a man of considerable contradictions. For example, how does a businessman who lays such store by treating people well and has such a demonstrably fine record of practising what he preaches in that regard, reconcile those humane qualities with his highly instrumental role in condemning thousands of Fleet Street workers and their families to the miseries of unemployment?

This was an element of the Wapping dispute described by union official Barry Fitzpatrick (in The Observer's 20th anniversary article) thus:

" Week in, week out I attended the demonstrations and as the weeks turned to months I watched the lives of people I'd known and worked with for years unravel. Twenty years may have passed but those sacked overnight - secretaries, researchers and cashiers as well as printers - still bear the scars of Wapping today."

Christopher Pole-Carew's answer?

"'The background was the corruption of the unions. Any print worker who became a member, with voting rights, was tacitly condoning the corruption, whether or not he took advantage of it himself. In addition, the holding of such a job was very valuable and was passed down through generations, so no way did your innocent, hard working man apply diffidently for a job which was vacant, get it, then find himself kicked out.

" But that is the background, not the answer, which is that, for me, it starts with Drake's Prayer * , which is a very real factor in the way I have run my life: the commitment to do the job I had agreed with Rupert Murdoch to do 'until it be thoroughly finished.' I had said I would do it. I had committed myself to do it. So I would do it. Nothing left to discuss. As for ' the innocents within the union ranks' they did not enter my thinking at all but if they had; if someone had made a cogent case for them and their suffering, I would have been genuinely upset but, then, they started off as free agents and joined their unions with their eyes wide open. If you want a nice warm place in such a room you take the risk of being within range of sparks from the fire."

(* *When his ship 'Elizabeth Bonaverture was lying at anchor at Cape Sakar on May 17th, 1587 Sir Francis Drake wrote a letter - the words of part of which were adapted by the Dean of York in 1941 to produce Drake's Prayer: ' O Lord God when thou givest to Thy servants to endeavour any great matter, grant us also to know that it is not the beginning, but the continuing of the same unto the end, until it be thoroughly finished, which yieldeth the true glory; through His for the finishing of Thy work laid down His life, our Redeemer, Jesus Christ')*

Just as there are many, like Barry Fitzpatrick, who will never forgive Pole-Carew for his part in the Wapping dispute, the wounds of the

Nottingham Evening Post disputes back in the 70s are still sore for a lot of people.

His sacking of 28 journalists for obeying their union's strike call and his subsequent steadfast refusal to re-employ them in line with the nationally agreed settlement of the pay dispute became a huge issue which saw him elevated to national notoriety. In these days of infinitely less powerful unions it is perhaps difficult to appreciate the enormity of sacking workers for going on strike in the union dominated 1970's.

You simply did not do that !

To the Labour and trades union movement, then so dominant in British industry, Pole-Carew had abused the most fundamental and inalienable workers' right…to withdraw your labour. It struck at the very foundations of trades union belief. It was "what the Tolpuddle Martyrs made their sacrifice for."

The resultant mass picketing of the Nottingham Evening Post, which lasted for months, saw thousands of protesters from the entire trade union movement and scores of Labour Party politicians, activists and supporters laying siege to the newspaper's Forman Street headquarters amid frequent outbreaks of violence, with dozens of arrests - the National Union Of Journalists' newspaper, The Journalist, complained bitterly about what they claimed was police brutality towards pickets.

The claim was supported on one occasion by a dramatic picture showing punches smashing into a demonstrator's face as police officers waded into the picket lines.

And there was heavy innuendo that the police conduct was being influenced by Pole-Carew's position as High Sheriff.

An article in one issue of the paper in June, 1979 was headlined **Blood Flows As Sheriff's Posse Attacks** and gave the NUJ's version of events the day Pole-Carew and others had physically ejected protesters who managed to get inside the Forman Street offices to stage a sit-in. It read:

" Robin Hood may have been buried where his arrow fell many a long year ago. But his traditional arch enemy, the Sheriff, is still around to plague the good folk of Nottingham.

" These days, the High Sheriff of Nottinghamshire is Christopher Pole-Carew, the notorious managing director of the Nottingham Evening Post, who sacked 28 journalists during the Newspaper Society strike.

" His first public act last month was to gather together a 'Sheriff's posse' of bully boys to eject by force pickets who were peacefully occupying the Post's editorial floor in protest against the sackings. The 39 demonstrators had entered the building to seek a meeting with Pole-Carew, who had consistently refused to come to the negotiating table since the provincial strike ended.

"And the police, not normally known for their impartiality when it comes to Evening Post pickets, were forced to admit they could not shift them as no offence was being committed. That, however, did not deter Pole-Carew. Summoned from his country home, he immediately set about rounding up his own private army of company heavies to throw the 'trespassers' off his premises. Several men who had no connection with the Post were pressed into service from the Blue Bell, the Forman Street pub which has lost a potential fortune by banning pickets and which, as a result, has become a haven for management sycophants.

" What happened next is the subject of an official NUJ complaint which is in the hands of union lawyers and which may eventually lead to charges of assault and incitement to assault being laid.

" Pole-Carew, after dismissing the police witnesses and giving a final warning to the pickets, gave the signal for his men to move in. The pickets, who had agreed between them not to resist, found themselves under an attack of totally unwarranted force. Several found themselves sprawling on the floor.

" Mike Bower, the Northern regional organiser, was kicked on the nose and blood streamed down his face. NEC member Aiden White had to sit astride Bower's prostrate form to protect him from more violence. One woman was thrown down the concrete steps. A dazed and bloodied Mike Bower lay slumped by a coffee machine when Pole-Carew, who had been playing an active role, grabbed him by the lapels and threw him towards the stairs.

" Since the occupation, which lasted just over an hour, the firm has employed guard dogs and handlers to patrol the works entrances and is apparently installing thousands of pounds worth of sophisticated security measures.

" For many of those who took par , the occupation provided the first distasteful sight of Pole-Carew in action and gave them a renewed determination to carry on the Nottingham struggle until he is forced to offer reinstatement to the sacked staff."

Later, in May, 1981, The Journalist, under the headline *Are Rich And Powerful Above The Law* , reported:

" A forceful challenge to MPs of all parties has been issued by General Secretary Ken Ashton seeking their support for NUJ demands for an inquiry into the behaviour of Nottingham Evening Post boss Christopher Pole-Carew and the local police.

" Ashton has sent a detailed report to each MP of the developments of the union's dispute with Pole-Carew after the sacking of 28 members who took part in the 1978/79 provincial journalists' strike. He lists Pole-Carew's tactics against the NUJ and other unions and the police's apparent un-willingness to act against the former High Sheriff at any stage.

"Ashton concludes pointedly: ' There is no doubt whatsoever in my mind that if any of these acts or threats had been made by trade unionists there would have been immediate and subsequent action by the police against the perpetrators.'

" He asks the MPs : 'Are rich and powerful members of the Establishment above the law? '

" And he expresses his belief that it should be a matter of concern for all ' that Nottingham police and Director of Public Prosecutions appear to take so little action when a serious assault is made on non-violent demonstrators and continue their inactivity when the same person appears to urge others to commit similar and even more serious criminal acts.'

" The acts and threats Ashton refers to are the attack by Pole-Carew and a group of " heavies" on NUJ pickets who staged a peaceful sit-in at the Post offices in April, 1979, in which Northern Organiser Mike Bower was booted in the face and had to have hospital treatment; the failure of the police to follow up diligently Bower's official complaint; the illegal dirty tricks of Pole-Carew's 'pep talk' to executives of Portsmouth and Sunderland Newspapers; the failure of the DPP to take any action on those matters.

"An inspector who was assigned to investigate Bower's complaint has admitted that he submitted his report to the DPP without even interviewing Bower about the attack on him. Ashton points out to the MPs that the union has since decided to make an official complaint against members of the Nottinghamshire Constabulary. But, he says, in view of the repeated failure of the official machinery to act, there seems little prospect of success for this complaint."

Mike Bower became something of a folk hero to the protesters because of the fearless determination with which he went about his picket duties, including lying down in front of huge newsprint lorries.

Today, he is a leading Labour politician in Sheffield and is able to look back on those days with good humour, recalling:

" My outstanding memory among all the passion and turmoil of the dispute was being with the pickets one day and not much was going on when, suddenly, someone pointed out Pole-Carew walking down the street away from the offices. So, I went after him and repeatedly asked him for efforts, meetings, communication - anything to end the dispute amicably. He didn't respond to any of this apart from by lengthening his already huge strides, thus requiring me to be jogging to keep up with him. Eventually, he stopped, turned to face me as I stood there panting and bawled ' *Why don't you shove orf, you scruffy little man* ' then resumed his giant striding - leaving me speechless for one of the few times in my life!"

In an earlier issue of The Journalist a picture was published of Pole-Carew resplendent in the tight black stockings; gleaming patent leather, silver- buckled shoes; knee-length coat and assorted frills and finery of his ancient High Sheriff's uniform, alongside a caption story which read:

" The overgrown Lord Foantleroy figure in our picture is the High Sheriff of Nottinghamshire, Christopher Pole-Carew, the man who has embarked on a crusade against the print unions and the NUJ in particular.

" The picture was taken when he attended the annual judges' service at Southwell Minster.

" Our sacked members were there, mounting a silent vigil of protest against Pole-Carew's trade union attitude , which is as antiquated as the gear he was wearing.

" The dismissed staff stood lining a path inside the church grounds as Pole-Carew walked with other main guests from Trebeck Hall to the Minster. In previous years, this procession has taken a longer route along the main road through Southwell into the church, but the arrangements were changed at the last minute this year.

" The congregation, invited specially by the High Sheriff, included civic heads, magistrates and several Evening Post staff.

" Just before the service began Kevin Hill, leader of the journalists, had a three minute chat with the firm's chairman Tom Forman Hardy, in a nearby car park: ' I asked if there was any possibility of having talks, whether formally or informally, to try to seek a way round the dispute which is now in its sixth month. The chairman said it was too soon to say and referred to 'various outstanding things' such as industrial tribunals, which still have to be dealt with,' said Kevin."

The Journalist's passionate coverage of the dispute and its incessant personal vilification of Pole-Carew was either darned good campaigning journalism or disgraceful neglect of proper journalistic balance, depending upon which side of the debate you stood.

But it might just have been argued that its editor, Ron Knowles had forsaken some of the traditional discipline of objectivity, inherent in the craft of good editorship, when he was found guilty of obstruction and using threatening behaviour on the Evening Post picket line!

It was Ron Knowles who, in October 1980, had obtained the exclusive story of Pole-Carew's infamous indiscretions while addressing executives of Portsmouth and Sunderland Newspapers and the relish with which the editor produced his special front page ***Portrait Of An Extremist*** left no-one in any doubt how he felt about the man.

Knowles wrote:

" Directors and management of a provincial newspaper group have been taking lessons in lawless union-bashing from Nottingham Evening Post boss Christopher Pole-Carew. Documents which have come into me possession show Pole-Carew as an anti-union extremist and his newspaper proprietor chum, Sir Richard Storey as his eager student of management terror tactics.

" Storey, who inherited the Portsmouth and Sunderland Newspapers group from his Tory father, Sam, set up a special meeting of his managers to hear Pole-Carew detail his industrial warfare tactics.

" In his talk, given in London a few days after the settlement of the seven week strike of NUJ members in Newspaper Society offices, Pole-Carew...

* Advocates petrol bomb threats against union officials.

* Explains how he deliberately sets out to ' humiliate ' and 'discredit' union officials.

* Recommends a ' reign of terror' against union members after a strike.

* Considers, then discounts, the possibility of organising advertisers and members of the public to ' bully' strikers.

* Urges that strikes should be deliberately prolonged for three months.

* Explains how he bribes scabs to work during strikes.

* Suggests intimidatory driving of heavy lorries to deter trade unionists from tracing newsprint sources.

* Urges vetting of all new staff.

* Reveals that company medical checks are used by the doctor to snoop on newcomers and report if they are ' security risks'.

* Explains how new staff are 'needled' to test if they are ' security risks.'

* Gloats about how he ' forced' the police to become involved in controlling pickets.

* Outlines illegal dirty tricks he would use if he were a union official.

* Reveals that the salary of his editor, William Snaith, was then £19,500."

Interesting that Ron Knowles regarded that last bullet point as a crime, along with all the rest!

After Knowles had gleefully splashed his big exclusive story, readers vented their anger in The Journalist's Letters Pages, a typical reaction being the following, from Hugh Samson, a Life Member of the NUJ:

" Your report of the activities of Pole-Carew sickened me. Clearly, the man should be subjected to that shock treatment that Whitelaw (*Willie Whitelaw, Home Secretary in the newly elected Thatcher Government*) recommends for young offenders , shorn of his cuffs and furbelows and subjected to some rigorous discipline. What is sauce for the goose could well be sauce for this objectionable gander. Reading about people like Pole-Carew points up how necessary it is to have a union that is strong and can fight to protect the interests of its members."

However, it was much to editor Ron's credit that , in the same issue of his paper and on the same Letters Page, he published a letter headlined **Pole- Carew Extremism: I Blame Knowles**, from Peter Black, a London freelance journalist, who wrote:

" Your lead story, **Portrait Of An Extremist**, made sad reading. You have not the moral or intellectual capacity to understand that Knowlesism produces Pole-Carewism, just as fire and wind increase each other. Anyone who reads The Journalist knows that its editorial stance (not to mention the slant of its news) is one of aggressive and fatuous confrontation with managements,whom it sees in the crude terms of a Pravda cartoon, all top hats and gold watches.

" The current crisis at The Times marks the latest triumph of this thinking and though I am writing well in advance of your next issue I do not doubt that somewhere in it you will be accusing Lord Thomson of broken faith, betrayal of promises and so on.

" Add to these efforts the constant misuse of power by the dishonoured London print workers of the NGA , who sign eleventh-hour agreements with management and break them at their earliest convenience, and you have an improvable blueprint for producing employers like Christopher Pole-Carew, who have come to see newspaper unions as enemies who must be beaten down , and are much better equipped to win the war than their opponents.

" It's some comfort to know that you and he are in a sense mirror images of one another. He does not represent management attitudes any more than you and your sort represent the bulk of journalists."

In March, 2009, all but four of the 28 Nottingham strikers sacked by Pole-Carew for going on strike in 1978/79 met for a reunion to commemorate the 30th anniversary of their ordeal.

Barrie Williams

Reunion of the Nottingham 28 - Picture: Rebecca McKevitt

The reunion was organised by striker Terry Wootton, who went on to become one of Britain's most highly respected tutors of young journalists. As Head of Journalism Studies at Sheffield University for many years, he lectured to hundreds of aspiring youngsters and nurtured many of today's top journalists in newspapers and television.

Said Terry: " It was fantastic for us to be back together again after 30 years. So emotional. A real night to remember.

" In sacking the 28, Christopher Pole-Carew lost some very talented, gritty newsmen and women. But in a strange way, it did us all a favour - because everyone became stronger and we all did better things with our lives. It was very rewarding to discover how everyone had gone on to tip-top jobs in the industry."

Another of the 28, Peter Anderson says he was proud to be one of the journalists pioneering ground breaking new technology with Pole-Carew in Nottingham before the union's strike call left him and the others with that conflict of loyalties.

Says Peter : " When people discuss new technology in journalism, they always say it was Eddy Shah and his regional group of newspapers which introduced it, before Shah's *Today* newspaper took it to the national stage. They are wrong. It was Christopher Pole-Carew and the Nottingham Evening Post journalists who were the real pioneers.

" I arrived at the Evening Post a complete innocent. I wasn't politically involved and I wasn't involved in the union. My friends at the Lincolnshire Echo, where I worked previously, had warned me that the Evening Post was ' an anti-union paper' but the wages were good and I had a young wife and child.

" The wages were good because the print unions were out of the picture. Christopher Pole-Carew already had the unions beaten. Direct input by journalists wasn't the writing on the wall for the print unions - it was the wall collapsing on top of them and burying them!

" We journalists were there from freedom of will to benefit from the new terms and conditions and the new profitability brought to the Nottingham Evening Post and because it was a very good newspaper to work for. Direct input was the bee's knees.

" Having already beaten the unions and got the journalists on side, Christopher Pole -Carew was wrong to let all that journalistic goodwill go down the plughole by treating his journalists as the same common enemy as the printers. He didn't need the printers but he **did** need us journalists.

" I think that after despatching the printers he'd got the taste for the hunt and ran full tilt after the smell of blood, recklessly, foolishly throwing away all his gains and taking it one chase too far.

" It wasn't a case of not knowing when he was beaten. It was a case of not knowing he had already won."

Terry Bowles was an ambitious young sports reporter on the Nottingham Evening Post when his union called him out on strike. He now runs Bowles Associates, a successful Sports and Communications Agency, which grew from a partnership he formed with another striker, John Lawson, in 1979.

Says Terry: " I was one of those who 'stayed in' initially but we were under great pressure to join the strike. Virtually every night, the NUJ would send top officials to Nottingham for a chapel (*branch*) meeting and they made it very clear that if we didn't agree to go out, they would take away our union cards and do everything in their power to prevent us from getting another job. In those days, if you didn't have a union card you couldn't get a self-respecting job within the newspaper industry. So, basically, by refusing to join the strike, we were pretty much committing ourselves to the Nottingham Evening Post for life.

" Pole-Carew and his henchmen had made it plain that if we **did** go out, we would be sacked. The Union claimed that would never happen. They said it had never been known in the industrial history of this country for people to be sacked for joining an official strike and if we **were** sacked, the other 30,000 journalists who were out on the streets across the country would refuse to go back to work after the strike ended until we were re-instated. But, when the strike did end, they all went back to work - and left **us** out on the streets.

" The bottom line is that Pole-Carew was true to his word, but you couldn't say the same about National Union Of Journalists' officials. I do believe that they honestly thought we wouldn't be sacked but when it came to the crunch, they didn't have the power to change anything.

" Dennis McShane (*later to become a New Labour Government Minister*) was President of the NUJ at that time and he was so convinced that he gave me a letter saying that if we were sacked, I would be guaranteed nett wages for life!

" I was in the process of moving house and when the Building Society wrote to the Evening Post asking for confirmation of my wages, they wrote back saying: ' We do not employ this person.' That's how I came by Dennis McShane's letter - to try and persuade another Building Society to give me a mortgage - and I still have it because I've always kept it to convince myself that it really did happen!

" It was a time when it was easy to feel bitter and twisted, made worse by the fact that it just happened to be the worst winter for many years. There was snow on the ground for weeks.

"A lot of the 28 were under the impression that it would all blow over but I must admit that I was convinced from the outset that Pole-Carew meant what he said. To be honest, I cannot recall ever exchanging a single word with the man so it's hard to say how I feel about him on a personal level. But he certainly had a profound affect on my life and on reflection, it just might have been for the better.

" It certainly took me into areas that I never expected to experience and was character building to say the least: When the 28 strikers started our own newspaper, a weekly called Nottingham News, I suddenly found myself as circulation manager with Gary Moran as my assistant. (*Gary Moran had been a news reporter at the Evening Post then spent many years in radio and is now General Manager of Nottingham Panthers ice hockey club.*)

" We had to meet the printer's van when it arrived on a Thursday night and drive around Nottingham dishing out copies to newsagents. Although most of the newsagents were very supportive, it wasn't easy for them because they had been told that any of them caught selling the Nottingham News would have their supply of Evening Posts cut off.

" I had my own selling pitch outside Marks & Spencer and I stood there for most of every Friday, shouting at the top of my voice. It was good fun for the most part - but worrying as well because we knew there was no future in it. Between the 28 of us, we didn't have enough expertise to run a newspaper and we certainly didn't have any capital to support it. But from an editorial point of view, it was actually a very good product.

" Largely through his relationship with John Lawson, who was the Nottingham Forest correspondent, Brian Clough was incredibly supportive. At a time when Forest were the European Champions, Cloughie refused to speak to any journalists in the country except for John and me and the first-ever front page lead in our Nottingham News was a world exclusive :' *I'm going to pay £1million for Trevor Francis'*. The following day, Francis became the first £1 million player in the history of English football.

" After several weeks on strike, John and I decided that we would have to do something positive about changing our lives and it happened one morning after we had completed our stint on picket duty. I lived at Long

Eaton at the time, while John lived in Arnold and my wife was at his house. When we pooled our resources, we hadn't got enough money to pay for two bus fares so we trudged through the snow for about four miles and along the way, we agreed to set up a business together. We were partners for 18 years in a freelance communications agency, specialising in sport… and I suppose you could say that was all down to Pole-Carew.

" There's no doubt that he changed people's lives with the stubborn stance he took. It was a good thing for some - and I can count myself among them - but not everyone was so fortunate.

" What I would say, though, is that there are ways and means of doing things and Pole-Carew didn't need to create the bitterness and resentment that lingered in Nottingham for a very long time and affected a lot of people. I hope he has that on his conscience."

Though it is not difficult to sympathise with the Nottingham 28 over what they went through back in 1979, the majority, if not all, of them appear to have gone on to build successful careers.

When all 28 were offered their Evening Post jobs back as part of the deal struck with the NUJ in 1984 only **one** took up the offer.

(*That one was Lynne Curry, who had been a junior reporter in the Evening Post's Newark district office for just* **two weeks** *when the strike call came. Lynne went on to become a prominent member of the Post's very successful, award -winning editorial team through the 'eighties before marrying her husband, Martin, a journalist with The Independent and joining him in Fleet Street in the early ' nineties. The couple them moved to Somerset, where they restored a beautiful old mill house and Lynne became a popular columnist on the Western Morning News for nearly 10 years before she died from cancer, aged just 48.*)

That the talented 28 eventually did so well outside the Evening Post is proof that they were right to want to hold on to their union cards - though, ironically, owing to Margaret Thatcher's subsequent union reforming legislation, they hadn't needed to.

And was Christopher Pole-Carew right to sack them?

Views on that will always be as mixed as they are passionately polarised.

At the time, the majority opinion throughout the industry was that he was wrong and that prevailed in the boardrooms as much as it did in the union meetings, especially since the Newspaper Society / NUJ settlement agreement had guaranteed a return to work without victimisation for *all* strikers.

But in the white hot heat of that bitter, violent dispute and given that more than ninety Evening Post journalists had rejected the strike call and chosen loyalty to the Company, is it fair to ask : What else could he have done? By re-instating the 28 in the aftermath of the dispute, wouldn't he have been belittling the support that the majority of the Company's journalists had given him (sacrificing their own union cards in the process) and breaking faith with them after they had been subjected to venomous verbal abuse and ugly threats; vilification and hatred in print and appalling intimidation as they crossed the picket lines?

And one hugely significant point was, either by accident or design, consistently overlooked in the welter of national publicity about the sacked 28….because of Pole-Carew's pay policy at the Nottingham Evening Post, they had been instructed by their union to go on strike in support of a national claim for a lot **less** money than they were already earning.

Whether you regard Pole-Carew's resolute refusal to accept that as a reasonable circumstance under which to withdraw their labour as overly simplistic or sound common sense, neither wild horses nor a million violent pickets a day for the next 20 years could have dragged him to any other conclusion.

In any event, it is not a debate which Pole-Carew would ever have even contemplated entering into at that time. What he did, by sacking the 28 in the first place was to ensure that there was no way the NUJ would secure majority support for a strike at the Nottingham Evening Post; they were the victims of collateral damage in his determination not to be pushed around by anybody. But, more fundamentally, his hugely controversial stance was a dramatic manifestation of his own strict code of **two way loyalty.** Breaking that code would simply never have been an option for him. And - as Terry Bowles points out - whether you think that sacking the strikers was right or wrong, Pole-Carew remained steadfastly true to his word while, on the other side, crucial promises made to them by the union which had forced them out on to the streets by threatening their future careers, proved to be infinitely less durable.

There had been calls for the national strike to continue beyond its seven week duration until the Nottingham 28 were re-instated but they failed (*it would have been futile, anyway*) and after the rest of the NUJ's 8,000-plus strikers had gone back to their jobs, those 28 people - several of them with families to support, many of them with mortgages to pay - were left high, dry and jobless.

Today, while a few among them also blame the union for the plight in which they were left , the flames of anger and resentment towards Christopher Pole-Carew still burn within them after thirty years.

It might appear incongruous that in rationalising the conflict of his professed regard for people with the apparent callousness with which he conducted his battles with the trade unions, Pole-Carew invokes *Drake's Prayer* but religion has always played an important part in the life of Christopher Pole-Carew.

His mother was strongly religious all her life. She started as an Anglican, flirted for a while with Roman Catholicism then became a Christian Scientist, in which faith the young Christopher was brought up. *

He describes his commitment to religion in typically direct terms: " Dartmouth Naval College took religion properly and seriously, including Divinity Instruction twice a term. Every morning we had Divisions (ie. parade) during which we Closed for prayers (ie. Marched closer, including good hearty hymns). Saturday morning had Congregational practise, when the music master took us through the hymns we would sing the following day. Sunday was a full blown service after Sunday Divisions, which was non-stop inspections in best uniforms. One of the more amusing aspects on weekday Divisions was the order before prayers - ' *Fall out the Roman Catholics* ' - when all non-Anglicans of whatever denomination fell out to stand in a huddle. The true Romans would cross themselves and mutter some foreign prayer or other. The rest, the occasional Sikh or Hindu, would stand around bored. I always liked the way the Navy recognised only two religions: Anglicans - and the others!

" At home, I was transferred from Anglicanism to become a Christian Scientist with Sunday School every Sunday for an hour and on every Wednesday evening, Testimony Meetings, when the devout would stand up to tell about something in their lives that was of religious significance.

" My mother was very devout and when she broke her leg, never saw a doctor or a nurse; simply bandaged it up and walked on it as soon as she could. I reckon she was amazingly tough as well!

" I believed in Christian Science (and still do believe) but I abandoned it when I was confirmed, at the age of 17, by the Bishop of Barbados whilst a cadet in the Training Cruiser, HMS Devonshire.

" My reason was definitely not that I didn't believe in Christian Science but that I was not capable of achieving the religiousness to be a true Christian Scientist. In other words, I simply wasn't good enough to be one, so I left it. The rest of my family, in one form or another, remained Christian Scientists. My sister, Loveday, confirms that her views are identical to mine, except that she didn't formally ' leave ' Christian Science but she feels that her positive and very happy outlook life stems from having *been* a Christian Scientist. This applies to me, also.

(* *Christian Science is a religious belief system established by Mary Baker Eddy during the 19th Century. It asserts that humanity and the universe as a whole are spiritual rather than material; that truth and good are real, while evil and error are unreal and that through prayer and spiritual comprehension these facts can be spiritually achieved and demonstrated.*)

" In the Navy, church-going on Sundays was voluntary, except that it was taken for granted that officers went ' to set a good example' to the sailors. On leaving the Navy, once we eventually settled down to village life in Great Chesterfield, I rapidly went onto the Parochial Church Council and have been on various church councils without a break for the past 60 years or so - and still am.

" Yes, my faith means a lot to me; it is the standard of love and tolerance that welds a good family, or a society, or a nation, together in the actual practice of loving one's neighbour. To me, it is only too obvious that the mess our country is in today is paralleled by the decline in Christianity in England..

" Do I believe? Most certainly. Yes. There was a man who showed us the way to 'overcome the sharpness of death' (ie. To immortal life, or maybe to become a ' Time Lord') His path was horrific and no doubt there are other ways, but they are not for me because I know that I am simply not good enough - although I do genuinely try constantly to live my life as a Christian; I can only ask God to help me to live a good life. I try hard. But I am not impressed by my results.

" Is there a God? Of course there is. Whatever atheists may say, they miss the point that something/someone created the universe way back forever ago and that thing/person/force we call God, who by definition has unlimited powers.

" How does my faith affect my life on a day to day basis? I am governed by two principles.

" The first: To me every single day is a personal gift from God to spend as I think fit. At the end of every day (yes, almost without exception) I go through what I have done to examine whether I have made good use of it. On occasions, if I feel that I am wasting the day, I will consciously do things to make up the missing requirement not to have wasted it. I don't mean religious things nor necessarily being nice. It could be making a shelf, sorting out books, hanging pictures - something that leaves a sense of achievement. God's gift of that day is too great to be wasted or frittered away.

" The second: Is the belief that everything one does should be treated in the context of Drake's Prayer."

Christopher Pole-Carew's strong belief in a good family has never wavered. Throughout the years when his business career was at its most controversial, most physically and mentally demanding, most exciting, stimulating and time consuming, he **never** lost that belief nor failed to practice it.

It has been a constant, unfailing love and devotion to his wife and three children, Delia, Camilla (*'Milly'*) and Peregrine. And that is appreciated deeply by those children. The happy home and the parental love and guidance that Gill and Christopher provided for them is remembered fondly by all three.

' Milly ' says:

" My first memory is, at about two years old, of sitting on my father's shoulders looking at a large grey house and past to a view of the barren, craggy Derbyshire moors. He held my legs firmly and I felt safe. I don't think I have ever lost that feeling.

" When we settled in Nottinghamshire, I was four and until the age of 11, when I went to boarding school, I travelled to school with him daily and then again when I returned at 18 to go to Trent Polytechnic to study art.

" There was never a dull moment.

" He constantly fired questions at me: ' What kind of tree was that? What bird had just flown past? Had I seen that stoat scuttling across the road? What instrument is that playing on the tape? '

" He got me to discover Binary numbers long before I was taught it at school and, of course, he talked excitedly about computers. I was always trying to keep up with him - and he did the same things on a walk. He would stride out (with me jogging to keep up) with his mind working at the speed he was walking, so one minute you would be searching the sky trying to recognise a bird's flight pattern, the next deciphering animal tracks, then suddenly stopping to identify fungi or wildflowers.

" It was exhausting, sometimes frustrating, but such fun and it has influenced me throughout my life. I am a sculptress and to an artist, observation is essential. Without daddy's input and 'training' I wouldn't work the way I do - observing nature for inspiration to create forms from stone. In particular, shells. We spent many holidays along various European coastlines hunting for cowrie shells or for totally round pebbles on Chesil Beach. I'm sure part of this was to give him and my mother some piece and quiet from squabbling children, but it was inventive and kept us amused for years!

" Daddy worked on Saturdays as well as all week at T. Bailey Forman , so when he was at home his form of relaxation was to create and maintain our home and our way of playing with him was to help re-roof the house, do the gardening, chop the wood. I kept bees with him. They were French bees and he said you had to talk to them in French and tell them what was going on or they would swarm. I was in charge of creating a fire with bellows and while the bees were pre-occupied saving the hive from the fire, Daddy would scrape off the propolis, clean up the hive and then we'd check the queen and at the right time of the year, collect the honey. It is a wonderful process. When I was stung, he would gently scrape out the sting so as to reduce the amount of poison pumped into me, then he would mourn the loss of one of his bees (they die when they leave their sting behind) which had lost its life protecting the hive. We always took gifts of honey from our bees and eggs from our chickens when we visited other people.

" During the strike in the '70s he got stung while tending the bees and had a serious allergic reaction, which I imagine was worsened by stress and exhaustion because he was never really at home during that time. I remember going up to my parents' room with a cup of tea for him. He was lying in the dark. His skin glowed white in the half light. He was all puffy and his hands were like boxing gloves. I passed the tea to him and he dropped it. It is frightening for a child to see a parent weakened…especially when I had received death threats on his behalf. I thought maybe the wishes of the man on the telephone were coming true. What sort of people use a child to relay messages of that sort? I have no time for cowards.

" Daddy is *always* creating something. I remember him spending a few hours every evening in his workshop from which he produced three mahogany boxes - one for each of his 'girls.' When he gave me mine, he said it was my character. It is a cube and as a teenager at the time, I was distinctly un-amused to be thought of in this way! I should have known better, because on further investigation, I discovered it wasn't quite as straightforward as that: Each side slides up to reveal six little drawers, each with a brass handle. They can only slide back into their own slot. Only two drawers open on each side because they are all different sizes and interweave internally. I am incredibly lucky to be the inspiration for such a beautiful thing."

(*In addition to these lovely, intricate and unique boxes, which Gill, Delia and 'Milly' treasure to this day, Christopher also produced for each of his 'girls', three incredibly dainty wooden spoons, with delicately curved handles - wonderfully tactile creations which must have taken amazing skill and patience to make.*)

" When I rang from France," says 'Milly', "on a holiday paid for by Daddy, to find out my 'A' Level results, he gave them to me - and they were appalling! But instead of berating me for wasting my education and his money, he asked me if I had been happy at school and when I said 'yes' he told me that was all that mattered.

" I didn't deserve that generosity of spirit and I think I realised then just how much he had done for us - and continues to do for us. It is not about financing us; bailing us out, but always being there with well-structured advice, love and a great deal of tenderness.

" When I got married, Daddy spent hours dead heading all the roses in the garden. He was determined that the garden would be perfect and not one rose petal would fall on my Wedding Day. He organised a jazz band, too. We went to the Blue Bell in the Old Market Square in the centre of Nottingham - a low ceilinged, smoky, historic pub packed with people - and fought our way through to the back where Derek Winters and his band were playing. They were great and they put on a fantastic show for my wedding reception. The guests danced and one got up and sang a few numbers, then we had a Mardi Gras finish through the corn fields to a helicopter, which Daddy had organised to take us away. He had shed a few tears after my sister's wedding as he confessed that although he was gaining a son, he was worried he was losing his daughter. I don't think he has lost either of us.

" Although he was a tough businessman and sometimes stern father (occasionally a bit frightening) he always kept the door open for negotiation. " Recently, when my husband and I separated and the divorce proceedings became acrimonious he helped me attempt to keep the lines of communication open and expressed a wish to stay in touch with Dominic.

" I consider myself to be lucky in many ways but above all in having Mummy and Daddy as my parents. I love them very much."

Son Peregrine looks back on a very lively childhood as the off-spring of the Pole-Carews:

" Delia and Charlie Joly loaded me into a large brown Silvercross pram and launched me down the garden of The Gables, Great Chesterford in North Essex - now sadly bisected by the M11. The pram was heading for the drive and the open gates onto the road and then for the open gates of the abattoir opposite. Luckily, there was a large tree trunk just before the drive and the pram hit a bump in the grass and careered into the log. I was fine. The pram wasn't. I was given a bollocking from Daddy and Mummy was deeply upset as that was the end of the pram. Camilla had yet to be born so I was certainly under five. Delia and Charlie were nowhere to be seen!

" That pram had featured earlier in a photo taken at Kingston Hall. I was sitting up, tied in by a harness, holding a pair of coconut maracas. There was snow on the ground. Apparently, shortly after the picture was taken, I had thrown one maraca over board and as Daddy picked it up I cracked him across the back of the head with the other.

" Another memory of Great Chesterford is when we made the most fantastic den in the asparagus patch. I couldn't understand why we got into so much trouble. It was just a lot of tall fluffy green weeds. It must have been July. It was hot and the sky was very blue. I can recall a couple of holidays. One in Dartmouth when we went on a fabulous teak decked, navy blue hulled yacht. It was cold, so Delia and I were wearing Daddy's submariners polo neck sweaters; they were very itchy, particularly under the chin, but they kept us warm.

" Then there was the walk on Dartmoor - we were coming off the moor down a rutted shale track, when we came to a brick hut. I suppose I had been a bit annoying as Daddy told me that was where little boys who were annoying were locked up. If I listened carefully I could hear them crying, he said. And I did. A shrill squealing was coming from the high windowed lock up. Mummy told Daddy to stop teasing me, as what I could hear was the squeaking of a wheel in what was actually a water pumping station. I'm not good at being teased - even now, nearly 50 years later.

" We had a holiday in Pembrokeshire in a three roomed wooden hut on a cliff overlooking a windswept beach. There wasn't a tree in sight. The hut smelt of damp and the lino floor always crunched from sandy feet. There was the heady smell of meths from the little primus stove. We went to St. David's and in the cathedral saw the casket that held the bones of St.David.

" Some years later we had a slightly more updated holiday in Eire in a Norwegian style chalet house overlooking a stunning sandy bay. We had plywood surfboards and rode the waves in for hundreds of yards. One day, wandering along the beach looking for shells, I saw a green globe half hidden by seaweed on the high water line. It was a fisherman's float that had broken away from the nets and been ground by the surf in the sand to give it a sandblasted look. I was so proud. I carried it carefully up to the house, hiding it behind my back to get everyone to guess what I had found. Daddy had found one in pristine condition a couple of days before. But mine was better. Daddy made a net to enclose them in. From that holiday on, those fishermen's floats have always decorated the downstairs loos of the homes we've lived in.

" We moved to South Wales in 1964. Delia and I went to the local school in Dynas Powys where we were taught Welsh. I can still remember counting - ' een, dai, tree, pedooar, pimp.' We lived down a long bumpy drive in a little red bricked farm house in Michaelstone-le-Pit. Halfway down the drive there was a ford across a brook, then the drive wound round a field in front of the house to a flint covered copen yard. We had a ginger haired Nanny for Camilla, Barbara - 'Bada' as Camilla called her." Granny and Granddad decided it was time they took Mummy on holiday without the family. They went off to France to see the Lascaux cave paintings. They came back with table mats depicting mammoths and cavemen. We had them for best for years. 'Bada' looked after Camilla and Daddy dropped us at school each day.

" One morning, Daddy decided to indulge in his favourite breakfast - tinned herrings in tomato sauce (fond memories of days living under the seas in a tin can!) I had some - I think Delia must have found rice crispies more to her liking - and in the playground halfway through break, my herrings re-appeared. Daddy had to leave work and bring me home. I've never had a herring since. I think Daddy was pleased to see Mummy safely home."

Elder daughter Delia remembers:

" I was eleven when my parents announced that we were moving again. It was quite a shock to the system. My brother, sister and I had settled down in Buxton and were enjoying the space and freedom of the house, the garden and the surrounding fields. In no time at all, we found ourselves in a tiny red brick house in the middle of acres of ploughed fields. It was winter and there was nothing but mud and it was so flat. Where were the hills and the valleys?

" I had moved from the local PNEU in Buxton to Ockbrook, a Moravian school just outside Derby, where I was a weekly boarder. The drive from Buxton every Monday morning during the autumn and winter had been wonderful …through the Pennines down the Via Gellia to Derby and then to Ockbrook where Daddy dropped me off on his way to Nottingham.

" Ockbrook wasn't easy. I spoke with the wrong accent and was a good seven or eight inches taller than my contemporaries, most of whom thought I should be in the sixth form. Having had a terrific education in a very small school, I was considered bright and came consistently top or near the top in most subjects, so the school thought I would benefit by being moved up a year. In retrospect, I think they wanted to even out the class sizes as five of us moved up. Missing out a whole year of schooling put me so behind I never caught up and remained in the bottom four for the rest of my time there. I think it knocked my confidence a bit, too. Winning the hurdles and the 100 yards for my house helped a bit - but I never really fitted in.

" However, when I was about 14, one of the girls in the sixth form came up to me and told me she thought my brother was really good looking. This really surprised me as my brother was 12 and at a boarding school. Eventually, the penny dropped and I realised she was talking about my **father** - you should have seen her face fall when I told her! From then onwards, the mistake was made over and over again. My father, of course, loved it!

" Because my parents married and had me so young, I am one of those rare people who can remember their parents clearly when they were in their twenties. My mother was very slim and glamorous and my father very tall and very thin. I remember sitting on a sand dune beside my father and thinking how thin his arms were. I remember him at St David's, racing up the cliff path to the coastguard's cottage, where we were staying, with my brother on his shoulders, taking enormous strides. It was our first ever holiday; we spent hours on the beach making enormous sand castles with moats and swimming in the rock pools. When we got back, Peregrine walked around for days holding his shorts up by the legs in case they got wet in the sea! We had another holiday in North Wales some years later and went to a beach where people had used the rocks at the bottom of the cliff to make wind breaks. Daddy made a huge one, three feet high. A job very well done. Later in the holiday we went back to the beach and another family was in our shelter so we built a new one. They came along the beach and offered us the shelter back, but we said we were very happy building a new one, so not to worry.

" In the very hard winter of 1962/63 Daddy was sent to Wales to do a managerial course on the South Wales Echo - and we got a telly! Daddy had been worried that Mummy would be lonely, so the TV arrived. Up until then, we had listened to the wireless or gone next door to the Joly's to watch Dr Who. Every Saturday in the winter we'd have tea and crumpets or toast by the fire in the drawing room listening to the wireless. When the telly arrived, we watched the wrestling with Kent Walton. We liked the tag teams best. And Mick McManus. We still have tea in front of a big fire in the winter - it's nice that some things don't change.

" One bright, clear Monday morning in the height of the cold weather we all got into the car - a pale blue Triumph Herald - to take Daddy to the station and Peregrine and me to school. 'Milly' was in her red carrycot taking up most of the back seat and I was squashed in beside her. Peregrine was sitting on Mummy's knee in the front and Daddy drove. The roads were thick with ice, snowdrifts had narrowed the roads and towered above us. We went round a corner…and straight into a van coming the other way. Daddy was bent over the steering wheel, moaning, with a handkerchief to his face. Mummy seemed alright. Peregrine was dazed and bleeding from a deep cut on his forehead and 'Milly' had been sick on the collar of her coat. I think I bit my lip. I climbed out over Mummy and went to see what had happened. I can't remember much about what happened after that, other than we had the day off school and we borrowed the Joly's car, as ours was written off. I think Daddy went down to Cardiff the following day.

" Very occasionally the great treat was for us to go to London to see Daddy in his office. I have a very vague memory of going to London by steam train and being taken to the Daily Express building - lots of chrome and marble. When we were older, we used to go to Manchester and Stockport and were allowed to start the presses rolling. The type-setters would print our names in metal for us to take home. There was a wonderful smell of hot oil and newsprint and the noise of the presses starting to roll was terrific. We thought it was tremendously exciting - still do!

" Daddy is *always* doing things and one of my first memories is of running across the drive at Kingsdon Hall to help him wash the car. I fell over and cut my knee and I still have the scar! Peregrine, 'Milly' and I were always (*and still are*) roped in to help him. We carried tools, spades, hammers and endlessly held things in place. He made us a gym in the orchard at Great Chesterfield, with a scots pine he'd cut down slung between two apple trees; a rope with a monkey's fist knot at the bottom, a swing and an old tyre hung from the branches. We spent hours playing there with our friends - Charlie Joly from next door could climb anything! We were the 'Monkey Club' and climbed every tree we could get up into. Daddy made me stilts when the craze took over the school and he taught me to jump on a pogo stick. He built the kitchen at Newfield; he made my mother, sister and me beautiful marquetry boxes; he panelled the hall at Newfield in oak. It nearly broke his heart when he went back to Newfield after they had moved and found all the panelling in a skip.

" He made beer until they legalised home brewing (he stopped then because he said they had taken all the fun out of it !) and I had my first beer at the age of two ; He let me loose in his workshop and taught me to saw and to hammer properly. I made my own doll's furniture. One year, when I was nine, I made my doll a bedroom out of an orange box and my granddad, who was over from South Africa, helped me put in carpets and electric lights. Granddad was so impressed by my sawing he gave me a fret saw for Christmas.

" Just before I took my 'O' Levels when I was 15, my parents realised that after four years I was still unhappy at Ockbrook and asked if I wanted to do my 'A' Levels elsewhere (at Queens gate). London was the immediate answer. My head was full of pop songs, clothes and Twiggy so I couldn't imagine a better place to be! The summer I took my '0' Levels, my friend Jane and I went to stay in Didcot with our friend Caroline, one of the few people in the school almost as tall as me. We slept late, emerging about lunchtime, jumped on the train and went to Oxford every afternoon. I have vague memories of hot days wandering happily around the shops and colleges, just mooching about as teenage girls do. I bought a dress that I wore most days. Mummy was horrified when I came back.. .the dress was no more than an overgrown shirt and only just covered my bottom! I was the bees knees! One evening we wandered into one of the colleges where a big marquee had been erected and was being set up for one of the college balls. There were masses of people milling about so three girls weren't really noticed. We wandered over to where the band was setting up and eventually got chatting to the roadies. They were very nice and invited us to stay for the party, but being well brought up girls we said we could only stay until it was time to catch the last train back to Didcot, which we duly did. The following day it dawned on us that we had been chatting to the members of Deep Purple * and my date for the evening had been Roger Glover, the bass guitarist!

(* *Deep Purple were a major rock band, at the height of their popularity in 1970*)

"As we got older, Daddy talked to us more and more about what he was doing. I remember him explaining about computers. In his mind, there was a little man with hundreds of little boxes and he rushed from one to the other posting information !"

So that is *This Man, Pole-Carew* as seen through the eyes of friends, foes and family.

At least , hopefully, it will have succeeded in broadening perceptions from the blinkered bias and ignorance upon which hundreds of opinions of this controversial character have been based for 35 years.

At best, maybe, it will have achieved some understanding of an exceptionally talented, deep and extremely complex man.

8
RETIREMENT - SORT OF!

Was it just luck that brought so many of you, with the skills to save my life, to where we had crashed ?'

ONE Sunday morning in 1989 Christopher Pole-Carew and his wife Gill were lying in bed at their Nottinghamshire home reading the Sunday newspapers - a product of the industry which, to its own huge loss, no longer provided a proper place for one of its greatest ever pioneers.

The telephone rang and Christopher answered.

On the line was his cousin Sir John Carew Pole:

" Hello Christopher. It's John. I thought I should let you know that the lease on Shute has come up. Would you be interested in taking it? "

Shute – the ancestral home

Shute was the substantial Devonshire manor house home of their ancestors the Poles from the 16th Century onwards. And Sir John was suggesting that Christopher might care to re-establish the family presence in the stately old pile.

The timing of the suggestion was opportune.

With retirement in mind, the Pole-Carews had been looking for a new home. Their search had been concentrated on Lincolnshire - close enough to all their Nottinghamshire friends and especially to daughter Camilla, who lived in Grantham, and with the added advantage of offering lovely houses at very attractive prices.

There were other reasons, the Pole-Carews reckoned, to move from Newfield, the home they had enjoyed for so long: " Development of the east coast had made the Fosse Way (A46) an overloaded thoroughfare, passing just forty feet from us, and Nottinghamshire County Council had ensured that they wasted the equivalent of a small town's annual electricity needs by putting lights all along that length of road."

Shute is the remains of a substantial manor house in a lovely village near Axminster in East Devon.

Christopher Pole-Carew describes it thus: " It was built originally in the 1380s by the Bonneville family; from them it had passed, after an unfortunate beheading in the Wars of the Roses, by inheritance to the Grays (*Lady Jane Gray, Queen of England for nine days - also beheaded, plus her father*) and was bought in 1560 by my family, the Poles. We held it until cousin John gave it to the National Trust in 1959 when he attached two conditions to the gift: that the house should be used as a home (*ie. not as some lifeless 'museum '*) and that whenever the lease came up it should be offered first to members of the Pole-Carew family (*ie. descendants of my great grandfather, William Henry Pole-Carew*) at the going commercial rate.

"And here we were being offered it in 1988!

" Well, why not?

" Was it exciting to move to one's, in inverted commas, 'ancestral home'? Yes, it was - even though it's a pretty poor 'ancestral home' which your immediate family has never lived in, nor owned and now, anyway, belonged to the National Trust.

" Plus, the shooting's much better than it is in flat Lincolnshire; the fishing is, even in these days of pollution and neglect, passing fair; the Exe is good for a salmon or two ; nearby to Shute is the Axe, with a respectable run of sea trout - and Shute had the added attraction of re-connecting with one's roots.

" So down to Devon we went; found Shute (*its name having been changed by the National Trust from Shute House to Shute Barton*) and immediately wondered if we hadn't made some terrible mistake!

" The house was empty and suffering from chronic neglect; water was leaking into every bedroom and at one point ran from behind the battlements to the ground floor three stories below. The plaster throughout the house was ' blown', ie. needing complete replacement. There was no central heating; the whole house needed re-wiring and re-plumbing ; the garden was a complete disaster."

Clearly, Shute Barton presented yet another huge challenge for the indefatigable Pole-Carew. But he was ready for it…

" The time had come for me to admit that my chances of getting a worthwhile job in newspapers ever again were almost non-existent; I had too many enemies at all levels. So if I was to retire, how would I survive without something to keep me occupied 16 hours a day?

" And here was the answer.

" What a challenge!"

And so it was , in the Autumn of 1988, that the Pole-Carew's moved lock, stock and barrel to Devon.

Their journey across England was an extraordinary sight - with a convoy of assorted vehicles laden with all manner of accumulated possessions trailing slowly southwards like some wild-west Wagon Train.

Among the conspicuous cornucopia of chattels conveyed in that convoy from Nottinghamshire to Devonshire were Christopher Pole-Carew's entire workshop, with circular saw, planer and lathe and masses of miscellaneous bits of timber, including the remains of a massive elm tree which he had lovingly stored away after chopping it down when Dutch Elm Disease struck in the late 1970's and from which, working entirely alone, he has since produced four splendid huge dining tables and two smaller ones.

They arrived and - despite the appalling state of Shute Barton - moved straight in, Pole -Carew exercising his theory that " the only way to make builders finish a house is to move in on them. It works. But not all wives welcome it!

" We had one bedroom in use - albeit with water coming in - and a kitchen with no heating, the elderly Aga in the middle of being converted from coal to oil, no cupboards and a sink with no draining boards.

" And so began a 20 year love/hate (*actually it was the other way round*!) relationship with our landlords…that august body, the National Trust.

" No-one has ever accused the National Trust of being fast movers on any matter and we soon found out that they had no plans to break with tradition for our sakes! "

Pole-Carew says the fact that it was to take so long before the house in which he and Gill were living could be considered fully habitable, was due in no small measure to " interminable arguments" with the National Trust, its experts and advisors…

" For example, they viewed with horror the suggestion that we should have central heating and the idea that the 15th Century windows should be adjusted to make them at least a little bit less draughty was met with puzzlement - even though, incidentally, all of this was to be done at my own expense.

" Eventually, I found that the best way of moving forward was simply to do things for the good of the house, tell no-one and with reasonable luck nothing would be said - or even noticed.

"A good example of this was when we had a visit from the interminable National Trust experts one Friday. Over the weekend I removed a wall - an ugly 1950s utility addition to the house - between a bedroom and a passage. On the Monday, they returned and passing through, they eyed the outline on the walls and ceiling where the wall had been. Not a word was said.

" However, some two years later, John Channon, my National Trust agent, said : '*Christopher, did you ever put in for planning permission to remove that wall?*' 'You can't be serious,' I replied. He said:' *It's fine for you to do that sort of thing but we are the National Trust and we simply can't get away with it*'

" It was a fair point. It was OK for me to ride roughshod over stupid regulations but not the same for a very large Establishment organisation. I believe my attitude towards the National Trust changed at that time; somehow John had shown me how the fact that, despite all the aggravation and frustration, I had actually really liked every National Trust person I had met could be reconciled with their being bureaucratic to their very eye balls, the kind of person that I instinctively despised, because they had no choice. Such is the power and influence of the Establishment on those within its circumference!

"Another example of the overlapping rings of bureaucracy that dominates everything that the National Trust does (whether they like it or not) was a visit we had to discuss the changes that I wished to make to Shute to make it more habitable and up to date - without, of course, damaging its wonderful atmosphere and character.

" On this occasion, John Channon and I were joined by a lady - let's call her Miss X - from English Heritage and a chap - let's call him Mr Y - from Devon County Council. As we went in detail through every point of what I wanted to do, entirely at my own expense, John agreed in principle with every suggestion I made while Miss X said 'No' every single time and every single time, Mr Y said he thought she was right!

" Eventually, when Miss X turned down my proposal to put a bath in a particular place in a room off what was to be our bedroom, I lost my cool, turned to her in anger and demanded to know :' Well - where would **you** suggest it goes? '

" She said :' I'm not paid to give advice.'

" To which I replied sarcastically : 'Oh, I'm so sorry. I hadn't realised how you did things in English Heritage. Give me your home address - I'm sure I can sort that problem out for you!'

" I didn't lose a friend, because I couldn't imagine her having any.

" But I certainly added another enemy to my substantial list!"

With typical resolution Pole-Carew - as always supported, encouraged and more than ably assisted by Gill - continued to work long and hard in often trying circumstances and frequently, since he did so much of the work himself, in conditions that were desperately tiring physically until Shute was in a fit state to live in.

It had taken them three years.

Three years in which they lived, day and night, in the house they were striving so hard to make fit to live in!

Now, it was not only fit for them but fit to be opened to the public - a condition of the lease arrangement with the National Trust - with all that entailed.

Few who know Christopher Pole-Carew (prone as he is to the occasional irascible outburst!) could easily envisage him playing polite and tolerant host to visiting strangers invading the privacy of the ancestral home which he had spent three years lovingly restoring and many ask him :" What's it like having people traipsing through your home. It must be awful?"

But, as is so often the case with this man of so many contradictions, his answer (given absolutely honestly, for he knows no other way) is not what they expect:

"It's not awful at all," he says..

"The practice of opening houses to the public goes back to the 18th Century when the wealthy used to like to show their fine new homes to anyone that might be interested, so the tradition is well founded.

" Plus, almost all those who come round are decent people who are genuinely interested and it is a real pleasure to show them round while incidentally enjoying the delights of listening to one's own voice talking to a captive audience for some forty minutes!

" The number who come because 'Wayne wants to use the toilet' are very rare - and anyway, our 'toilet' was not available to visitors. So there!"

Neither did Pole-Carew's frustrations with the National Trust prevent a good relationship with their guides, who showed those visitors around: " They are delightful, almost all well educated and genuinely interested in the house and its owners. Over the years, some became close friends.

" Plus, they all believe in the National Trust and all it achieves - as do Gill and I. All in all it's true to say that while we welcomed the end of every 'Season' - seven months from Spring to Autumn - we equally looked forward to the beginning of the next one.

" We chose to open on Wednesday and Saturday afternoons, which we felt was the minimum amount whilst playing fair with visitors. Our attitude towards visitors was that the most important thing is for them to enjoy themselves. When I took people round (not often, because the National Trust guides would say that was what *they* were there for) I let them look in the cupboards and go into the bits that *aren't* open to the public – ie. all the places people *really* want to see because they aren't allowed to. Much more fun!

" It's the little things that people like. For instance, Shute has the largest fireplace in the UK - in the *world* , I reckon; the only one 'where Father Christmas can park his reindeers under cover while delivering presents!'

" Gill also made visits more fun for children by sticking replica ladybirds all around the house for them to find and count. If they got the number right they got a sweet at the end (no child ever failed to get the right number. Fancy that!)

" Before that, we used to see so many children being dragged around, bored almost to tears, but not any longer. And for the brighter ones there were frogs and fish and tortoises to be found as well!

" Making people happy is truly a great pleasure."

For all they were happily at ease with the visitors, there continued to be episodes of friction with the National Trust…one such concerning a huge beech tree in the garden.

" My cousin by marriage, David Tudway-Quilter from Wells, a well known expert on trees, warned me that if I didn't cut a huge limb off it, the tree would be blown down when next we had a serious gale.

" I told the National Trust and asked if it was OK for me to cut off the limb. They said '*No - not you. We'll send someone to do it.*' then never did and 18 months later, in the storms of 1990, the whole tree was blown down. Typical!"

In 1994, Christopher Pole-Carew had what he describes as ' the only serious quarrel' he had with the National Trust…

" This concerned a letter I wrote to the Daily Telegraph about an article in that paper in which Lord Scarsdale who, not long before, had given Keddleston to the National Trust, complained of the Trust's attitude towards him and his wife regarding the house, its decoration, etc and the Trust's plans for its future.

"Francis and Helen Scarsdale, who lived in a wing of the house, had been invited to attend the planning meetings, at which the Trust's experts aired their views on what should and should not be done to the house.

" Naturally (since they lived in it!) Francis and Helen expressed their own views as well. These, they said, were listened to in silence - and then ignored, despite the fact that Francis Scarsdale had been brought up at Keddlestone and had lived there for a great number of years, which made *nobody's* knowledge and experience of the house more relevant, nor love of it more deeply felt and genuine.

" History does not relate whether he regretted his decision to give his lovely house to the National Trust, plus the very substantial endowment always required, but the article left one in no doubt that the way it was run annoyed and saddened him.

" I read the article and responded with a letter to the Daily Telegraph because I felt it touched on an attitude that I believe the Trust had, and still has, towards those who have made it the organisation it is today - namely its habit of ignoring, almost airbrushing out, those they call the 'donor families.'

" So I weighed in… and oh, dear. You have no idea how many people were upset!

" It seemed as though a string of people from Sir Angus Stirling down were horrified that anyone could possibly criticise the National Trust or, more to the point, manage to find anything about the National Trust that could possibly be criticised. They wrote and they visited and they all, in their different ways, said the same thing: ' You are mistaken; the National Trust is right and caring without stain or blemish - so what you have said cannot possibly be true.'

" I was astonished by the response. The letter I had written was simply to support Lord Scarsdale's resentment of the way he and Lady Scarsdale were treated by the National Trust people involved in caring for his home. He told me that they would attend committee meetings to discuss matters such as what colour a room should be painted or should some trees in the garden be cut down. He would tell those present what colour the room had been over the years from his childhood, assuming that they wished to keep the house looking as it had in the past. They listened - and then continued the meeting as if the irritating little interruption had not taken place!

" Should those trees be cut down? Lord Scarsdale remembered them being planted in his youth, specifically to provide a screen to block the unsightly view of industrial Derby from the house. Now that they were mature trees they were doing the job extremely well, which seemed a good reason for leaving them alone. This opinion was graciously allowed to be given before the committee agreed without further ado that the trees should come down - thus destroying the otherwise rural view.

" My knowledge of the National Trust indicated that they tended to ignore criticism. I thought, therefore, that if I were to write a letter to the Daily Telegraph supporting Lord Scarsdale's comments there might well be a chance that his concerns would be heeded. How naïve of me to think that the National Trust could possibly acknowledge criticism from anyone - let alone someone living in a National Trust house and therefore in regular contact with them and well aware of the way they did things!

" It is, though, important to keep this spat in proportion and context. It is a fact that the Trust is staffed by people who I have found to be thoroughly nice; who on balance look after their properties well. But they are, sadly but inevitably, deeply and incorrigibly bureaucratic which, considering their size and reach, is not surprising."

Meanwhile, relationships with the National Trust not withstanding, Shute was now home to the Pole-Carews and this meant that Christopher had to find ways in which to ' fill the time'…"otherwise, how could I finish each day having put it to good use?

" The loss of a formal focal point for one's raison d'etre, which is what a job has a way of providing, makes a substantial hole in one's existence which can be hard to overcome. It used to be quite common for people to give up and die when they retired and no longer had their work to sustain them. I found it took three to four years to adjust, in which time I cast around spasmodically for the possibility of employment - anything, so long as it could give me a focus for my energies - until one day it occurred to me that I had spent decades fighting to achieve successes for the benefit of others and now, as I looked back on it, **what on earth had it all been for?**

" Suddenly, none of it mattered any more.

" T. Bailey Forman - the company for which I had laboured so long and so hard - had been sold off, with all its staff who had mattered so much to me, to an organisation that seemed motivated mainly by the making of money.

" So?

" What was it to me?

" The answer was **nothing.** Not any more.

" So it was goodbye to a working environment and hello to good red blooded retirement, with lots of opportunity to fish and to shoot and to garden and to fiddle about making nice things out of wood."

However, Pole-Carew had not long settled for this new way of life before necessity forced him back into work.

He was a Lloyds ' Name ' and had invested his pay-off from T. Bailey Forman in that organisation. When Lloyds ran into extremely turbulent waters, Christopher lost £350,000 to £400,000.*

(* *Lloyds of London - a British insurance market in which multiple financial backers ; private investors, known as 'Names' , or corporations came together to pool and spread risk - suffered huge losses in the early 1990's, incurred mainly by asbestos claims in the United States. Thousands of 'Names' lost their money.*)

" I lost enough money to mean that I had to do something about getting some work," he says. " I chased around and by chance, Derek Winters said to me:

'Hey, have you seen this new free ad magazine called 'Loot' in London.'

" So, I got a copy and looked at it on the train coming back from London and thought 'Bloody Hell'. Someone had cracked it! The advertising business had come full circle so instead of people paying for their ads in a free sheet, you now had paid for sheets with free ads. Clever. I thought: ' This is good news'. It had originated in Canada and had been started in London by a chap called David Landau. I called him and told him I thought Nottingham would make a good place for one.

" I saw him and we agreed we would start a 'Loot' in the Nottingham area. It took some time to sort out exactly when it would launch and, unfortunately, by this time, another one called Ad Mag had opened up in Derby and was spreading across into Nottingham.

" The wholesale newsagents, who I knew of old, said that their experience was that whoever starts first wins. We started second and it never really got going as it should have."

Among Pole-Carew's team as managing director of the Nottingham 'Loot' were two star performers from his days with T Bailey Forman, David Williams on computers and Shirley Campbell on sales.

" I really enjoyed being back at work and getting stuck in and running something again. But we were on a hiding to nothing. We had missed our slot. It had taken too long to make the decision to go into Nottingham and when we did it was too late because the Derby AdMag had beaten us to it, otherwise we'd have eaten it!

" I did it for two years but there was really no point in my staying after that so I left."

Temporary financial difficulties sorted, it was time again to settle for the good life of rural retirement:" I became a member of Richard Marker's very pleasant shoot at Coombe, near Honiton and shot with him for several years until I joined another shoot that I had known originally in the late 1960's/ early 1970s from a connection that went back to when I had been at the Naval Base at Portland. So here I was completing a circle and coming round again some 25 years on. Lots of shooting - and Devon is as fine a place to enjoy the sport as you can find.

(" I first enjoyed shooting during my prep school days at Great Walstead but I didn't get many opportunities to pursue the sport in the Navy - *you don't shoot sea gulls. They're the souls of dead sailors!* - nor in my early civilian life. However, in Nottinghamshire, Tom Forman Hardy rented a lovely shoot in the north of the county, where he most generously invited me to shoot many times a season. Also, in the newsprint world, your suppliers would entertain their customers rather than waste money on advertising to such a minute number of people and so I would be invited to shoot with Charles de Selincourt and Michael Pelham, both of whom became close friends. We also fished together. I rented a shoot from Andrew Buchanan, who later became a highly effective Lord Lieutenant of Nottinghamshire, at his ancestral home of Hodstock Priory. It was small but compact and great fun and gave me enough days' shooting to be able to repay all the invitations I received. Shooting is an expensive sport; for example, an invitation to a medium day for eight guns planning to shoot a bag of, say, 150 pheasants would today cost around £400 to £500 a gun and it would be pro-rata in the 70s/80s so if you accepted such generous entertainment from someone you would naturally plan to return the compliment and that includes business invitations. Not good to be beholden.")

" One of my first truly Devon days was at David Hoare's lovely shoot at Luscombe. The first drive was not far from the house and the guns lined up down a valley which fell steadily from the right end of the line, where I was, to the left. The pheasants were being driven from the hilltop in front of us and as they moved further along so they flew ever higher above the guns, who were lower and lower. And there was I - nearer to the birds than anyone. After years of shooting in flat Nottinghamshire and Lincolnshire I looked up with horror: ' They can't possibly be within range,' I thought and then: ' If I miss them all (*as I expected to*) then I might as well go home straight away!' Fortunately, two or three pheasants did me the favour of coming down when I pointed my gun at them, so my reputation was saved. As the drive went on and the birds were driven over the rest of the guns, I noticed with deep relief that they ,too, were finding them at the limit of their range. What an introduction to shooting at its very finest!

"And so, I shot with Richard Marker for some happy years, which included achieving a right-and-left with woodcock and - very much to the point - witnessed, so that I could claim membership of the select Woodcock Club!

" I had, though, been asked if I would like to join the Minterne Shoot, just north of Cerne Abbas in Dorset. I knew Eddie and Dione Digby (*Lord Digby, who owned the Minterne Estate, his son Harry owns it now*) and many of the guns well - among them Harry Ross-Skinner (*H-J to everyone*) , a dear friend from my Portland days. I could not manage to shoot at both places so one had to go and I sadly left Richard's delightful shoot for Minterne.

" It was run in those days by Neil Lothian, very ably supported by (*Lieutenant- General Sir*) Richard Vickers, and was very much a military shoot. I think H-J and I , both being ex-Navy, were only allowed in to prove that the soldiers took a broad view on life and were prepared to mix with anyone!

" It was reckoned that you had to be a Colonel to get into the beating line, but Brigadiers were accepted as guns!

" Indeed, there was Brigadier Lipscombe (father of Sue, a close friend who incidentally married a Brigadier) who in the early days shot in the line then gave up shooting so went beating for the shoot and finally, when his knees were no longer what they had been, was driven to fixed points on the shoot where he acted as a 'stop' (*ie. standing where he would tap a stick against a tree to discourage pheasants from running past him. Then he would be moved to another place for the next drive and would tap away again.*) He was a delightful; person and totally dedicated to the sport.

" Neil Lothian died (*inconveniently during the Shooting Season* !) so Richard Vickers took over complete control and the Shoot continued happily until he decided to call it a day in 1999. But no-one wanted to take his place.

" The Minterne Estate has the most wonderful terrain for a shoot: it occupies the valley that runs north from Cerne Abbas beyond the Cerne Giant * and so has the continuation of the escarpment onto which the Cerne Giant is carved.

(* *The Cerne Giant - also known as The Rude Man - is a figure of a giant, naked, club wielding man carved into a steep hillside near the picturesque Dorset village of Cerne Abbas. One hundred and eighty feet (55m) high and one hundred and sixty seven feet (51m) wide, the ancient carving cuts through grass and earth into the underlying chalk.*)

" What a wonderful place to develop a ' high bird' shoot. I offered to run it and by default was accepted. And so began seven happy and fulfilling years influencing my favourite sport.   .

" The Guns in Richard Vickers' shoot were his contemporaries - and generally mine also, which meant that they were getting on a bit. If the Shoot was to continue, younger blood would have to be brought in, but tactfully. This turned out to be no problem thanks to the good nature of the current Guns most of whom, with increasing years, preferred the less challenging (but arguably much more sporting) Boundary Days that Richard organised.

" My first aim was to make better use of the Cerne escarpment which had never really been exploited to its limits. We no longer stood on the hillside around the cover that held the birds but down on the plain below, where they would come over us gliding, dropping and accelerating at a height of up to 150 feet. Mind blowing. But what a challenge! Get just *one* of those pheasants and you would dream about it for ever! I deliberately started each shooting day with one of the high drives in the hope of limiting the number of birds shot by destroying the Guns' self confidence, to which they objected and insisted on a lower 'warming up' drive first (*which by normal standards were themselves quite high.*) In fact everyone rapidly became used to these amazingly high birds; one found they caused the opposite effect - namely it became difficult to cope with low birds, which seemed as if they were on top of one.

" Another advantage of standing on the plain below the escarpment was that there was open space behind the Guns before the pens down the valley, which made for ideal conditions for picking up. It does seem to me that very few shoots pay proper attention to this aspect of the sport. There is nothing clever in dropping birds into places where the Pickers-up have a terrible job getting their dogs to the birds - or, indeed, so far back that it takes for ever. Nor is there any satisfaction in leaving wounded birds unpicked to die slowly or in the mouth of a fox. A nice open area gives both the Guns and the Pickers-up's dogs a fair chance to retrieve. They are all there to enjoy themselves as well!

" Shooting is such a fascinating sport with so many facets and enjoyed by all sorts and conditions of people. Dog lovers have the best of it because they can progress through beating to shooting to picking up, all the time having the joy of working their dogs. Those who cannot afford the very considerable expense of driven pheasants or partridges or grouse can belong to small self-run shoots with the Guns taking it in turns to beat or to shoot, or can go to Beaters' Days (*with the paying Guns beating for a change*) at the end of the season, a thank-you for having been with the Shoots through it - and that, incidentally, is where the 'experts' can see some amazingly good shooting!

" The Minterne Shoot became quite well known; in fact one to which visitors were delighted to accept an invitation, which is the ultimate justification for all the hard work in creating it - particularly the Keeper's. Our Keeper, Bob Scaife, has the ideal temperament including that essential deeply pessimistic approach to his job based on a certain knowledge that predators, misguided members of the public, disease and the weather work together in close harmony to ensure that his birds would achieve their ambition to die somehow, anyhow, before the season started! Bob and I got on extremely well on the basis that I could not his do *his* job, nor had any intention of trying to, and that he had a free hand as long as he never failed to ask *me* for the help I was there to give him. This way he would be able to give of his best - which he certainly did.

" Included in Bob's skills was the knack of ensuring a good supply of competent Beaters and we had a first class team amongst whom I am proud to number some good friends. I have always sought to keep the 'gap' between Guns and Beaters as small as possible; hence we lunched in the same room. The Guns table was the Wardroom; the Pickers-up's the Petty Officers' Mess and the Beaters' the Lower Deck - recognisable instantly by the silver candelabra on it! My shooting days started long ago with Guns and Beaters eating their packed lunches together, sitting on bales of straw in the stack yard with the dogs milling round. I never really took to 'smart' lunches for the Guns, which is very much the norm of course, with most of them not even acknowledging the existence of the Beaters. It is, I suspect, the penalty that Shooting has to pay for its costs increasing so dramatically over the years to the point where many shoots depend on Guns with high paying jobs in the City or equivalent, so that inevitably a smaller proportion have a country background - however good shots they may be.

" For all that, though, I shot for several years on Lord Lambton's lovely grouse moor where one lunched in a little vale high up on the moor with a gypsy caravan and a Range Rover full of delicious delights; with a long table covered with a white linen cloth and loaded end to end with silver and his Lordship's butler superintending everything impeccably, including a murmured query to our leader, Keith Darby, as to whether the gentlemen's dogs would care for the oxtail bones! *Who was it who said he liked eating a packed lunch on a straw bale?*

" I have stayed in an exquisitely appointed shooting lodge, where there wasn't a single bottle of wine to be seen. They were all magnums of the best vintages! (*Fond memories of Luton Hoo with Michael Pelham!*) And driving down to Beaulieu on a Friday evening with Charles de Selincourt and writing poetry on the way. Charles, incidentally, came to Minterne with his 16 bore loaded with No 1 shot - about nine pellets - and proceeded to slaughter our highest pheasants, occasionally muttering to himself that he wasn't killing them as cleanly as he would like!

" Sadly my shooting days were brought to a somewhat abrupt end by a serious injury sustained in a road accident on a fishing holiday in New Zealand in 2007, though in fact I think had really shot enough by the time the accident happened so the ending was, in a way, convenient. It was harder to break with the people than the sport. Farewell Bob, Keith and Mike and Jackie as representing the Beaters, and the Guns, H-J most of all, and the wonderful Pickers-up: Susan and Sue and Ursula and Gay, run so brilliantly by Richard Vickers and David Cunningham. I'm certainly not walking out of their lives."

Though ruled out of shooting by that injury, Christopher Pole-Carew maintains an active involvement in fishing," a sport I came to rather late in life."

He recalls: " My first serious fishing venture was to Canada with Charles de Selincourt to the Miramichi in New Brunswick, the Rocky Brook, to be precise. This was one of a number of trips that the newsprint manufacturers organised for the 'top brass of the newspaper world' who were their customers. For years I had resolutely refused invitations on the grounds that I couldn't possibly repay such hospitality, as I did with shooting, and would therefore feel beholden and compromised in my buying of newsprint for the Nottingham papers. Eventually, I realised that I was almost certainly the only newspaperman to refuse suce invitations and that I was missing wonderful occasions to meet off duty with one's fellows, including the Fleet Street bosses, who one normally met only very rarely.

So I said yes '... but don't think it will affect my newsprint buying.' To which the reply was: ' Don't be stupid, Christopher. You're only on this earth once. Come on! ' So I did - and so started a passion for salmon fishing that has taken me to fish in Canada and Newfoundland; Oregon, Pacific North-West; Chile and Argentina; South Africa and New Zealand and, of course, England and Scotland. Largely on holiday with an uncomplaining Gill, who likes to cast a line herself.

" With the delightful Canadian Ronnie Blair I went to Labrador and the Hunt River; with Michael Pelham I learned what a wonderful river the Spey is (and had a five pound grilse leap spinning in the air eleven times - *and I got him!*); On the Cree one morning, Gill caught a large stone, she told me (she knew for a fact that she didn't catch salmon!) but it kept on moving. I went to help her and we reeled in enough line to take the fish down and out to sea - but she'd got it. **Seven pounds!** What do you do when you have achieved an ambition like that? You celebrate, of course. So Gill took the afternoon off to go shopping. I took her rod with the same fly on; went to the same place and caught another. The fly was a Blue Charm and the water was falling after three days of rain. In South Africa, we went up into Drackensberg Mountains to a Game Farm, which also had fishing. They had an adorable tame otter who would come into the restaurant and cadge sausages off the guests, lying on its back to eat them. In the middle of the night it left its lake outside our window, jumped in and dried itself on Gill's blanket! In return, I managed to catch a medium sized trout from its own lake - but nothing from the river.

"All fishermen can tell stories and go on and on until it bores people - non-fishermen who don't know what you're talking about (*what is a Blue Charm, anyway*?) and aren't interested and fishermen because you are taking up time that could be much better spent telling their own stories. So I try to avoid telling them!"

To Christopher, living at Shute in glorious Devon, it seemed that retirement would not be complete without acquiring a bit of fishing of his own…" very difficult indeed to achieve. So I got myself appointed Secretary and Treasurer of the Axe River Fishing Association. They were thankful; nobody wanted either job under any circumstances! This way, I surmised, I would be one of the very first to learn about it if a bit of the Axe came up for sale. It worked! Bill Knapman was selling his land at Middle West Water north of Axminster, up the Yarty, the main tributary of the Axe. He knew I wanted some fishing, so it never got within a mile of the open market or an estate agent. It was mine - plus 10 acres and a totally derelict 15th Century cottage. Either I did up the cottage and let it or I had a half a mile of seriously expensive fishing on the Yarty!

So I did up the cottage, which is only a few yards from our bit of river.

" The Axe isn't a particularly good river for fishing, although it was once famed as one of the finest small salmon rivers in England. That was before chemical fertilisers poisoned the water and the Labour Government forced the sale of so many estates to their tenants who had never had to care for the river and had no intention of starting; and their cattle broke the banks down; and the earth settled on the bottom in the redds and killed the salmon and trout eggs before they could hatch. This happened all over the Westcountry, so it wasn't special, but the Axe was blessed by being a fine enough river to merit the attention of no less a body than the

Ministry of Agriculture, Fisheries and Food. So they put a trap on the river in 1963 (*number of salmon recorded passing through:* **747**) and by 1983, in spite of massive restocking they were all but extinct: Destroyed by Government interference.

" Never mind. We do our best for our little river. We stock, though doing so until the water is cleaner and the banks stable enough is a waste of time and money but it matters to Andy Locke, the Environment Agency's incredibly dedicated and knowledgeable water bailiff, so we do it..

" I managed eventually to off-load being Secretary and Treasurer after many years, but in the meantime I had become a committee member of the South West Rivers Association (the 17 rivers of the South West) and also a trustee of the Westcountry Rivers Trust and I'm now President, via being Chairman, of the Axe Vale Rivers Association.

In 1998, when he was Secretary of the Axe Vale Rivers Association, Pole-Carew published an article entitled ' *A Little Bit Of Axe History.*' Some would say that only Christopher Pole-Carew could write **controversially** under such a heading and typically, the article pulled no punches.

He wrote:

" In 1844 George Pulman published his famous work, The Book Of The Axe, and in it he tells us of the weir at Coaxdon, one and a half miles above the Weycroft mill: ' *At Coaxdon Mill weir, about the year 1820, two salmon of ten pounds each and one of fourteen pounds, with a cart load of salmon fry, were landed at one and the same haul in a trammel net. I myself remember that on one occasion fifteen or sixteen years subsequent to 1820, the fry were at the same weir destroyed in such enormous quantities that after supplying the tables far and near the residue were thrown about the fields for manure.*'

" In 1860 evidence was taken (in fact, from the same George Pulman in the case of the Axe) on behalf of the Government about the state of the nation's rivers with the intention - which came to pass - of setting up Boards of Conservators, generally one for each river. This was the first organised governmental attempt to protect or conserve our rivers.

" The section on the Axe tells us about the rebuilding of the mill weir at Coaxdon in 1842 and how it totally blocked the river with a perpendicular structure 12 to 14 feet in height, so that the 30 miles of abundant spawning grounds above were completely denied to returning salmon, leaving only the 10 miles below Weycroft. In addition , ' *the miller thinking he was privileged to kill fish* (in the pool below the weir) *at all times.*'

" In 1872, the Inspectors of Salmon Fisheries (England and Wales) reported that salmon ' *had diminished greatly, the cause unaccountable unless it be the supposed pollution of the river Axe, near its mouth, by the sewage of the town of Seaton, which is its chief - if not only - cause.*'

" Let us journey down river to Axe Bridge, near Colyford and come forward in time by about a hundred years, to 1956 - but before taking up at that point, let us refer to a promise made in the 1930s by the Ministry of Agriculture, Fisheries and Food to the National Association of Fisheries Boards that a full scale investigation would be carried out into ways and means of improving salmon rivers.

" My next source of information is a paper by Derek Braggins, our Vice Chairman, on the MAFF trap: ' The Axe and its Problems', written about six years ago, which concisely sums up that critical period in the river's history:

" In 1956, the Ministry of Agriculture, Fisheries and Food (MAFF) belatedly, thanks to the War, honouring its promise, decided to place a trap on the Axe in order to tag and study the salmon population of that river for the benefit of the country as a whole. Indeed, it was considered that the research would be of international importance.

" Assurances were given to riparian owners that fishing rights would not be adversely affected and in fact there was a secondary aim to these researches - namely to carry out an experimental stocking with the intention of doubling the Axe's salmon population.

" What then happened?

" In **1963** the record showed that **747** salmon had passed through the trap. In **1973** the number had fallen to **179**. By **1983** the salmon were all but **extinct**, in spite of massive restocking from Scotland.

" Contemporary accounts tell us that some Axe tagged salmon were found in various West Country rivers, presumably having abandoned their native home, tributaries below the trap were crowded, whilst a few managed the journey up river by going round the trap during floods.

" **In twenty years the Axe had had the last of its once bountiful salmon population completely destroyed - this time by an apparent ally.**

" This is not to place to examine in depth what went wrong: many factors contributed to the decline of salmon all over the West Country at this time and there is no reason to believe that rivers with similar agriculture within their catchment areas (eg. the Piddle or the Tone) were any less polluted. But they kept their salmon, albeit reduced in number. The Axe was the only river to have its salmon stock totally wiped out and the only river to have been blessed with a MAFF scientific study - and trap.

" In 1961, the Axe Vale Fishing Association (now more accurately called the Axe Vale Rivers Association) was set up with the aim of restoring the river to its condition before the placing of the infamous trap. This today continues to be the Association's first and overriding objective.

" For many years nothing worthwhile was or could be achieved: MAFF preferred to withdraw their staff from the river, they ceased to support the restocking and hoped that all would be conveniently forgotten - which is better and more lasting than being forgiven and clearly cheaper!

" Meanwhile, the official guardians and protectors of the Axe had become the South West Water Authority: the river's largest water abstractors, also owners of the aforementioned Seaton sewage works and, like MAFF, part of the Government network. What hope of a chance did the poor little Axe have?

" No saga is complete without some good news to offset a story so far filled with unrelieved disaster. In 1989 a Good Fairy waved her political wand and the Water Authorities were privatised (bringing solid happiness to some and higher water bills to many) and in the process their responsibility for protecting the rivers was taken from them and given to the newly formed National Rivers Authority : the first true friends in officialdom since the setting up of the Conservators in the 1860s.

" Time has passed and the NRA has now become just a division of the Environment Agency with a field staff reduced, like the salmon they strive to protect, to scarcity level. Not on balance good news for the rivers, but mitigated by the retention of some of the very hard working and dedicated NRA people, with their deep knowledge and love of our rivers (more especially, we like to think, of the Axe!) The Axe may not yet be getting the support that we of the AVRA still consider it is clearly entitled to, but with a much revitalised Association combined with the support of the South West Rivers Association, we have now for some three years seen small but authentic indications of success in the restocking programme; our very own Axe salmon returning from sea to spawn in their redds. A 12 pound cock fish with a telltale clipped dorsal fin has already been caught earlier this year, on its return from the sea, and released without leaving the water!

" If I have harped on the salmon to the exclusion of all other inhabitants of the Axe it is because we believe that if a river is healthy enough for salmon (next to the grayling, the most fastidious of all fish) to thrive in it continuously then the surrounding environment must by definition be in good shape. If a river can support a goodly stock of salmon and trout then you will find that it can and will support, for example, the elusive otter, the water vole, mayflies, kingfishers, rare grasses and so on – but, please, not all those insatiable newcomers, the cormorants, so apparently beloved by the RSPB , a mere twenty of whom consume in a year more fish than the Axe's entire annual stocking programme.

" In 1994, the Axe Vale Rivers Association spent from its then 59 members' pockets and by their and the Axe Fly Fishers' labours the equivalent of £33,700 - the only private individuals who spend a single penny or actually work a single hour on our Axe Vale's rivers physically to care for them; a figure, incidentally, that very comfortably exceeds the Environment Agency's comparable expenditure.

" If all the legions who dictate to us, or give us so much ' un-researched' advice were to join in actually working alongside us in caring for our little Axe, what a wonderful river it would once again become!"

Today, as combatant and intolerant of bureaucrats as ever, Pole-Carew still cares passionately about his local rivers and says proudly:

" Owning a bit of river is great fun. Anyone can fish, but to few of us is given the opportunity to change a river; to make pools; put in weirs; plant trees, which I do constantly, though it's best not to let the authorities know of your activities. Those who spend their lives telling us what we may do from the comfort of their offices do so largely from a basis of near total ignorance. English Heritage are, in my experience, among the worst, with English Nature close behind. The Environment Agency are pretty bad, but whilst they may not know what (*with the exception of their very fine field staff*) they are doing, they do actually in their hearts care a lot about our rivers and it shows: the Axe has had a lot of help from them on a broad front – but if you want to improve your fishing in simple, time-honoured and practical ways, don't tell. That way, no-one gets upset.

" It will, therefore, come as no surprise to anyone to learn that the 'concrete pool' on the Yarty is considered to be one of the best sea trout pools on the Axe System and can be found at Middle West Water.

" Making weirs also keeps grandchildren happy!"

And so, caring for Shute, playing host to visitors and occasional VIP guests; falling out with bureaucrats; shooting, fishing; DIYing on a scale to turn lesser men white with fear; being an active church member and a church warden; serving on Rivers organisations and parish councils, with several stints as Chairman; travelling extensively and always being ready to help his children and grandchildren, all eventually passed for **retirement (?)** for the incredible Christopher Pole-Carew.

In retirement, as throughout the rest of his life, was able to satisfy his strict mantra to **Get Something Definite To Do** every day to such an extent that his mentor, the eccentric Great Walstead headmaster RJ Mowll, who drilled that discipline into him when he was a small boy, must have looked down from his study in the sky with great satisfaction – though it could be argued that, as Pole-Carew has now obeyed that order **every single day since 1939** (ie. More than **25,000 times**) it's high time old Mowll allowed him a day off!

Life in retirement at Shute was everything Christopher Pole-Carew would have wished for himself.

But two seismic events were to shatter the relative calm of that life.

In 2004, Christopher and Gill's youngest daughter Camilla ('Milly'), her husband, Dominic Welby and their children Maria,17, Octavia ('Tavy'), 14, and Hector, 11, were spending Christmas at Galle, on the southern tip of Sri Lanka. On the morning of December 26th, Camilla, Dominic and Hector were just getting up in their beach hut, some 20 yards from the water's edge. Maria and Tavy were in an adjacent hut. Up a tree nearby, their hut boy Ranga was getting coconuts for their breakfast. He happened to glance seawards and to his horror saw an enormous wave sweeping in towards the beach.

Galle was about to be hit by the Indian Ocean Tsunami, which killed 225,000 people in 11 countries.

Young Ranga was so astonished by the sight of the giant wave that he fell out of the tree. Normally, that fall would have injured him. It didn't. Because what should have been dry land below was already deep in water pushed ahead by the wave.

His immediate concern was for the huts that were his responsibility and for their occupants. He dashed down to the nearest one, got Maria and Tavy out of bed and rushed them inland to safety with his family.

In the other hut, Camilla was woken up by water bursting through the door and then the floor of the hut 'exploded as if a grenade had gone off.'

The wave had hit them. The hut was totally destroyed.

Camilla grabbed Hector but he was swept out of her arms seawards. He caught hold of a wooden stump, all that remained of the framework of the hut, and hung on until the wave subsided.

In the pause before the next rush of water struck, Camilla, Dominic and Hector took refuge in a concrete shower hut, between two destroyed wooden ones.

The next surge hit the concrete hut with such force that it crumbled on impact. Camilla, Dominic and Hector were tossed around in the swirling water along with pieces of shattered concrete, one of which pinned Hector under water by his leg. Another slashed Dominic's leg down the shin bone as if it had been filleted.

The water retreated, shifting the lump of concrete holding Hector and he was released. The surges then steadily reduced in strength and in a suitable gap, they pushed Hector through a window so he could run up the beach to safety.

Eventually, calm came. Camilla and Dominic left their shelter and made their way up the beach. Dominic, who was in complete shock, insisted on searching the beach for their possessions but the only thing they found was an ipod, which had been a family Christmas present.

Curiously, Camilla's sunglasses, lensed because she is short sighted, had stayed gripped in her hand throughout the ordeal and as she walked up the beach, they were the only thing she was wearing.

(Camilla recalls how, later, she was often asked : *'How did you feel walking up the beach naked?'* To which she replied: ' **When you have lost all of your possessions - clothes, passport, money, credit cards, identity almost; your husband is badly wounded and you've lost two daughters, who are possibly dead, what you look like is not exactly your main concern!'**)

At the top of the beach the local people, despite their own horrendous ordeal, gave them love, kindness and clothes. Camilla was given a sarong by Ranga's aunt, with whom he lived, a precious garment that was 'quite possibly the other half of her entire wardrobe.'

Maria and Tavy were there. They were safe and unharmed. Hector, too, had made his way to safety. The family had survived a disaster in which many thousands of others had perished.

There were no doctors available to treat Dominic's injury, only a German visitor who gave rudimentary First Aid, and Maria tore the

'Somebody Had To Do It'

bottom off Camilla's sarong to make a bandage for her father's leg. The gash he had suffered did not bleed until some four hours later - the result, he was told, of his system being in shock.

The locals were convinced that more waves would come, so everybody moved up into the jungle, onto higher ground.

A close friend of Camilla and Dominic, Henri(etta) Tatham, managed the Sun House, one of the most luxurious hotels in Sri Lanka. She had sent people down to search for the Welbys. When they were found, they were taken up to the hotel where another family, who were occupying a suite in the Sun House annexe, moved out so that Camilla, Dominic and the children could have space together.

At supper time, all five of them trooped into the dining room - three of them covered in scrapes and scars and wearing whatever they had been given down on the beach; Camilla, who is six feet tall, draped in a sarong meant for a considerably shorter Sri Lankan with the bottom torn off, wore no shoes. She was unable to get any until she got back to England. Two Indian girls from Delhi moved up to give them room to sit down at a table.

Camilla's main aim was to get the family back to England. Dominic's leg required medical attention but there were so many Sri Lankans desperately needing hospital treatment. There was nothing they could do to help. So far better, she reasoned, to get out of the way.

Henri organised a taxi to take them to Colombo. She had managed to book a flight for the five of them and the British High Commission were helping. When the taxi arrived, Camilla says she put Dominic and the two girls on board then went, with Hector, to say thanks and farewell to Henri. When she got back to the taxi, she found that two people had occupied the remaining space, with their luggage - and refused to budge. **They** were going to Columbo, they told her, and had no intention of getting out. So it was **her** taxi? Too bad!

Camilla stayed behind and helped with the influx of displaced tourists flooding into the hotel until some journalists offered her and Hector a lift in their van. Driving out of Galle, they saw lorries piled high with dead bodies.

Dominic and Maria and Tavy went to Columbo and found themselves a small hotel where they waited until Camilla and Hector joined them two days later. They had missed their flight and struggled to get another one - but eventually they got home.

Back at Shute, Christopher and Gill Pole-Carew heard the news of the disaster on Boxing Day and knew that Sri Lanka had been hit, but - says Christopher: " I went into ' don't want to know' mode and convinced myself and half convinced Gill that Galle was too far round the southern tip of Sri Lanka to have been affected."

It was not until the Welbys got home that the full horror of their experience hit Camilla's parents and Christopher will readily tell you of his deep gratitude for the people who helped his daughter and her family.

" Everybody helped, wherever it was needed. Good Samaritans don't understand about differences: local or visitor, rich or poor, creed or colour. They only understood that people were hurt and in need of help - and that they gave in abundance, regardless."

All five of them were emotionally scarred by the experience. It took Hector many months to recover from bad nightmares; Tavy gained a few grey hairs and denied anything had happened. Maria had to face her AS Levels having lost most of her notes. Camilla, with typical Pole-Carew resolve, strove to ensure that, as a family, they stuck together.

The emotional effect on Dominic Welby was particularly intense, as can be gathered by reading an account of the experience, which he was encouraged to write "in order to get a handle on what had happened."

Dominic's version of events differs, in part, from Camilla's, upon which the story as told above is based. That's possibly a result of the terror, stress, chaos and confusion which must abound in such a dreadful catastrophe.

Dominic wrote:

" Some hours after we had escaped to higher ground I had Peter Gabriel's refrain 'when the flood comes, you get no warning' locked in my mind and then I am stumbling again, tears predominate, sentences will not be finished.

" He was right. We had the shutters on our beach hut closed against the night-time mosquito raids. The noise of the sea seemed loud to my drowsy post-Christmas senses. But that's OK, big full moon, high tide, perhaps every now and then the sea would run up beyond its usual range.

" The next wave lapped up over the verandah and leaked into our bedroom. I was quite cross at the inconvenience, picked a few things off the floor and stomped back into the bedroom ,closing the door.

" The next wave changed everything. Suitcases and clothes were swimming. Milly screamed 'come over to the concrete' and as we did so (

Hector, aged 11, was inside with us) the water lifted the floorboards and we had no more bedroom. We made our stand in the concrete shower room, with two air vents and each other to cling on to. Milly saw our daughters escape but her screams for help could not be heard over the din. I am very cross by now, which is crazy but gives me strength. Hector is screaming now. I don't know why. The last wave had landed concrete on his toe, trapping him and submerging him. As he screams and the Tsunami inhales again, he is freed and for a sickening moment adrift, then our hands lock.

" As the next wave strikes Milly points out the pane of glass in the roof which is big enough for Hector. We survive the wave and anger helps me to slide the glass out of the way. Apparently we then pushed him onto the roof, though I can't remember. I remember the waves stopping. I knew they were safe. Two of the family looking after us asked where the children were. I could tell them that all mine were safe.

" I looked out at the now vast expanse of beach and reef that the returning waters had exposed and had an admin moment. I found and put on a soggy sarong, then went on a mission to find our belongings. First is a single purple paper chain from our beautifully decked-out cabana of the day before. Then I look out onto the reef and spot a six inch cube which, unbelievably, turns out to be one of the Ipods which was everyone's duty free Christmas present. It is still sealed when Maria (17) opens it later in the hills. The contents are dry, pristine. Tsunami-proof packaging. Well done guys!

" I keep looking, although now I am being advised to desist. But we need passports, something, anything. Milly has returned. She had thought I was dead. 'What's that?' as she points to muscles in my leg which normally I prefer to keep covered. 'Oh, shit.' And now I do desist.

"Apparently there is another wave to come so we cross the wrecked railway line and coast road into jungle and higher land. I see no other injuries. I alone will be slowing others up if we have to move at speed again. We meet up with a small group of tourists and Sinhalese and decide we have come far enough for now. There is a phone, but it will only receive. We share a cigarette. Hector is convinced he's going to die. I start humming my tune.

" Precious bottled water is poured over my wound, which is covered with aloe vera and bandaged. My leg rests on the seat of an old tricycle. My new friends, Jerome and Flick, survivors from the cabana next to ours, lie on the ground beside us. His leg is bleeding and I wonder, absently, why mine is not.

" In the few days we have been in Sri Lanka we met Zoe, who is rebuilding a house close to where we are now grouped. I am helped down to what is three quarters building site, but Zoe has offered her bedroom - a beautiful sanctuary for the remaining daylight hours of Boxing Day. Then fruit arrives. Then tea.

" Of the many angels who aided me that day and in that place, the most recurring was a German tourist who consistently offered up his medical expertise regardless of his own discomfort. Before I went down to Zoe's house, he had aggravated his hiatus hernia by tying cloth across the arms of a chair so that my leg could do better than the tricycle, to which I had got rather over-attached.

" Shortly after I had been deposited on Zoe's bed, he arrived with two friends and - amazingly - a mosquito net which they then ingeniously rigged up around ceiling fans and shelving, keeping the dread leg safe from further predators. Then he asked for a torch - and it was inspection time. The mantra was 'fleisch wound - no problem' which was fine by me, especially when accompanied by pain killer and anti-biotic. I lost my precious aloe vera but it seemed a small price to pay for the western bush medicine taking me under its wing.

" Outside my sanctuary the mood was not so sanguine, yet my medic angel seemed confident enough. If there was to be another big wave it was most unlikely to be so high as to cause us trouble. I would stay where I was for the night unless the wound deteriorated, in which case we would get to Galle hospital. This was wishful thinking because we would never get transport; because Galle hospital was manic inside and because the crowds outside Galle hospital looking for relatives within were so intense that you couldn't get in. Still, we didn't know any of that so it seemed like a pretty good plan.

" Unfortunately, as darkness fell the perception of risk changed and I was to be moved to higher ground ' as a precaution.' Even here, we were again given a mosquito net for protection by people yet again putting mine and my family's needs before my own. Not that I'm especially grateful at the time - three cushions and a concrete floor and no light was not my idea of where I wanted to be on Boxing Day.

" Many Simbalese had moved on a further kilometre inland and had taken refuge in a Buddhist temple. I wanted my children to do the same but it was too dark. This felt like our last stand and after a difficult conversation about reincarnation and finding each other again, we started singing - Gilbert & Sullivan, Tom Lehrer, Christmas carols, Beatles. And we waited.

" Then to our complete amazement two more angels, Kokila and Smithy, appeared at the doorway. ' Come on. We've come to take you to the Sun House ' - a hotel nestling in the heights outside Galle and run by our close friend Henri. How had they got to us? ' There's a mini-bus waiting for us. Let's go.' I went to say goodbye to my German rescuer and we left. Part of me is dreading another journey after the last appalling climb uphill, but going down is almost entirely painless - for which I am extremely grateful.

" The main road was still blocked so we took an intricate route through darkened but peaceful villages. I just hold Kokila's hand. I don't have any words. Eventually, we reach Galle and I get my first glimpse of the bigger picture. The fish market no longer exists, the town is a mess and pretty much deserted apart from police getting on top of sporadic outbreaks of looting. I am spared the horrors of the bus station where water levels had risen too high too quickly for escape. I will learn later that only ten per cent of Simbalese can swim.

" But now we have reached sanctuary and Henri's warm embrace. She is still running a fairly functioning hotel without power or mains water. Amazingly at this time the phone is working and we talk to and reassure parents. We find ourselves back in the hotel where we had been 24 hours ago enjoying a Christmas feast. Tonight some guests are superb and one family even hand over a room for us to use. Others give us our first taste of indifference. They are here to have a good time. We are an embarrassment. Well, we do all look terrible. We're too tired to care and Henri gets us away from that ugliness.

" We hear Smithy's tale of a yoga class that ended up in the trees, of rescuing children and of making choices no-one should have to make. Milly, Smithy and I sit with our legs up on a coffee table. They're not pretty but it's quite funny. We giggle a bit, smoke a bit and eventually call it a day. Milly and I lie close together for as long as we can then we too must attempt sleep in our own ways.

" Next day the phones are down, we cannot reach the High Commission. Maria is desperate to leave. My agenda is different and basically consists of trying to persuade someone to agree to stitch up my leg. There is plenty of vodka, which apparently is for the wound and there are a few glum faces at this mis-use of resources. Mid- afternoon I am told a doctor is coming so I anticipate her work by downing whisky fast. But it is not to be. The wound is not clean and so must not be closed up. Get to the UK on the next flight is her prognosis.

" This means splitting the family up as Milly looks like she is getting blood poisoning and must rest where she is. A mini bus arrives to take our new friends, who have given us their room and a bunch of clothes, to the airport. There is space for three of us. Hector and Milly stay behind. For the next seven hours I am guzzling pain killers like sweets and then we have reached the airport. The flights are full. Yes, but surely, this man is injured. I'm sorry the flights are full. If surgery is so important it'll have to be in a Colombo hospital. Only one had appropriate facilities and, no - obviously the government can't foot the bill. Unfortunately for me the banks in the UK are closed on both December 27 and 28. Suddenly I'm worried again .

" Happily Tookoo, an angel from the High Commission, finds our sorry party at the airport and takes us under her wing. We are taken to the local hospital, given mattresses in a conference room for the night and a room next day. It's a very long day spent next to the phone watching CNN and getting a still wider picture. By eight that evening we've managed to sort a flight for Maria, who was due to fly that night anyway, but nothing else. Our middle daughter Tavy, who has been extraordinarily strong and upbeat throughout the crisis, is now beginning to crack. Transport which had been arranged for Milly and Hector to get to us from Galle is sabotaged when their seats are stolen by others. I'm beginning to lose interest.

" Strange things then began to happen. I call Henri at 10 to give her the news that Maria is confirmed to fly and discover Milly and Hector were now travelling on another bus. I do the time calculations and establish they will get here after the two London flights have left . But amazingly this is wrong, they complete the seven hour journey in four and arrive just as we are about to leave with Maria and attempt to beg for seats for us too. Our luck is bouncing up again as we discover that Thomas Cook have chartered a flight to rescue the needy (all unpaid volunteers cutting short their Christmas break) and we are squeezed onto the flight by wonderful Peter from the High Commission who has clearly got calm-in-a-crisis well figured out and gave us steadily improving odds as to our chances of getting home that night.

" We got to Bahrain and all applauded the efforts of the flight crew. The refuelling was fast and then we reached Gatwick and for me a series of hospitals and reunions. Some can understand what we've been through, some cannot. Would I be able to if it was friends of mine? I just don't know. I do know we have been amazingly lucky and I feel a strange responsibility not to waste that luck. I have found out that, at bottom, I'm not the coward I thought I was and that feels good, too.

" I confess I have always led a fiercely independent life and my motto has always been never to be beholden to anyone. I now recognise this was a mistake. I have learnt to trust and to receive and I feel much better for it."

Six weeks later, Dominic again committed his feelings to writing - this time with a very great deal of poignancy. He wrote:

" Our bodies are 95 per cent water. My body has retained the memory of its sister wave. Sometimes I feel crashing against my back, sometimes the swell becomes a calm. At 9am on Boxing Day morning the intangible was stripped out of me as the water forced its way through my earthly form.

" To start off with I felt ghostly in crowds. People walked through me, shattering my fragile soul into unattached particles. I am finding it hard to gather them back together and I do not feel that I have the right to exist on this plane. Now I am an empty shell of bone and pulp that functions soullessly.

" I understand all that I do have. I am lucky. I did not lose my loved ones. I am alive. I am at a loss and I need to grieve. But what for? In quiet moments I cry for my friend Mike Hearn, he has gone. But for myself? For my family?

" I went to the edge and knew the moment of acceptance as the waves passed through me. It's not a matter of giving up the will to live because when the opportunity arose to survive I took it. It's the sure knowledge that when Death reaches out you must take his hand and walk his path.

" You might tell me to look on the positive side, that perhaps part of me did die that morning, that I was scoured clean and that I will rise again with new purpose. But for now I am empty, devoid of emotions that I need to function in the world in which I have been washed up.

" Friends are loving and giving everything they have. When they hug me I pull my stomach in because my Hara has been dried out by sea salt. Each day is taken on gently and lived and breathed with thanks.

I don't sleep well. I rest and let events wash over me. Calm and silence are important, natural sounds are beautiful. I am waiting for time to heal the scars and for my body's memory to absorb the wave."

As the world started to come to terms with the horror of the Tsunami, friends of the Welbys in Sri Lanka banded together to organise a charity which concentrated on restoring people's lives; particularly getting businesses up and running again. Practical help, such as putting a fridge into a resaurant behind where their huts had been so that the owner could open it up again; getting a brickworks going; organising the design and production of fishing boats to replace those that had been lost; organising camps for the homeless; rebuilding a Muslim village, which had lost 500 of its community of 3,000; dealing sensitively with cultural issues, like the need for widows to stay indoors for 30 days' mourning - not easy when houses had been wiped out.

Then, when the anniversary of the disaster came around at Christmas, 2005, Camilla and Dominic wondered how they could express their gratitude to Ranga, the young lad who had saved the lives of their two daughters and whose aunt had clothed them in their hour of need.

Should they give money?

However big the sum, it's a tip, whatever it might be called - and that would be degrading; you don't buy off a Good Samaritan.

Ranga was an orphan, brought up by his aunt. He had no prospects; his family being at the bottom of the social system. His chances of getting a decent job of any sort were remote. His role in life was destined to be no more than helping out, here and there, perhaps once or twice a week. But Camilla and Dominic found out that Ranga had a wish which was less a realistic ambition, more an unattainable dream - to drive a three-wheeled motorised taxi (driver in front, two passengers side by side behind) called a Tuk Tuk, after the sound of a two-stroke engine.

So, they sent enough money to Ranga's family for them to go to the Tuk Tuk factory where Ranga chose his own green 'Reggae' Tuk Tuk - with the biggest speakers south of Galle! Camilla has been back and ridden in it, speakers blaring out, fare waived, of course! It is apparently a huge status symbol among his friends and it has allowed him to land a job ferrying around clients from smart beach villas and bringing money in for the family.

Sadly, for Camilla and Dominic themselves there was not such a happy ending. They split up and were divorced not long after.

Christopher Pole-Carew and Gill believe that it might well have been the Tsunami " that caused our much loved son-in-law Dominic to change and turn away from Camilla, leading to their divorce."

The next event to shatter the routine of life at Shute occurred in February, 2007.

Christopher and Gill took a holiday in New Zealand, via Sydney, Australia, where they were pampered by Christopher's Crane, Saville and Raffles cousins for a week. Christopher had a hankering to visit Christchurch because two of his ancestors (great grandfather William Henry Pole-Carew and great, great grandfather William, Lord Littleton) had been founders of that city.

The main object of the holiday, however, was fishing.

They stayed with friends, the Dentons in the middle of South Island before setting off on their fishing trip, planning to stay at B & Bs as they worked their way around the island.

" The first was at Arrowtown," says Christopher, " comfy and very pleasant; no fishing that day, just a little enjoyable retail therapy….

" The next day, I took myself off, complete with guide, to fish the Tekapo river; crystal clear water, nine to ten feet deep, with rainbow trout cruising around just off the bottom looking like miniature sharks. Not easy to catch. The fish weren't stupid and visibility, up and down, was perfect. I put a dry fly, a bomber - large, brown and fuzzy - onto the surface above a trout. It moved up and down the river beneath and came a foot or two nearer the surface. Another cast - nothing happened. Then, **wow!** The trout came from eight feet down like an Exocet and took the fly clear out of the water. Hooked and fighting! Seven minutes later I had him: five and a half pounds of fighting rainbow trout. It was a fish to remember. A fish to lie in the bath and dream about. A special fish."

It was also the last fish he was to catch on that trip.

And very nearly the last fish he *ever* caught.

The next day, after a lazy morning driving and fishing and a gentle lunch before proceeding, the Pole-Carews were driving sedately along the Hast - St Joseph road, a very quiet stretch which normally carries very little traffic.

Gill was at the wheel. Christopher was dozing. And Gill fell asleep.

Their car careered off the road and came to rest, leaning on its right side, in deep undergrowth. Christopher had been knocked out. Gill was unhurt, apart from minor bruises, having been saved by an airbag. But she was trapped and was only going to be able to get out by clambering over Christopher, who had clearly not fared so well. He came to long enough to say: " Gill. Turn off the engine!" Then fell back into unconsciousness.

His neck was broken.

Gill, realising he was very badly hurt, dared not clamber over him to get out of the car.

There then ensued a series of the most incredible and fortunate coincidences.

Despite the usually near-deserted nature of this stretch of road, they had been followed by a car carrying two Turks (*"from Chippenham - where else!"*) who, despite being a very long way behind, had managed to see the Pole-Carew's dark green car disappear into the undergrowth.

In another accident, just a few weeks later, on a similar stretch of that same road, a car left the road and was not found for four days - but on this occasion, the Turks were able to flag down another motorist soon after they had stopped.

And this car contained a qualified nurse from Holland.

Two strokes of exceptionally good fortune. Then came a third.

Along came another car. And this car contained two paramedics from a local film unit.

Then, amazingly, yet another car appeared on the scene.

And at this stage, the dramatic sequence of events began to qualify as a miracle: This car contained a doctor from Seattle.

Someone obtained a machete and that was used to cut through the dense undergrowth which was preventing Gill from getting out of the car.

Then, with extreme caution , they lifted Christopher out of the vehicle and carried him to the road. He was drifting in and out of consciousness and told his rescuers he needed a whisky. As they worked, with immense care, around him,very gently lowering him down and laying him on the road, he told them that he was fine and they could all go now - except for one of the Turks who was thoughtfully holding a sunshade over him… " because he's doing a grand job!"

He and Gill were taken by ambulance to a helicopter which flew them to a hospital in Greymouth. There, Christopher was examined and x-rayed before medics decided he was too badly hurt for them to cope with so he had to go by plane and ambulance to Christchurch Hospital. For this journey, which was very risky in his condition, he was wrapped up in black plastic, bound with brown sticky tape so that he couldn't move and in one of his few moments of consciousness on the trip, he remembers thinking : " What a great way to travel - as a parcel! "

In Christchurch Hospital, he spent six days in intensive care while a collapsed lung, which had been punctured by a broken rib, got well enough for him to be able to take anaesthetic.

Then came a complex major operation. Two broken vertebrae in his neck were mended and bolted together. The surgeon, Mr Jeremy Evison, went in through the front of the neck. (" So nine grandchildren can now say that *their* Grandad has had his throat cut and lived!")

There followed 15 days in the Trauma Ward - " a very happy time and really a wonderful experience"- during which this miraculously irrepressible man (then aged 75, let's not forget) recovered so rapidly that he is, with typically animated enthusiasm, able to take up the story himself...

" The doctors, the nurses and the ward staff were so kind and the other patients were delightful - most of all Trev Rickard, who managed to laugh at all my jokes! It was a mixed sex ward but why do people in the UK make such a fuss about that? It 's nice to have some feminine company and anyway, the curtains are drawn round one's bed whenever a nurse or doctor comes to see you. No-one in that hospital seemed to think it was wrong or unsuitable.

"After 15 days Trev was discharged and so I thought maybe it was time for me to go, too. I was getting bored and the damaged arm and another cracked vertebrae seemed to be mending as well. So they let me out. With hindsight, maybe I should have stayed another week but there is a limit on the amount of time you can lie in bed and ,anyway, there was a lovely world outside to go back to!"

And what of Gill all this time...

" She, poor thing, had all the remorse and worry of having been at the wheel of the car at the time of our accident which is as bad, possibly worse, than being the damaged one. She visited me daily and brought members of Trev's family with her. The wonderfully kind Dave and Aynsley Denton took Gill in and what was originally intended to be a four day visit turned into a four week stay. That really is true friendship. Imagine if Gill had had to sit in a hotel room all that time.

" New Zealand really is a most wonderful country; glorious scenery, plus good wine and fishing. What more could you want? But it's the **people** who make it so very special. It's like England was 50 years ago; no-one locks their front door; if you're walking across farmland and the farmer comes up you and asks if he can help you, he truly means it.

" One day I remarked to Clifford, a friend: ' I could happily got to New Zealand and never come back.' He replied: *'You very nearly did!'*

" Wonderful people. Wonderful country. I pledged that when my neck was better we'd go back." And they did.

Eventually, the time came when Christopher was deemed fit enough to be flown home to England. But it was not to be under normal conditions. He had to lie flat out, on oxygen with a nurse in attendance. Back at Heathrow, an ambulance was waiting to take him home to Devon, where he wasted no time in writing his heartfelt 'thank you' letters to all those who had contributed towards saving his life in New Zealand.

From Police Constable Robin Manera, who had taken control of the accident scene, he obtained the names and addresses of his rescuers who, with such extraordinary coincidence and good fortune, happened to be on that normally deserted road on that fateful day.

Then he wrote to tell them:

' Without the help of you all I would have been dead or, worse, paralysed for the rest of my life. Just think!

There was a time, though, when the pain was a bit much, when it occurred to me that lying in bed being waited on hand and foot forever sounded like a pretty good option. But then they would probably have stopped my evening whisky, so I went off the idea.

Right. So what happened? Let me tell you the bit I know…The time from your taking me out of the car, with (my wife Gill tells me) unbelievable gentleness, to lying in bed in Christchurch Hospital Intensive Care Unit has a lot of gaps in it. I think I was lucky to pass out for the bit from the car to lying on the road, but I do remember telling everybody that the most useful person there was the one holding the sunshade and don't let him go under any circumstances. Lots of thanks, then, to the sunshade man - as if the rest of you had done nothing at all! I also remember being bundled up like a parcel for the journey and thinking what a good way to travel !

My first five days in Christchurch Hospital were spent in intensive care, staring at their ceiling, which was incredibly dirty - so much so that one of the ceiling tiles kept sagging under the weight of the dust on it to the point where it nearly touched me, lying below it. The dust then fell off and back up the tile went again, only to repeat the process all over again - and none of the staff ever noticed. There's no question: Morphine certainly helps to pass the time!

'Somebody Had To Do It'

I had another hallucination that the staff of the Intensive Care Unit were all Chinese and that they had kidnapped me for ransom. Luckily, I have no memory of how, I managed to escape and the staff gave up being Chinese and became their normal selves again!

Mr Jeremy Evison operated on me on the fifth day and, I understand, did a masterly job pushing the vertebrae back into place and joining two together, with a bit of titanium and four screws he happened to have to hand, using a Black & Decker drill, or some such tool. Result: a rejoined spine and a seriously cool scar on my neck to impress the grandchildren. Honestly, not many grandparents get this lucky!

Nine days after the operation were spent in a section of the Trauma Unit with five other sufferers, would you believe it, nearly all from road accidents. My views on the police being so strict on speeding, etc have changed dramatically. Imagine, if everyone drove carefully and safely, the hospitals would be half empty.

Sixteen days after the operation they let me out and after resting up with friends we have now flown back to England, first class (because of having to lie out flat) plus my own nurse in attendance (I needed oxygen for most of the flight). How smart can you get! Finally, the 150 miles home from London to Devonshire in an ambulance that, would you believe, exceeded the speed limit almost the entire way and didn't use his siren once.

Now to the hardest part of this letter: to express in words the overwhelming gratitude I feel for all of you; so many people who came to my rescue and with your skill and gentleness helped me back to my lovely, happy life when I could have ended up either dying very painfully or being paralysed.

Was it just luck that brought so many of you, with the skills to save me, to where we had crashed or was it statistically bound to happen once in every million or so times? To me, it's much simpler. I thank God that there are so many wonderful, caring people in this world, although I'm not sure why so many happened to be concentrated on that day in South Island, New Zealand.

Someone should write a Kiwi version of the Parable of the Good Samaritans…

A certain Pom was left badly wounded when his chariot came to grief on the Haast Road. In a flash, some six Samaritans downed tools and dashed to help - even before either a Levite or a priest had a chance to pass by on the other side - calling in their friends and lifting him up *and carrying him on wings and things to the hospital in the city. They said to the landlord of the hospital: "Fix him up proper and when we are next in town, we'll settle up." The landlord of the hospital said: "No way. This Pom was in an accident. It's all on the house." To which, a Samaritan said :"I'll drink to that." And so, the wounded Pom and his wife were able to stay a little while longer in that wonderful land and then return safe and (nearly) well to their home across the seas.*

Thank you from both Gill, my wife, and me from the bottom of our hearts for all your care and kindness.'

To the staff of the Intensive Care Unit at Christchurch Hospital, he wrote:

' This is to all the wonderful people who work in the Intensive Care Unit at Christchurch Hospital from Christopher (Chris) Pole-Carew who, from February 28th to March 6th was one of your patients.

I came to you with two vertebrae damaged and out of alignment in my neck and another one cracked halfway down my back. You fed me morphine, put me on my back with sand pillows round my head and gave me the most interesting part of the Intensive Care Unit's ceiling to study in depth for five days (and whilst doing it, to learn patience. I did!) I can't remember much of that time but, being me, I must have managed to make a nuisance of myself. Was it Di who sternly asked me where I was ? Of course, I knew perfectly well where I was…in the disused, clapped out mini supermarket where you (who were all Chinese) had kidnapped me and were holding me to ransom . Not that I was going to let Di know that I knew this, so I fooled her by pretending I was in Christchurch Hospital! I remember happy talks with Mick and other faces I knew at once when I came to say goodbye to you all.

What more can I remember? That I will never forget feeling so safe and, in your care, knowing that I was wrapped in love and gentleness. Not just thinking it; it was a feeling so strong that it was almost tangible.

It is almost impossible to express my thanks and gratitude to you all because these words cannot do justice, but in my heart they are there.

I enclose a modest sum of money, with the request that it be spent as and when, to show kindness to members of your staff. I hope it will remind you that half way round the world there is someone who will never forget you and your skill and care and loving kindness.'

To the staff of the Trauma Unit at Christchurch Hospital, he wrote:

' *On March 6th last, Christopher Pole-Carew was moved from Intensive Care, having been operated on for a neck injury by Mr Jeremy Evison and transferred to the Trauma Unit until he was discharged on March 15th*
That is the simple record, doubtless one of many such incidents, not particularly special - but it wasn't at all like that to me, Chris. It was so comforting to share one's pains and worries with fellow sufferers; to know them as people who had also met with misfortune and were facing up to it: Trev, in the next bed, was suffering more from deep depression than the injured back and lungs that had brought him in; dear Mary, with her broken leg, had to wait in patience through five days for her horrific operation to have it mended all over again. Was I a difficult patient ? Almost certainly - and firm words were uttered to tell me to do as I was told, but never once a single cross word. At 75, I don't remember names as I used to, but Ross from the Army and Judy and Mary Anne and Pete are still clearly there with all the others whose faces I can still see. And please tell Tala that nobody makes coffee, or smiles as sweetly, as she does.
I felt that for those nine days I was wrapped in a cosy blanket of love and gentleness. I think it must be built into the very atmosphere of your hospital because I was acutely aware of it in the Intensive Care Unit as well.
How does one express one's gratitude for such kindness 24 hours a day, every day, even when one woke frightened and in pain in the small hours of the night? These words are a poor attempt to convey my feelings.
I enclose a modest sum of money, with the request that it be spent, as and when to show kindness to members of your staff. Whatever the uses, I do hope that they will remind you that there is someone half way round the world who will never forget you and your skill and care and your loving kindness.'

For the next two years, life continued as usual at Shute - though some years earlier, Christopher and Gill had resolved to prepare to leave the historic house which had been their home since 1989.

" There was a sensible realisation that we'd reached the point when, sooner or later, it was going to be too arduous running a house that was open to the public because we'd be too old; so we'd better do something about it; so we did."

Their new home, they had agreed, would be the cottage they owned at Middle West Water. Since Christopher rescued it from complete dereliction and effectively re-built it in 1995 the cottage, part of which dated back to 1410, had been let to Sedgemoor College for use by children in care. They wanted somewhere for particularly difficult children; those who, for one reason or another, couldn't be in a communal environment.

" They were seriously mixed-up girls," says Christopher, " who had been put into care by court order and this had been contracted to Sedgemoor College, a good organisation, by the county council. They were very good tenants. They looked after the house well. One carer would live in with two girls so that they were under constant supervision. Then New Labour, hell bent on creating jobs, decreed that you couldn't have less than two carers in any given situation. So, I doubled the size of West Water and took it up to a six bedroom house so that they could have two carers and four children. In doing that, I made sure that it was to be done up in such a way that it would eventually suit Gill and I to move into. For example, the dining room in the extension was made precisely to accommodate the huge dining table I had made from elm; upstairs, the dividing wall between two of the bedrooms was built in such a way that it could be taken out to make a big bedroom for us, etc.

During this work on the cottage, Camilla paid her parents a visit and saw a strength in her father which helped her in overcoming the horrors of the Tsunami:

" When I go to stay, we sometimes talk about the miracle of being alive. We have both been through traumatic events, Daddy breaking his neck and me surviving the Tsunami along with my then husband and three children. The result is a firm belief that having survived such events, one must surely be here to give something back for the gift of life. There is certainly something very spiritual about surviving under incredible odds

" It was just after the Tsunami when I went to stay with my parents and they took me down to see how the work on the cottage was progressing.

" I was still in shock. I sat in the car with the comforting sight of the back of my parents' heads in the front seats and we set off the back route to free wheel down the hill, just as we had done as children. I felt safe, like the little girl on his shoulders in my first memory of Daddy. It takes a while to feel safe after a wall of water going 500 miles an hour has hit you!

" We arrived at the house, which was alive with builders and workmen. The electricians were running wires all over the place and my father was chatting to them, asking after their families; how the job was progressing, when a thick grey flex looped itself around his feet and he tripped and hit his head on a pile of planks.

" His head was bleeding and he had gone quite pale, but he refused help of any kind, except a glass of water, then he got up. It frightened me just as much as his allergic reaction to bee stings had back in the days of the newspaper strike - but this time it also showed me just how determined he is not to give in or to show weakness.

" It helped me get through the after effects of the Tsunami ordeal and the heartbreak of a divorce I didn't expect."

In the 13 years in which his cottage was used for children in care, Pole-Carew saw social services at work at first hand and gained huge respect for them...

" Let's face it," he says, "social services in this country have got a pretty poor reputation for incompetence so it's no bad thing to be involved with social services at ground level - then you realise that they are decent hard working people doing their best. OK, there will be some who are not hard working and don't do their best but our lot did, consistently, over all the years I saw them at close hand."

The Government, however, did *not* earn his respect in the same way...

" New Labour liked making laws for the hell of it, I sometimes suspect - and the laws relating to children in care in these kinds of properties became unbelievable. For example, there was no way that anybody could come into the cottage without being signed in and out.

" There was no longer any way, that I could see, that the girls were being disciplined at all. If one of them didn't want to go to school, she didn't go to school.

" The carers were extremely decent and conscientious people but it seemed to me that they were hidebound by too much legislation. I suggested that maybe the girls might like to come to tea at Shute to give them a day out. After all, going to tea in a castle is not something many children get the chance to do and they could have had a nice wander around the battlements - but it was never done.

"There didn't seem any longer to be much concern for little loving touches. After they had left, we wanted their addresses so that we could send them Christmas cards. '*Oh, No. Sorry. We're not allowed to give you their addresses. Someone will come over and collect the cards, so that they can get them.*' But no-one did.

"I really thought that all the legislation made the place into a prison - but maybe the whole object of New Labour's idea of social services in such cases is that in their childhood they should be fitted for their future lives - and they were, because when they went to gaol they would have no problem in settling in!

"It was so sad, because they could have enjoyed it so much. I provided chickens for them to look after - but that lasted no time at all before a reason was found for not having them. But children *need* animals.

"I could have taught them fishing, happily. But of course, I would have to be investigated, wouldn't I, if I was going to have anything to do with the children.

"It's all so very sad how too much legislation has changed places like that from being homes in which children can be given some kind of loving care into individual little prisons."

Sedgemoor College then went out of business and that provided the timely opportunity for Gill and Christopher to move out of Shute and into Middle West Water - but not before 1001 DIY jobs identified by the tireless Pole-Carew had given him many more days of 'finding something definite to do' in and around the lovely old cottage.

The move eventually took place in June, 2008 - and the fact that they were still in chaos did not deter Mr and Mrs Pole-Carew from hosting a family Christmas for 18!

After Christmas, there was yet more work for Christopher and Gill to do with the cottage and in and around its ten acres - in particular Christopher's proudly owned stretch of river before, in late January, they went back to New Zealand for their promised return visit.

Both felt they had unfinished business in New Zealand; Gill to complete a holiday that, first time round, had become a nightmare; Christopher to catch the fish that were still waiting for him!

But, more seriously, more importantly and more emotionally, for both of them, was a real need to see and thank the people who had saved Christopher's life.

Two years had passed before he was fit enough to travel so far but he was unshakeably determined to go back " to thank those wonderful people who had shown such love and kindness to me in my time of need."

And so, on January 28th, 2009, they flew to New Zealand (*via Hong Kong ' for Chinese food and retail therapy'*) for a first stop at North Island , which they had had to miss completely on their last visit.

While, back home in England, people were having to cope with bitter cold and a blanket of snow, the warmth of North Island was very acceptable - apart from just one impediment…" It was too hot for fishing!"

They stayed at various Bed & Breakfast establishments "…. so nice, especially the rural ones, that it was like staying with one good friend after another."

But one overnight stay brought a touch of real luxury :

"We had a night with Geordie and Margaret Fergusson at the High Commissioner's residence in Auckland and it was a much appreciated high spot," said Christopher. " Whisky and soda brought to you on a silver salver by the butler tastes so much better!

" Geordie's father and grandfather had both been Governors-General of New Zealand so it was not surprising to find him there as High Commissioner. He and I both had great-grandfathers who had been founders of Christchurch, in South Island, so it was by way of a family visit."

The Pole-Carew's found South Island, 2009 to be suffering from drought, with pale brown mountains everywhere. There was a very real risk of serious bush fires (Australia was suffering appalling fires at the time) so all tourism had been banned in the Molesworth area, which is noted for its wonderful fishing. It seemed that the fish population of New Zealand was determined to avoid Pole-Carew on this occasion, though he did eventually find some fishing, catching a trout in the Mangles river weighing close on 6lbs : "….Not particularly large by New Zealand standards and then rain set in, largely ending the fishing part of our trip."

They stayed again with their friends Dave and Aynsley Denton, who had been so kind and helpful after Christopher's accident and as the holiday neared its end it was time for the pilgrimage of thanks.

On Thursday, February 26th, Christopher and Gill went back to Christchurch Hospital to which he had been taken, his neck broken and so near to death, two years earlier.

At the Intensive Care Unit he was greeted by the Nurse Manager, Nikki Ford and the Charge Nurse of the Trauma Unit, Karen Wilson.

Said Christopher : " They were both clearly delighted to see me, which prompted the thought that maybe not many people bother to thank hospital staff in this way. But why on earth wouldn't you after all they've done for you?

" They took me to visit my ward, where I correctly identified my bed and the ceiling above it - hardly surprising since I had spent six days studying it intently while waiting for a lung to mend sufficiently to take anaesthetic for the operation on my broken neck. Then, on to the Trauma Ward, where I spent 15 days; the occupants of the beds seemed to be the only obvious changes.

" We lunched with the nurses in the hospital canteen, where Gill had had so many lonely meals in the time before my operation when I was unable to acknowledge her as she sat for so many long hours beside me.

" We would have liked to have taken the nurses out for a meal in a fancy restaurant but there was no time between shifts for them to do that. We so enjoyed being with them.

"What wonderful people they are. And how very much I owe them."

There was one more pleasant surprise before this very emotional visit came to an end…" One of the staff, Marianne Scott, who had come in on her day off to see us, took Gill and I on a tour of Christchurch; not only looking at fascinating famous buildings but also up into the surrounding hills for truly spectacular views of the city.

" What a wonderful way to end our second visit to this lovely, lovely country."

9
THE POEMS OF POLE - CAREW

Carpentry, bricklaying, plumbing, beekeeping. Many and surprising are the skills of Pole- Carew. But poetry?

WHAT IS LOVE?
(On our Golden Wedding Anniversary)

What is love? Can anyone say?
You'll only know when it comes your way

How **wide** is love? As wide as the sea?
Or as close as the ties between you and me?

How **high** is love? How high can you go?
To heaven and back, as we both know

How **deep** is love? Like an endless well?
As deep as our feelings; as we can tell

Can you **touch** love; does it have a face?
We know it's there by its warm embrace

Can you **see** love; does it wear a crown?
You can hold it close, so why put it down?

Can you **hurt** love? You can, alas
And the pain and remorse will never pass

Does love mean **bed**? What a **narrow** thought
To those whose Cupid's darts have caught

How **strong** is love? Like tensile steel?
The strength of our love is what we feel

What **colour** is love? You can't see it, though
After fifty years it has a golden glow

Does love **hold tight**? It binds like twine
It makes me hers and it makes her mine

Is love the **greatest**? We must agree
With faith and hope, she's the first of three

What do you do if love has gone?
I think you mourn, for the days are long

How **old** is love? What do you mean?
My love will always be sixteen

What **name** has love? Call it what you will
That short sweet word to me spells **Gill**

FOR OUR GOLDEN WEDDING PARTY
(July 2004)

As we all sit here together
Well-watered and replete
I think we ought to ponder on
The reason why we meet

The story is quite simple
It's a tale without a flaw
How Gill and I have lived and loved
For fifty years and more

Our secret is to compromise
On everything in sight
As you must know, I'm always wrong
And Gill is always right

*"But Christopher, there's something wrong
I really cannot see
In you the attribute they call
The soul of harmony"*

You know I'm self-effacing
It's Gill who rules the roost
It only takes a smile from her
My confidence to boost

*"You say you've lived for all these years
Sans hindrance or let
And not one quarrel's passed your lips
How boring can you get !"*

No. that's not true, you cannot say
Our life has been a bore
Exciting, thrilling - that's the word
We couldn't ask for more

With friends like you around us
Let me say before we part
How much I'd like to thank you
From the bottom of my heart

I'd like a finish that will mark
This moment in my life
So fill your glasses, raise them high
And drink to Gill, my **wife**

MY FAVOURITE SPORT

Oh, I see the pheasants flying
As they stream across the sky
And I see the pheasants falling
And I sometimes wonder why

The keeper has his bantams
And he rears his birds from birth
When he sees his pheasants dying
How does he rate their worth?

And the beaters all are marching
In a line out in the brash
Do they do it for the pleasure?
Is it really for the cash?

Behind the guns are pickers- up
Their dogs are thorough bred
They prefer to track the wounded
But I wish they all were dead

I shoot the pheasants flying
And still I wonder why
We kill those lovely creatures
With such terror in their eye

Oh, we're all in this together
Beaters, keeper, dogs and gun
When we face the Day of Judgement
Will we say 'twas just for fun?

(And an attempt to answer the above....)

*" So did you go on shooting, then: for better or for worse
Did nothing change within you since you composed that verse?"*

God made us men who hunt and kill a million years ago

These are the ways of countrymen, why should we change them now?

A DAY OUT
By Tara

It's seven o' clock on a late Autumn day
It's time for the gun and the dogs - and *away*!

Creedy snores there in dreams of the past
Delta is circling, her tail wagging fast
And Tara is frantic: the great day at last!

But breakfast comes first; will he *never* be through?
Stick close to his side; he could leave without you

Get into the car, lie down and don't roam
If you climb on the seats he might leave you at home

The journey is boring; it's *such* a long way
Just anticipation to heighten the day

Oh Heaven! We're there! Lots of dogs I can see!
Black things they call labs and smart spaniels like me
While a dashing young pointer lifts his leg on a tree

Over there is young Barb, sneaking off to the wood
I've given her tips so she'll soon be quite good

Ugh! Here comes that Lottie to spoil the fun
That superior bitch is the keeper's best one

Why *do* they wait so, just standing about?
Lapping up something called coffee no doubt
As if pheasants and partridges counted for *nowt* !

We're moving at *last* and the sport has begun
If we'd waited much longer we'd have missed all the fun

I must squat for a moment for relief; you can guess
    All this excitement can give me *real* stress

I'll take barely a moment; I'll be just a tick
If I weren't being dragged by my neck I'd be *quick*!

We're all in a line now; they're ready to go
He says he likes high birds; they make such a show
   Hmmm, Delta and I see it differently, though

Here they all come and well, what do you know?
    It's *really* too bad: he's missed three in a row

Wow, high birds are coming, they're all over us
    He's missed nearly all, so why such a fuss?

I've been known to run in; it's *serious* fun
So many birds round you, I chase every one!

The keeper says I'm the worst dog on the Shoot
  If he had half a chance he'd give me his boot
    Master won't have it, so I don't give a hoot!

A new drive has started, let's hope for the best
    We came to retrieve, not enjoy a good rest

Over one comes, good heavens - it's *down*!
It's the person next door, with no dog of his own
    Not one of us, he must live in a town

It's the last of the drives and our master's got four
If he'd shot a bit straighter he might have got more

We've managed to get all our mouths round a bird
One partridge, two pheasants - and I got a third

Well, so much for shooting; that's all for today
    Now that it's ended it's *home* right away

Back in the car and too tired to think
I hope he won't stop at the pub for a drink

My master's my master when all's said and done
But I'm *sure* I'd do better if I had his gun!
Fair's fair, though, we've *all* had our share of the fun

The great day is over for all of us three
At last we're back home for a nice meaty tea
Creedy and Delta and Tara -

That's me !

(In the Spring of 2008, there had been complaints about the use of grazing sheep to control the grass in the churchyard of St Mary's in Stoke Abbott. This row prompted Marcia Astor to write a poem in defence of the graveyard sheep. In reply, Christopher Pole-Carew offered an alternative poetic point of view!)

THE SHEEP
By Marcia Astor

We've erred and strayed like all lost sheep
Yet when, at last, we die
May we, forgiven and asleep
Here in the churchyard lie?

Should mowers roar and shred our peace
Or strimmers flake our names?
The rural idyll soon would cease
To suit suburban aims

We hope that sheep may safely graze
And neatly trim the sward
We much prefer the ancient ways
The parish can afford

Oh, please Good Shepherd of the flock
And parish council too
No more fast forward of the clock
Preserve the noble ewe!

THOSE SHEEP
By Christopher Pole-Carew

Who eats my flowers, mocks my grave
And with a munching sound
Disturbs the peace I dearly crave
Leaves droppings all around?

My wife's a gardener, God wot!
She loved to till and hoe
But now she decorates my plot
With things that do not grow

A plastic daff's not fit to see
Upon my breast, alas
And all because the PCC
Keeps sheep to mow the grass

My latter days were marred for me
When deafness took its toll
The strimmer's gentle hum would be
Like manna to my soul

I know some love the bleating sheep
And I respect their view.
But when you're dead and six feet deep
You have your feelings, too!

ODE TO A FAVOURITE SALMON FLY

For fishing flies to give their best
And lure the salmon from its rest
Their colours can be gold or black
In running water, or in slack.

*But quite the nicest fly I've seen
Must be the dainty Green Machine*

What flies are they that work so well
In Scotland's rivers; who can tell?
The Burrach on the Spey is great
The Stoat Tail when the burn's in spate

*But salmon fat or salmon lean
Will all rise to a Green Machine*

Blue Charm is favoured along the Dee,
The Buck Bug on the Miramichi
When fish are jumping, water's warm
A Bomber on your line's the form

*But when you weary of this scene
Turn to your faithfull Green Machine*

You cross the ocean, bridge the gulf
Your guide insists Natural Wulff
Poor fellow simply doesn't know
His range of flies will surely show

*Do not be selfish, never mean
Present him with a Green Machine*

If flies could fly across the seas
And mate with whomso'er they please
From West: McDougall, East: Jock Scott
It wouldn't matter which was what

The finest offspring ever seen
Would be a hybrid Green Machine

When nights are long and days are short
And fishing just a dreamy thought
When rods are packed for better times
With clean and shiny flies and lines

There on its own rests in between
Your sleepy little Green Machine

SAME MESSAGE
By Christopher Pole-Carew

Will You Hear Me?

Can you hear me, will you hear me
Do you want to hear, my dove
When I come to you a-courting
Singing songs of lasting love?

When I tell you of the wonders
That can bring such joyous bliss
Will you listen to me, spellbound
Seal our trysting with a kiss

When I tell you of the passion
That can come with love divine
Will you hear me, listen to me
Say that you'll for e'er be mine?

Hey Listen!

Hey, chick there and waddya know
I've got the hots for you - let's go!

You know I'm switched: I've found a pad
I'll get the money off me dad

D'ya hear me, babe, I'm telling you
We'll be an item - just us two

Wots gotcha hon? Quit mssn me
n text me now wile im stil 3

THE FORMAN STREET MARTYRS
(December 1978)

It's the Company what matters and that's the golden theme
Its great and glorious future is what we always dream
But 28 reporters thought it wasn't really right
To put T. Bailey Forman before their brethren's plight

The NUJ was calling for 60 volunteers
To join the ranks of martyrs to their fellow workers' cheers
They knew what stood before them and 32 held back
They didn't like the options: employment or the sack

The weeks have passed unnoticed, including Peace on Earth. Amen
But 28 reporters had a different Christmas then
The union's found agreement with the papers through the land
Yet no-one seems to care about that hapless little band

Their notebooks have been copied, their desks have been cleared out
What should have been a victory has turned into a rout
The NS and the Management and SLADE and NGA
Will always make good copy because they always have their say

In Forman Street it's snowing hard and charity is thin
In Acorn House they haven't time for pawns that didn't win
So find yourselves another job and next time round you'll know
Compassion doesn't pay the rent - the wise always lie low!

(NUJ - National Union Of Journalists; Acorn House - NUJ headquarters; NS - Newspaper Society, the regional press trade organisation; SLADE, NGA - two other print unions)

EXPENSES
(June, 2009)

I'd like you to note
I don't pay for my moat
My chandelier's totally free
My expenses are long
But I've done nothing wrong
Don't you see, I'm a Tory MP?

My friends and I all flip around
The money mounts up pound by pound
My second home's where I will be
Because I'm a Minister
There's nothing that's sinister
Don't you see, I'm a Labour MP?

I think I am holier than thou
But my colleagues aren't holy - no how!
That's the way of the House, don't blame me
My wife's brother's fences
We're repaired on expenses
Don't you see, I'm a Liberal MP?

AN HONEST RACE
(January, 2008)

Dear Lord I love this world so much
That I can see and sense and touch
Such kindness you have given me
I've fought my fights, I've had my wins
And so to counteract my sins
I have my loving family

My time will come, as to us all
And I will wait your last clear call
Lord, give me strength that I'll have run
An honest race across this place
Please help me with your loving grace
To mend the wrongs that I have done

Please let me stay awhile, I pray
I know I cannot choose the day
So much I've done; much more to do
Such happiness on earth below
Such love I have, such friends to know
Ere I return, My God, to you

10

THE THOUGHTS OF POLE-CAREW

*He's been called outspoken, blunt, belligerent, forthright, infuriating, amusing.
But **never** boring...*

ON POLITICS :

I have never been a true Conservative, because they do seem to be the Party of vested interest. At heart, I think I am a Liberal (19th Century style) but, then, I don't believe in supporting failure. When Tony Blair came to power I welcomed him because I thought his New Labour formula would mean the end at last of ' no alternative' politics , meaning that you voted for the Party that was not unacceptable to you, whether or not they showed any likelihood of competence or ability. In 1997, at last, a moderate, middle-of-the-road ' Conservative' had a genuinely acceptable alternative to the disastrous mess that the Tory Government had become - without having to settle for even more nightmarish Socialist policies, with their unbroken record of bankrupting the economy, increasing bureaucracy and destroying entrepreneurial initiative.

How wrong can one be? With Tony Blair what we got was a self-seeking spin artist and his dyed- in -the-wool Scottish buddy, Gordon Brown who, as Chancellor, destroyed our nation's wealth (gold reserves and pensions - just for starters!) then our competitiveness with over-taxation, then created so many state employees that they are now a significant voting factor in Labour's favour. This is a variation of the old Labour policy of subsidised council estate ghettoes to ensure control of local councils - but writ larger! Margaret Thatcher destroyed those old political ghettoes - but who will get rid of the vast army of state employees that grind us down today?

Brown, initially with support from Blair, has ruined our country. He has attempted to break the Union apart, with England made to foot the bills; he has virtually destroyed our Armed Forces with under-funding and over-stretching; and so the same story goes, through Education to the National Health Service.

But is David Cameron, a kind of pallid, right wing Blair lookalike, the answer ? Get real! What this country needs desperately is another Margaret Thatcher: ruthless, far - sighted and generally dedicated to our country's well-being and with a contempt for the gravy train ambitions of most of our MPs.

Currently I support the United Kingdom Independence Party - not because I think it will ever manage to form a Government but because it is the only Party that is wholeheartedly and single mindedly pursuing our nation's interest, albeit on a narrow front. A significant UKIP would mean that the three main parties would have to stop ignoring the wishes of the people of this country regarding Europe and learn to behave themselves - belatedly.

At least UKIP is honest about what it stands for. Which other party is ?

ON POLITICAL CORRECTNESS:

IN Cromwellian times there was an equivalent to today's infuriating Political Correctness; a form of Puritanical Correctness that ground down the pleasures and freedoms of the people to do their own things.

And it ended with the Restoration of the Monarchy.

So is there any hope for us today for a Restoration of Sanity without petty restrictions? I doubt it. Not with Brown's one million extra state employees existing - and being rewarded handsomely - to make Political Correctness ever more oppressive, year in, year out.

What hope is there of a return to normality?

ON SOLUTIONS:

There's only one solution to all of the above for any freedom loving person in this country: **emigrate.**

Get out of here because it's finished.

Go, instead, to where good English principles are still held : Australia, or New Zealand, or Canada.

England is beyond recovery.

Our European neighbours (*all the nearby ones, as any reading of history will confirm, have old scores to settle*) will ensure that we never rise again.

Indeed, we will be split into regions so that we truly cannot.

But there will be no question of splitting up Scotland or Wales, of course!

ON TRADES UNIONS:

Contrary to general belief, I have never been anti-Trades Unions, nor have I ever discouraged anyone who worked for me from joining one.

In fact, I used to tell all new joiners at the Nottingham Evening Post that they had complete freedom to join any union of their choice should they so wish.

Most people don't realise that it was the unions of the 70's and 80's who attacked **us** for daring to know how to run things, including caring for their members better than they could ever have hoped to.

Unions are, I believe, a necessity in Industry.

What hope has the individual worker on his own of facing up to greedy, unfeeling and self-interested employers? And there are many of those to be found. In fact, I would argue that they are the majority.

My personal philosophy has always been that it is the unarguable duty of any employer to see to the welfare of his employees. This stems mainly from my Naval upbringing and is reinforced by my belief that anyone who professes to be a Christian should demonstrate it in how he treats his neighbours, ie. Those with whom he has dealings or comes into contact..

At T. Bailey Forman, after the 1973 strike, I found that my duties of care for our staff increased considerably. With unions having abandoned them, who else was there to look after their interests but their Managing Director?

Remember, I had joined that company when it was paying the minimum union wage rate and had only recently (*as a result of taking in employees from Westminster Press in a merger* – **not** *from a change of policy decision*) stopped sacking people as they neared retirement in order to avoid paying them pensions!

There was no pension arrangement. When an employee came up to retirement his pension was decided at a board meeting. Just that. No wonder I had learnt from many people at all levels in the firm, including my predecessor, that once you were over 60 (*55 for women*) you had to tread with incredible care!

The trouble with the print unions in those days was that they were all-powerful, basically badly run, politically motivated to a ridiculous extent and prone to corruption - albeit less so in the provinces than in London. Intelligent concern for their members' welfare was, in practical terms, non-existent; the interests of their leaders came first. Likewise, intelligent concern for the changes that were inevitable in our industry never entered their minds.

I do so deeply hope, some 30 years on, that the unions have recognised and taken up the vital role in industry that they really should occupy.

Their members' interests are best served by well run, profitable companies that look into the future and prepare for it; make the money to pay good wages and provide proper training. It is worth noting that **only in Nottingham** did print workers' training move with the times – because I required **all** apprentices to learn not one but all three basic trades, running smack across all union demarcations – on the grounds that in their working lives they would see a minimum of two of their skills disappear without trace.

Unions should be **good** news for a well run company and should aim to be the salvation of a badly run one. I would see much good in union leaders sitting on the boards of companies to help achieve the most efficient and profitable use of labour and unions taking into their executive structures successful industrialists to help them understand how to get the best results for both sides. This would rely on the union leaders having the right motivation and on the industry leaders being not the money-obsessed exploiters but the Harvey-Jones type (*maybe I'm biased because he was a submariner, too* !) who inspire and give their employees reasons to look forward to their working week - which is not a bad point from which to start.

Success should never be measured solely in money.

ON THE STATE OF OUR NEWSPAPERS:

NEWSPAPERS held sway as the dominant communications medium from around 1900 up to the 1960's, when television started cutting into them, with the damage becoming serious in the 70's and 80's.

Could the damage have been prevented? Not really. You can't un-invent television, nor the computer which, in the last decade, has allowed the Internet to inflict even more serious injury on the newspaper industry.

Could the damage have been mitigated? Probably, yes. But it would have required much more sensitively alert managements than the industry even remotely possessed.

Free newspapers, with their blanket penetration, were hammering at the provincial industry's advertisement income bases and providing editorial content, albeit of varying quality, for nothing ; the free-ad papers with their revenue coming from cover price but their classified advertising free, hit them where it really hurt - in their small ads which, arguably, rated equal to editorial content for reader interest.

Their decline was inevitable.

Or was it?

How come the national newspapers survived?

Certainly, the nationals lost sales but the best of them recognised that while they had lost out to TV for news they had retained the market for informed opinion, which matters a great deal to all newspaper readers of whatever intellectual level - a point that few provincial paper managements even appeared to have recognised.

Instead, they pushed for higher profits by reducing editorial staffs and increasing advertisement rates when the market was demanding the opposite in both cases.

The declining businesses still managed to generate good money - but the price was steadily falling quality generating fewer worthwhile jobs.

To survive and succeed provincial newspapers needed to be embedded into the hearts of their readers' communities, which is what really good editorial content is all about, with advertisement rates that could fight off competition and keep their advertisers loyal.

This, in turn, meant not being greedy for excessive profits.

The ever improving new technology should have been seen as providing the means for better, more competitive local newspapers.Sadly, it was used to destroy jobs in order to generate ever greater profits whilst the burgeoning opposition steadily ate their foundations.

When the Internet arrived, the health, strength and ability of the newspapers to respond vigorously to this huge new threat had been seriously weakened by the pursuit of greedy profits. So what did the newspaper managements do?

They went for even bigger profits.

Greed and insanity both come before a fall!

ON BUREAUCRACY:

GORDON Brown and Tony Blair have much to answer for in their steady (*perhaps deliberate ?*) destruction of the bulwarks of our Anglo - Saxon and Victorian heritages.

A fine Civil Service has been swollen to the point where its prime function seems to be to sustain itself in ever increasing numbers while burdening those it purports to serve with ever more restrictions and interferences.

This has come about because of our political masters' determination to control, from the centre , every facet of our lives.
And it is inevitably and obviously having disastrous results.

ON THE NATIONAL HEALTH SERVICE:

THE National Health Service seems to be obsessed with targets that have little practical significance but imply successful achievement.

It has become a black hole into which more and more money is poured for ever dwindling results. Whilst the numbers of medical and allied staff decline in absolute terms (*as percentages of the whole*) the already swollen ranks of management and support staff continue to flourish and expand - at ever greater cost. And yet, Cabinet Ministers constantly boast about the money spent as if it were the *only* measure of success.

But why should this be so? Why should ever more layers of management make an organisation more competent or efficient? All my personal experience tells me that the reverse is, in fact, the case.

Will we *ever* have the political masters with the vision to undo the dreadful mess that strangles what is, at heart, a truly fine Health Service, staffed with so many people of wonderful ability and kindness?

Yet the solution is really so very simple: return control of their affairs and decision making to the hospitals and doctors' practices; Start by cutting out political and bureaucratic interferences of any sort, because the history of the nationalised industries show that they are the death knell of any business organisation of whatever nature or size. Indeed, there is ample evidence that over-centralisation is a prime reason for the decline of large companies.

Let the doctors and nurses, who – unlike the bureaucrats – know and understand the needs of the sick and broken, run their own hospitals, including the appointment of such managers as they need to handle the administration for them.

Let ***them*** also decide what limited records they need to keep and what limited returns they need to make to be truly efficient. Maybe my doctor would then stop taking my blood pressure every time I see him; ***he's*** not interested, but he needs it for the bureaucratic returns his practice has to make.

How many pointless jobs would then disappear?

How much wasted money would then be saved?

Maybe some could even be returned to the wretched taxpayers who foot the bills for Government's never ending extravagances. **But don't hold your breath on that!**

ON EDUCATION:

OUR Private Education system is of a quality that attracts the children of discerning parents from all over the world while our State schools are frequently derided for the disasters that so many of them have become. The surviving Grammar Schools bridge the gap - some even bettering the Private Education schools.

Can we solve this mess, including the collapse of the exam system, solely through unending Government interference and manipulation?

Can we end the pushing of half-educated youngsters into so-called universities to obtain meaningless and therefore worthless degrees, all to show how clever our political masters are while actually proving that they are anything but ?

Labour, old or new, has always preferred levelling down to levelling up and clearly prefers to suppress real ability and talent in favour of universal mediocrity. The Tories used to prefer the opposite, but now I really don't know where they stand – and I don't think ***they*** do either.

Brown has done everything to overload the private sector by burdening it with the State's responsibilities for so-called deprived children from the state schools, while forcing our universities to take students who have not been educated to the necessary level. There should be a solution to solve the gap between our systems, other than the Labour one of destroying the better of the two. More difficult is how to do it relatively painlessly, ie. without mass closures and re-openings, or mass transfers from some schools to others...

Firstly, give back to headmasters their **complete** authority over the running of their schools with the right to appoint outside individuals – a majority of them being parents – to their management boards. Secondly, remove **all** political interference from the exam system.

Let the universities jointly determine the exams they require their intakes to sit, which will set proper levels for the secondary schools to aim for. Let the secondary schools, private and state together, jointly establish the levels of education they require from the primary schools, again by examination. Different secondary schools and universities will expect different pass marks in the various subjects - quite naturally because they would all be looking for different calibres of students.

How about money - which tends to be closely linked to freedom of choice?

Let the Government funding be tied to the child, regardless of whether the child goes to a state school or a private school. This is not just a matter of long overdue justice, it would help by encouraging more children to be sent to private schools, which would help by reducing the numbers in state schools and that, in turn, would be to the advantage of the state schools.

By itself, though, this would risk causing mass closures and upheavals - so it needs to mitigated somehow. So, how about tax breaks to those who make donations to specific schools, payable each term across a specific number of years - the equivalent of a pupil's time at the school. The levels of tax relief, or the length of time they ran for, could be varied: the better the educational standard of the school the less the tax relief, probably starting at nil for private schools with full relief for inner city disasters. Above a total level of contribution to a school the contributor(s) would earn the right to be represented on the school's management board, either in person or by nominating someone suitable - as is standard practice in industry and commerce for shareholders. Should a contributor send his child to any specifically designated schools then his rights, or tax breaks, would be higher.

This ' outside funding' would be reserved for two purposes only, with no exceptions:

Seventy five per cent minimum to pay the salaries of **extra** teachers;
Twenty five per cent maximum to fund sports facilities.
What is one trying to achieve with this?

Firstly, to get the dead hand of politicians and civil servants well away from education - it is much too important for them to be allowed to continue to foul it up; Secondly, to encourage non-taxpayers' money into schools and further, to promote really effective links between primary and secondary schools so that, for example, a private school could well have one or more state primary schools as 'feeders' to it. Or, indeed, vice-versa. The aim is to blur the margins and differences between the two current systems. It is quite likely that such a system would encourage specialist schools in, say, music, art, science…whatever subjects higher educational establishments would welcome.

What I am proposing is not complicated; it emphatically does **not** require bureaucracy to make it work; it provides targets and standards to meet the requirements of those who will take the output from the different levels of schools.

And it motivates committed individuals to put their money and their talents into creating a first class education system for the whole country.

11

HE DID IT HIS WAY

*Controversial and enigmatic, people love him or hate him, but **what** a man!*

NOW, at the age of 79, Christopher Pole-Carew can reflect on a truly remarkable life…not that he's one for idle reflection, nor that he thinks it's time for him to do so!

Just as he did in his forties, fifties and sixties, he looks 20 years younger than he is, still runs everywhere, still stands ramrod straight to his full 6ft 5ins, still exudes indefatigable energy and still holds diligently to his lifelong creed of ' finding something definite to do' with every day.

There's always a new project; always something he ***must*** do in a tearing hurry; never time to relax - at least not in the conventional ways that you might reasonably expect for a man approaching 80.

To Christopher, " relaxation" means hauling a huge fish out of a river after an epic struggle; creating something beautiful out of wood, normally from a tree he's chopped down himself and dragged into his workshop, there to treat it with tenderness and respect as he caresses it into a form of his own imagination.

" Relaxation" is tackling the next big restoration job at Middle West Water (" so many of them – and all such fun!) such as do-it-yourself landscaping of acres of very difficult terrain. Gill tried as hard as she could to dissuade him from buying his own digger for fear that he may over-turn it! Gill lost - and so his latest ' boy's toy ' is a four and a half ton Hitachi machine about which he enthuses:

" *I need it for doing loads of things at Middle West Water and anything smaller would be a waste of time. It has a proper crane arm - two sections, outer and inner, with their own controls - with a bucket that you dig in and then turn it towards you so that it scoops; three buckets, five feet wide, for grading; 2ft 6" wide for every day work; six inches wide, a seriously mean bit of kit, for digging out tree stumps and a blade, which is what us in the business call the bulldozer bit on the front. Also it swivels round through 360 degrees. I'm hoping to hire it out a bit to be able to buy an attachment (cost £1000) so that it has a proper pterodactyl-like mouth and can pick up lumps of rock. That must be the ultimate!*

Thus, Middle West Water was recently the setting for the extraordinary sight of two octogenarian gentlemen lunch guests and their 79-year-old host taking turns on the digger, bulldozing and shifting earth as part of his landscaping project.

" *They were thrilled; best lunch party in many a long day!*" said Christopher.

" Relaxation" is engaging in stimulating, challenging, animated debate of issues of the day with guests at lively lunches or dinner parties, at which the Pole-Carews' generous hospitality - especially of the liquid variety - and Gill's prowess as a cook are renowned.

In short, there are still invariably a million and one **definite** things for Christopher Pole-Carew to do!

Gill, as she always has done, manages her hyper-active husband with good natured patience and tolerance while occasionally (and she is the ***only*** person in the world who can do it!) putting him firmly in his place.

Their love for each other, enduring since their teenage years, remains as deep as it is charmingly obvious.

'Somebody Had To Do It'

*Christopher and Gill Pole-Carew –
everlasting love.*

Old friends thoroughly enjoy Pole-Carew's company, finding him as gloriously unpredictable, outspoken and amusing as ever he was.

New friends, which he makes with genuine, full-on interest and exuberance, are as susceptible to his charm as ever they were.

His family love him to bits, especially his grandchildren with whom, when they were little, he carried on that rare gift which he had with his own children of being able to relate to young minds and to create for them, spontaneously and enthusiastically, little touches of magic.

Christopher Pole-Carew is a happy and fulfilled man.

He tells me:" What a wonderful way to spend one's evening years; lots of interests in the Westcountry river world; plus Shute Parish and Church matters; one's children with their children to visit us; my Gill of 56 years of marriage still with me; sea trout fishing twenty yards away from one's door; an unlimited amount of landscaping to be done and serious equipment to do it with.

"God has been so very, very kind to me."

Because he is such a controversial and enigmatic man with such a multi-faceted life, Christopher Pole-Carew will always mean different things to different people:

To hundreds who worked with him and stayed loyal to him through the tumultuous, pioneering years in Nottingham, he will forever be a fantastic leader; a good, thoughtful, considerate and generous boss who fought *for* them as well as *with* them to blaze exciting trails to innovative achievements which were 20 or 30 years ahead of their time.

They'll never forget that.

To hundreds of trade union members who got in the way of his single-minded visionary zeal in Nottingham and for thousands more whose jobs were wiped out in the bloody revolution that was Wapping, he will forever be ' that evil bastard Pole-Carew' who trampled over workers and their families, driving them into the miseries of unemployment without a second thought.

They'll never forget that.

To hundreds more in the newspaper business who know more of the myth than the man, efforts to explain that " he's really not like that at all and never was" are met with transparent incredulity.

They'll never believe that.

There are those with whom Christopher Pole-Carew has crossed swords, who think him arrogant, self-opinionated and callous.

There are those for whom Christopher Pole-Carew has shown great charity, who think him selfless, kind and tender.

There are many whose lives, if only temporarily, he has blighted.

There are many upon whose lives he has scattered gold dust.

THE END